A CHILD IS BEING BEATEN
The Psychodynamic Approach to Adolescence

This book is dedicated to our late father
JTRP
He tried to be a Christian

Head Master of St Thomas' Prep. School, Colombo 3, Ceylon
Warden of 'Glendale', Royal College, Bandarawela, Ceylon

He was an all-round man who in his youth was the North Ceylon and Nuwareliya Tennis Champion. As a boy he played cricket for his school, captained football and was Head Prefect of St John's College, Jaffna, Ceylon

A CHILD IS BEING BEATEN
The Psychodynamic Approach to Adolescence

Dr K. Sounthy Perinpanayagam

ATHENA PRESS
LONDON

A CHILD IS BEING BEATEN:
The Psychodynamic Approach to Adolescence
Copyright © Dr K. Sounthy Perinpanayagam 2003

All Rights Reserved

No part of this book may be reproduced in any form
by photocopying or by an electronic or mechanical means,
including information storage or retrieval systems,
without permission in writing from both the copyright
owner and the publisher of this book.

ISBN 1 84401 047 3

First Published 2003 by
ATHENA PRESS
Queen's House, 2 Holly Road
Twickenham TW1 4EG
United Kingdom

Printed for Athena Press

FOREWORD

I have pleasure in writing this foreword because I have seen evidence of the efficacy of the method used by Dr Sounthy Perinpanayagam.

His clinical experience was first in adult psychiatry, which was deepened and crystallised in his work with adolescents in difficulty

His views on how adolescents can best be treated as in-patients and outpatients are different from the ones based on authoritarianism which has characterised the last two decades before 1997. What Dr Perinpanayagam believes and practices is a much more balanced treatment of guidance between the adolescent who needs to develop skills in self- control, and the family and controlling forces of so-called law and order. This is in harmony with the Greek classical view of "Not too much and not too little".

In autumn 1971 I changed appointments. My new NHS Consultancy consisted of four sessions at the Tavistock Clinic -in the Adolescent Department and five sessions at Northgate Clinic, an in-patient unit for disturbed adolescent boys, where Dr Sounthy Perinpanayagam worked as a registrar. In watching and listening I was very impressed by the then young Dr Perinpanayagam. He was friendly with the patients, highly respected and liked, but more important still, was their trust in him.

From these initial attributes which he has retained, he has developed his skills with study and more importantly with a personal Kleinian training psychoanalysis.

During the time interval between these first impressions mentioned already, Sounthy Perinpanayagam has had experience at the Tavistock Clinic where I was the chairman of the Adolescent Department, and later as the first Medical Director of the Regional Adolescent Unit for the N.E. Thames region where he ran a very successful psychodynamically orientated unit for ten years. He has developed strong disagreement with the view that adolescents should be treated with severity. He believes that containment and understanding should be reinforced by understanding and firmness, and that, severity independently will only alienate adolescent youths even more. In other words there is likely to be a negative "therapeutic" response; a belief which is amply justified in his writing.

In his book Dr Perinpanayagam states very clearly and emphatically that boundaries of permissibility, behaviour-wise, are needed, but that negotiation, without compromising honesty and truth, is more fruitful and provokes much less destructive opposition. In other words a harsh regime provokes opposition even to the point of rebellion while no guidance imposes upon the young person (or group) a developmental process in which the boy or girl or group feels they get no help. This foreword does not do justice to the lively and refreshing illumination, which is shed by a study of the contents of this magnum opus.

A. HYATT WILLIAMS
Formerly Chairman of the Adolescent Department
of the Tavistock clinic, and Director of the London
Clinic of Psychoanalysis

FOREWORD

I am very pleased to have been asked to write a foreword to this book, for there are many qualities represented in it that I appreciate and admire. I value its straightforward language, its unaffected style and its passionate engagement with the problems of adolescence and adolescents. The author makes it quite clear where he stands -in pursuit of serious professional work with young people -the whole work enterprise being based on a humane understanding of the personal, family and societal dilemmas that young people have to deal with.

There are many books on adolescence on the market. Some are worthy tomes that give one a lot of theory, but don't really further practical application in the heat of everyday work with disturbed adolescents. Yet others give 'advice' as to what is to be done but with little clue as to how the individual 'pieces of good advice' might link together to put in place an overall professional approach to working with adolescents. This book falls into neither of these two traps. It gives the reader enough theory to enable the problems to be seen from a variety of perspectives and focal lengths, but it also gives a wealth of clinical illustration to make the book an invaluable tool for the worker with adolescents. But the whole point of work with adolescents is that it is about the work being kept in perspective -in the mind of the worker and also in external reality as it applies to teamwork. Nowhere is this more important than in adolescent residential settings. Here, understanding the adolescent is important, being aware of the staff dynamics essential as they invariably reflect the psychology and psychopathology of the client group, and managing the institutional pressures -in my view the only way of having a fair hope of therapeutic success and institutional survival.

It is particularly in this aspect of the book that the author's years of clinical, institutional and directorial experience shine through and enrich the reader. He makes it absolutely clear that caring for the staff is as essential and integral a part of running the institution as is looking after the adolescents. Without 'contained' staff in Bion's sense, it is not possible for the staff to contain the adolescents and for the process of growth for all concerned to proceed.

This book is a rich source of clinical, staff, institutional and managerial vignettes of the processes that occur in adolescent institutions; it is the intermingling and illustration of these strands that makes this book so gripping. Adolescence can be gripping for all of us, though it often leads to 'switching-off or 'burn-out' when the framework for understanding is lacking. The reader need fear no such outcome with this book, partly because it is the description of a personal journey of wonderment and discovery in the jungle of adolescence.

The author brings to the text a natural sensitivity, cultural awareness from having grown up in a multicultural, multilingual, multireligious community. Add to that real life experiences as International University boxing champion, medical school training, a personal psychoanalysis, and running an adolescent unit for many years, and you have a richness of practical and intellectual experience that is required reading for all working with disturbed adolescents.

ANTON OBHOLZER
Chair, Adolescent Department, Tavistock Clinic
and Chief Executive Tavistock & Portman NHS Trust

Contents

Introduction		xi
I	The Operation of Brookside Young People's Unit from 1975 to 1985	24
II	Both Psychodynamics and Behaviour Therapy are Needed	68
III	A Short History of the Adolescent Services from 1965	88
IV	A View of the Services Through Systems Theory	105
V	Psychiatry and Psychoanalytical Therapy – A Scientific View	116
VI	Objective-Subjectivism	139
VII	Individual Psychotherapy with Adolescents	149
VIII	Residential Treatment of Adolescents	190
IX	Some Common Phenomena	216
X	Some Interesting Cases	241
XI	The Alpha-Action	261
XII	About the Author	272

INTRODUCTION

An interesting thing about a good philosophical theory is that when it is finally postulated it feels as if you knew it all along, that it was always there to be seen. It just needed that person with the clear thinking to extract it from the surrounding mass of confusion. It is often made out of simple self-evident truths. Popper's formula, about how progress is made,

P1----> TS ---> EE --> P2,[1]

applicable to science and to any human endeavour, is one of these. Here, P1=the problem TS=Trial solutions, EE=Error elimination and P2=new problems arising out the solution of P1. If P1 and P2 are the same, then no progress has been made.

If one looks at the overall development of the adolescent services from the early nineteenth century, Popper's formula would show it as:

P1 -------Much activity---------P1

Where P1 is the question 'Does punishment solve the problem of juvenile delinquency and adolescent disturbance?' The 'much activity' in my formula above represents periods during the last two centuries in which it was shown that punishments and harsh treatment neither deter nor correct disturbed behaviour, and are followed by constructive changes and periods of real progress which last for a while but are then thwarted by changes in policy. This has been the pattern in the adolescent services from the early nineteenth century when Mary Carpenter fought passionately against the punishment and cruel treatment of young offenders. (Mays, J.B., 1975, *The Social Treatment of Young Offenders*, Longman, London and New York.)

The same question, P1, 'Does punishment and harsh treatment solve the problem of juvenile delinquency (synonymous with adolescent disturbance)?' is being asked today as it was in the 1850s.

ACTIVITY IN GREAT BRITAIN

In the mid-sixties there was a thoughtful and progressive move by the government of the day, following disastrous results in the control of adolescent misbehaviour and juvenile delinquency during the previous few decades. The Approved School system, with its harsh training for all delinquents together with *Behavioural* techniques, was abolished, and a White Paper, 'The Child, the Family and the Young Offender' was published, in which the many antecedents of delinquency were recognised and the notion of treatment being directed to the cause was favoured. It was the beginning of the idea of the Psychodynamic approach to adolescent disturbance.

Then in 1979, before Psychodynamics became widely recognised as a treatment method for disturbed adolescents, there was a change of government, and with it a change of policy and reintroduction of harsh treatment of delinquents. (See Chapter III 'A Short History of the Adolescent Services'.)

The new order culminated in a National Survey of the Adolescent Services by the Health Advisory Service (HAS), in 1985 and its report, *Bridges Over Troubled Waters* ([2]Horrocks). It was a devastating report for those few who were trained in Psychodynamics and knew its value. In a letter to the Bulletin of the Royal College of Psychiatry, the Chairman of the Association for Psychoanalytical Psychotherapy, in the NHS, ([3]Steiner), pointed out several deficiencies in the conduct of the survey. The chief of these was the composition of the steering committee, which contained a single psychiatrist who was not trained in Psychodynamics nor in Child Psychiatry, and there were the inevitable deficiencies that would follow. He noted the absence of the word 'Psychotherapy' (or any related concept), in the entire 77 pages of the document, and no recognition of the antecedents of adolescent disturbance. The overall conclusion, writing on behalf of some 200 staff of the NHS of all disciplines, was,

> …we have found deficiencies so glaring in the report that it would be a grave disservice to the needs of this group of patients were it permitted to proceed unchallenged, possibly to become a blueprint for a future national service.

It did become the blueprint for a future national service. Psychodynamics was wiped out of the adolescent services at a stroke.

Together with this, Brookside Young People's Unit, (YPU), the Regional Adolescent Unit for the N.E. Thames region, arguably the strongest psychodynamic unit in the country, was closed, on the *strong* recommendation of a review led by the same psychiatrist who conducted the national survey of the adolescent services for the HAS.

I was the Medical Director of Brookside YPU at the time. I too wrote about the National Survey of the adolescent services and its report (*Bridges Over Troubled Waters*) to the Bulletin of the Royal College ([4]Perinpanayagam). The staff and I had worked extremely hard in the regional unit and had carefully worked out and 'fine-tuned' policies and principles of management and treatment, which enabled us, with the minimum staff given to us, to operate as a second- or third-tier specialist service, treating the most disturbed adolescents in the region. The only complaints we had ever received were about the selectivity of patients we admitted, by disappointed referrers – we were a 20-bed unit operating in a region which required 74 beds according to regional statistical standards. We achieved an overall success rate of 70%. We were treating 17–19 residential patients at the time of closure, with no disasters of any nature. The closure of Brookside YPU, for those of us who knew it well, was something like the destruction of Cambodia by the Pol Pot regime. The details of the closure of Brookside YPU are in another book, *The Dossier of a Critical Closure: The story of an NHS Review* (Athena Press).

This book is my attempt to resurrect and share the thinking we did at Brookside YPU; a kind of thinking which is as relevant today as it was fifteen years ago. It is badly needed in the chaotic world of adolescence in Western culture, a culture which is progressively penetrating all parts of the world. The good intentions of the philosophy of 'Tough on crime and tough on the causes of crime', cannot be put into practice without the psychodynamic approach – it is the only method that seeks and attempts to deal with the cause.

PRINCIPLES OF MANAGEMENT AND TREATMENT

At Brookside we attempted common sense treatment of the youngsters by directing treatment to the cause. The principle of directing the solution of a problem to its cause pervaded every aspect of the work of the unit. It depended on honest discussion with the youngsters and ourselves, and trying to understand overt conscious expressions as well as the underlying covert unconscious communications – *Psychodynamic Treatment*.

We learned that this approach in combination with other relevant forms of treatment achieved quicker, better and long-lasting beneficial results, than methods which simply try to stop bad behaviour by restrictions and punishment in its various forms. It requires a degree of training of the Consultant and one or two senior staff in psychoanalytical thinking, interested conscientious staff, and regular frequent staff discussion.

COMPARATIVE SUCCESS RATES – TREATMENT OF THE CAUSE

In the Home Office document, 'Aspects of Crime: Young Offenders', compiled by the 'Crime and Criminal Justice Unit Research, Development and Statistics Directorate, April 1999, states, on page 20,

> The number of 10 to 17 year-olds sentenced for indictable offences has risen for four successive years. In 1997, nearly 41,000 males and 5,600 females aged 10 to 17 were sentenced in either magistrates' courts or the Crown Court.

and on page 26,

> Over four-fifths (88%) of 14 to 16 year-old males and 82 per cent of 17-year-old males were reconvicted within two years of release from prison. This is slightly more than older prisoners: 72 per cent of 18 to 20 year-olds are reconvicted.

> Among 10 to 17 year-olds, 79 per cent of those given a supervision order and 87 per cent of those who receive a probation order are reconvicted within two years. Conditional discharges and fines have the lowest rates of reconviction for young offenders. See figure below.

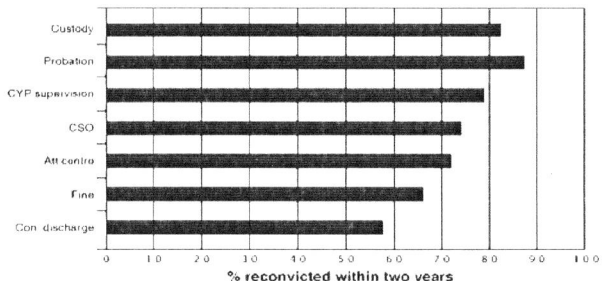

Reconviction rates after sentence of 10 to 17 year-olds: Sample of offenders sentenced for a standard list of offences in 1994 who were reconvicted of a standard list of offence within two years.*
From 'Aspects of Crime: Young Offenders', compiled by the "Crime and Criminal Justice Unit Research, Development and Statistics Directorate, Home Office, April 1999, page 27.

It is of particular significance that nowhere in the two Home Office documents I have read is there any mention of *the causes of the delinquency, and disposal being designed to meet the cause.*

A RECENT TREND

There is an overwhelming move in the academico-socio-political world today to rely on statistical evidence for answers to all problems. The cause is often ignored.

It is a self-evident truth, whether it be about a crack in the wall, a faulty motor car or a human condition, that treatment should be directed to the cause. Disinterest in the cause can lead to many far-reaching detrimental effects, apart from not solving the problem. It easily leads to fashions and rivalries in treatment

---

* One can see from this diagram that the reconviction rates are in the 80-90% range for those youngsters who have been convicted, whatever the disposal, and in the 50-60% range for those who have been given a conditional discharge. This seems to suggest the importance and power of *identity* especially for a growing adolescent. I think identity is a key issue for any human being anywhere in the world who seek to establish this after the basic needs of food, clothing and shelter have been achieved. How else can we understand the increasing ethnic conflicts all over the world and the demands for separate states?

methods, biases in favour of one treatment over another and polarisation, which can become very difficult to eradicate once it has been absorbed into the system, when a homeostatic resistance sets in. This is particularly so in a field like adolescence, which contains so many different kinds of specialists – parental, educational, psychological, medical, penal, and social services – each having a natural inclination to use and support their own particular expertise.

BROOKSIDE YOUNG PEOPLE'S UNIT
(BETWEEN 1975 AND 1985)

In Brookside we endeavoured to discover the cause of adolescent disturbance and then to direct treatment to the cause.

Firstly,

Of a random sample of disturbed adolescents referred to Brookside Young People's Unit, between 1975 and 1977, 87.9% were found to have damaged relationships with their parents. The other 12.1% were found to be suffering from a formal psychiatric illness. ([1]Perinpanayagam, 'Pathology of the Adolescent', BMJ, 1978; [5]Perinpanayagam)

The first group, (the 87.9 %), had no other causative factor. Many of those suffering from a formal psychiatric illness also had damaged relationship with parents.

Then,

Between the years 1976 and 1985 the unit was run as a psychodynamically orientated Unit, which dealt essentially with the problems caused by damaged relationships with significant people. The unit admitted only the most disturbed adolescents in the region, who had had failed treatment elsewhere – a tertiary service. All appropriate methods of treatment were used, except those that were in conflict with the psychodynamic approach. The rate of successful treatment outcome based on a five-year follow-up for recurrence of symptoms or offending, was estimated as around 70%. The average length of stay was nine months. ([9]Perinpanayagam)

INTRODUCTION

ADOLESCENT DISTURBANCE AND JUVENILE DELINQUENCY

There is no characterological dividing line between a conduct disordered adolescent and a delinquent youngster. One moves imperceptibly into the other. There is more of a difference between an emotionally disordered adolescent and a conduct-disordered one, yet one can switch from one into the other under the impact of forces that alter his or her internal state of mind. If one looks at the stories of these youngsters and the relatedness of events in their lives, it will be seen that there are many contributory causes for their disturbed and disturbing behaviour; the single underlying common factor however in all cases seen today *is damaged relationships with parents or significant people*. It is also the one cause whose effect is most detectable, and is the most susceptible to change for the better.

PSYCHODYNAMICS

I find myself in some difficulty when I am asked to explain what psychodynamic treatment of adolescents means because it means so many different things. It does not fall into any of the well-known stereotypes. It is not psychoanalysis, though the understanding gained from psychoanalysis is important. It is not behaviour therapy, though it incorporates behavioural principles in its practice, and it recognises the value of medically based formal psychiatry. I'd like to call the psychodynamics of adolescence *an attitude*, which recognises that the disturbed adolescent is the final product of his inherited qualities which have been modified by many years of painful disturbing experiences, within a frame which is bursting forth with indomitable creative internal forces – *the adolescent process*, which requires understanding and careful nurturing of the creative forces within him/her.

In practice it is a simple, sensitive, common sense treatment of the youngsters, which depends on discussion with them and trying to understand their overt conscious expressions as well as the underlying covert unconscious communications. It is treatment that tries to understand and deal with the cause of a problem.

While the definition I have given is simple, its practice has its difficulties. I think it will be useful for me to reproduce, at the end of this introduction, a slightly modified version of an article I wrote for the *British Medical Journal* in 1978 on the Psychodynamic Approach to Adolescence.

A BUILT-IN RESISTANCE

A key feature in psychodynamics is that it does not seek to alter behaviour through punishment. It is neither for nor against punishment. There are situations in which psychodynamics would recommend punishment if it is thought to be necessary for the resolution of a problem, for instance, when an offender's guilt over something he has really done is great and reparation is impossible.

One of the significant difficulties for the wholehearted acceptance of psychodynamics is its non-punitive aura which does not rest easily with an articulate majority. Human beings seem to have a deeply ingrained urge to hurt those who disturb/offend them, even though there has been ample evidence over the centuries (⁷Mays.) that harsh treatment and punishment neither deter nor correct offenders. Likewise, in spite of the daily events in our own lives and in those around us, which show that 'violence begets violence', the drive to retaliate, hurt, kill, and perpetuate a conflict, often seen in international situations, seems to supercede the far more profitable and wiser course of tolerance and understanding.

The observation of Sigmund Freud in his paper, '*A child is being beaten*' (⁸Freud) seems relevant to this human tendency. He speaks of many patients he had who as children of five or six had pleasurable fantasies of a child being beaten – fantasies which, he thought, could develop into sexual perversions of different kinds, or disappear in repression or reaction formation and sublimation. He said, '*very probably there are still more frequent instances of it among the far greater number of people who have not been obliged to come for analysis by manifest illness.*'

INTRODUCTION

THIS BOOK

In Chapter I, I have given a description of how the kind of work in Brookside YPU, till 1985, was developed. It contains an understanding of why it was eventually called 'Psychodynamically Orientated', even though we used all kinds of treatment.

Chapter II is about why Behaviour Therapy and Psychodynamics are both needed. Chapter III gives a short recent history of the Adolescent Services and how the service was deprived of the psychodynamic approach. Chapter IV gives a view of the service through Systems Theory as it has been for around fifteen years, without psychodynamics.

Chapters V and VI are about the validation of psychodynamics – A Scientific View of Psychodynamics and Accuracy of Interpretations. The rest of the book contains a more detailed and, I hope, a clearer account of psychodynamic work with adolescents. They include chapters on Individual Psychotherapy, Residential Treatment of adolescents applicable to both open and secure settings, and chapters on common group phenomena and some special cases.

The last chapter, which I have called The Alpha-Action, concerns an interpretation of some fundamental psychoanalytical ideas as described and explained by some of the greatest psychoanalytical thinkers of our time, such as Klein, Bion, Meltzer, and my teacher, mentor and friend, Arthur Hyatt Williams, to mention a few.

As I have always emphasised to the staff I work with and have taught, psychodynamics requires total honesty in the interactions between the treaters and the patients. There is no easy written down way to respond to the behaviour of the youngsters. The response must come from taking in each particular bit of behaviour and understanding it, and *giving back to the patient/offender the understood form of their behaviour*. It requires learning and development of the treaters.

Extract from the *British Medical Journal*, 1978, 1, pp288–289:

> THE PSYCHODYNAMIC APPROACH TO ADOLESCENCE
>
> *The world of adolescent psychiatry is something of a jungle. The*

different disciplines and workers often find themselves in conflict and confusion. Opinions about the most appropriate way of dealing with a disturbed adolescent differ and are held with conviction. Objectivity often becomes elusive, and feelings run high. The self-defeating intense emotional involvement of well-meaning but inexperienced workers is common in adolescent psychiatry, and even the most intelligent and skilled professionals can become irrational and deskilled when they become involved with a disturbed adolescent. At the other extreme some psychiatrists refuse even to see such patients. These phenomena rarely occur with psychiatrically ill children or adults.

Difficulties of adolescent psychiatry

Adolescents are confusing young people. Chronologically they are between children and adults; in truth they are both child and adult. They may feel and behave like children at one time and quickly switch to becoming adult. They deftly throw out a bit of pathology amidst a variety of normal developmental feelings and behaviour. They are highly adept at sensing the weak points of adults and using this knowledge to embarrass, attack, seduce, and manipulate adults. Even with the greatest objectivity it is difficult and confusing for those working with disturbed adolescents. It is even more so for the youngster, for he is often not aware of what he is doing.

The difficulties that occur because of the very nature of adolescence are only one aspect of the problem. A more important factor, and the one that causes the greatest problems in dealing with disturbed adolescents, is that the intense feelings experienced by him/her are similar to one's own more hidden ones. It is difficult for the adult helper to separate himself from the youngster and regard him/her clinically and objectively. Most disturbed adolescents do not look ill and cannot be placed in a diagnostic category with a recognised treatment. It is relatively easy to place a psychiatrically ill adult in a diagnostic category and to keep aloof, calling him ill and oneself well, and to look at him clinically. Equally, to separate oneself from a disturbed child is relatively easy; after all, he is only a child and the helper is an adult. But the disturbed adolescent is neither a child nor an ill adult: he is a youngster who suffers intensely from feelings of depression, anger, fear, guilt, and confusion – feelings common to all normal adults. His feelings are so similar to one's own that the boundaries between him and the adult helper are blurred.

It is a myth that adults grow out of adolescence into a state of sexual and emotional maturity, confidence, and independence with a well-crystallised identity. Many aspects of adolescence remain with normal adults in varying degrees of intensity throughout adult life, and when one is confronted by youngsters with problems one's own adolescent aspects are touched – often exacerbating any unresolved pathological aspects of the personality. It is this that creates the greatest difficulty and confusion in dealing with the disturbed youngster. Inability to recognise this confusion results in an 'acting out' and consequently an attempt to get rid of the adolescent, or a confused involvement with him/her that perpetuates one or more aspects of the problem. To be able to treat most adolescent disturbances, the psychiatric worker must experience and deal with the feelings aroused in him by contact with the disturbed youngster. If he attempts to avoid this painful and difficult contact or allows himself to succumb to the feelings engendered he will not give adequate help.

Nature of dynamic psychiatry

The term dynamic psychiatry is ill understood and often misused. Many believe it to be some impractical, ineffective, and esoteric exercise indulged in by people who have time on their hands and who play around in casual fashion with people and ideas. In fact, the dynamic approach is the only valid and practical treatment for most disturbed adolescents, though combination with other techniques and chemotherapy may be useful and necessary.

The basis of dynamic psychiatry is the fact that relationships with 'significant' people have an effect on development and current behaviour, and that behaviour can be altered by examining and understanding relationships and feelings. If the unconscious mind is acknowledged, then, in undertaking this examination, you must observe and take into account more than what appears on the surface in others as well as within yourself. Techniques used in this type of work vary from psychoanalysis – the most complex, deep, and subtle of them – at one extreme, to less ambitious and more practicable techniques, such as psychodrama and role-playing, at the other. Other techniques, such as behaviour therapy and chemotherapy, could be used to complement dynamic psychiatry provided that such combinations are carefully undertaken, well understood, and designed to meet the requirements of the individual case; otherwise they could work against each other and defeat the primary object of helping the patient.

Dynamic psychiatry is a form of thinking and an attitude that is unusual in the ordinary course of life. Whatever the form of society, everyone has been brought up to behave well, to be pleasant and nice, and to make himself and others comfortable and happy. Society's aim has been to curb 'bad' feelings and impulses and to create people who are acceptable to others. One has learnt, with varying degrees of success, to push away into forgotten corners of the mind one's 'badness' and nasty feelings, not only through social conditioning but also because these feelings are unpleasant. In some cases these 'bad' feelings have been inadequately dealt with and cause trouble. Dynamic psychiatry brings out the long-forgotten impulses and experiences underlying a patient's disturbance and makes them available for examination. It might then be possible to resolve the unconscious conflicts and problems, or at least put them away more effectively.

Dynamic psychiatry is difficult for both the patient and the worker. For the patient, at first, it seems as if life is being made even more difficult; he is being forced into owning unpleasant – perhaps frightening – feelings, the very thing he has been trying to avoid and hopes to escape from by coming for treatment.

For the worker, to grasp and hold on to the value of the concepts used in dynamic work – something that goes so much against his natural tendency – is not easy. To be touched emotionally by the disturbance of the patient makes him anxious and insecure. It is most difficult for the doctor. Doctors have had a specialised training in treatment based on antidynamic principles in which they have developed confidence over the years. They have also developed a feeling of security and an uncomfortable yet satisfying feeling of near omnipotence as a result of projections onto them from lay people. It is with the greatest difficulty that they abandon the security of these attitudes in the face of all the internal and external forces that work towards their retaining them.

Ever since mental illnesses began to be regarded as amenable to treatment, attempts have been made to classify them on some rational basis so that treatment could be administered in a simple, logical manner in accordance with such classifications. While efforts at classification continue, I believe that the human mind is increasingly recognised to be too complex and subject to too many variables to permit a simple medical model of mental illness. This is true of adolescent psychiatry more than any other branch of psychiatry.

Any rational and serious attempt to treat adolescent problems must take the causative factors into account. Adolescent disturbance usually results from damaged relationships with significant people in their lives. Treatment must take these factors into account and therefore must be on dynamic lines.

K.S.P.

REFERENCES

[1] Magee, B., *Popper*, London, Fontana Modern Masters, Ed. Frank Kermode, 1986, pp.65–66.

[2] Horrocks, Dr P, *Bridges Over Troubled Waters,* A Report from the NHS Health Advisory Services for Disturbed Adolescents, March 1986, ISBN 85197 053.

[3] Steiner, John, Bulletin of the Royal College of Psychiatrists, Correspondence, Vol.10, September 1986.

[4] Perinpanayagam, K.S., Bulletin of the Royal College of Psychiatrists, Correspondence, Vol. 11, Feb. 1987.

[5] Perinpanayagam, K.S., 1978, *British Medical Journal,* 1, pp.424–425.

[6] Perinpanayagam, K.S., 1987, Response to the Review Report, to the North East Thames Region.

[7] Mays, J.B., 1975 *The Social Treatment of Young Offenders*, Longman, London and New York, p.3.

[8] Strachey, *The Complete Psychological Works of Sigmund Freud,* Standard edition, Ed. James Strachey, 1917-1919, Vol XVII, pp.79-204).

Chapter I
THE OPERATION OF BROOKSIDE YOUNG PEOPLE'S UNIT FROM 1975 TO 1985

The Beginnings of Brookside Young People's Unit

The Opening and Development of the Philosophy of Treatment
Brookside YPU was opened in August 1975. It was the first adolescent unit in the North East Thames Region and I was appointed as its first Consultant Psychiatrist and Medical Director. It was a twenty-bedded unit serving a population of three and a half million, largely of social classes four and five. Till Brookside there was no NHS facility for the admission of disturbed adolescents. Adolescents who required admission were reluctantly admitted to General Psychiatric Hospitals. There had been huge protests about this from parents and even more from the professionals in General Psychiatric Hospitals. Every Consultant Psychiatrist in the region welcomed the opening of the unit and expected that the few adolescents who were admitted to their wards would easily be accommodated in the Regional Unit. In fact the regionally agreed norm for adolescent beds for its population of three and a half million was seventy-four.

The clinical staff given for twenty inpatients was: one Consultant, one Senior Registrar in rotation with the Royal London Hospital, one Nursing Officer and twenty nurses, of which ten were qualified Registered Mental Nurses and ten were unqualified nursing assistants; one social worker, one psychologist, and one locum art therapist. (I later negotiated with management to have that same art therapist in a permanent position by sacrificing one staff nurse.) There was a school attached to the unit run by the local educational authority, which had a headmaster and two specialist teachers. The unit was located in the grounds of Goodmayes Hospital, Goodmayes, Essex.

The school had been established a few months before I arrived. There is a brook running at the extreme end of the grounds and the educational authority had named it 'THE BROOKSIDE SCHOOL'. That it was a misnomer for the adolescent unit was readily recognised and together with the school authorities and hospital management, we jointly came up with 'BROOKSIDE YOUNG PEOPLE'S UNIT'. It was a good start.

The co-operation I received from the hospital management and the school authorities in setting up the unit in those early years was, I felt, extraordinary. I also had the unstinting support of the late Sir Desmond Pond, who at that time was Professor of Psychiatry at the London Hospital, where I had an honorary academic attachment. He had been on my appointment committee.

The first staff person to be appointed was the Nursing Officer, to be in charge of the nurses and nursing in the unit. A very experienced charge nurse from the Northgate Clinic, where I had worked for the previous seven years, was appointed to the job. I knew her well. She was comfortable in her position of authority and it turned out had a particular talent for choosing nursing staff who were well suited to the working with adolescents. We were also fortunate in having appointed a very thoughtful and experienced senior registrar and an enthusiastic young American psychologist, whose experience across the seas gave a refreshing input into the system.

The education authority wanted a ceremonial opening and, without consulting me, no doubt imagining that I would approve, had organised a gala opening with the Mayor of Ilford as chief guest. I thought gala openings were most inappropriate for the beginning of an adolescent unit. But the appointed staff and I joined the celebration, regarding it as the formal opening of the school. When I was invited to speak, I reminded everyone that the NHS part of the unit saw the opening not as an occasion for celebration and rejoicing but as the opportunity to emphasise our apprehension about the difficult task that lay ahead. We got ourselves into the Kleinian Depressive Position.

The management of Goodmayes Hospital, in their keenness to ensure that they would provide the best support for the unit, had built up a team of their toughest male nurses, to be called in for help when the disturbed adolescents erupted in violence and rioting. One of my first tasks was to ask them to dismantle this 'Emergency Task Force'. I had learnt that people and adolescents in particular had a tendency to live up to the expectations pushed into them by adults. I assured the Goodmayes Management that there would be no riots and no violence. The next thing I did was to ask them to remove the red 'emergency buttons' placed in each of the staff offices, for the use of staff to call for help when the adolescents threatened or attacked them. They did not remove them because they said it would have been too expensive to rewire the place. But the message from me to the managers of the unit, about a certain attitude and approach to the work of the unit, was clear. During the ten years that the unit functioned there was only one single occasion on which the emergency button was pressed, and that was by a patient who had become frightened by his own violent feelings.

Having worked in a residential adolescent unit for seven years I had learnt well that adolescent feelings, which often remain dormant in adults and staff, are inevitably touched by close association with disturbed youngsters. If these adolescent feelings in staff are not recognised and managed, there is the danger that staff will collude with the youngsters as if they were on equal terms or even instigate exciting, destructive, adolescent behaviour. I was acutely aware of how much more trouble and violence is caused among adolescents by staff reactions and counter-reactions to ordinary adolescent behaviour than by the youngsters themselves.

I brought in many ideas and knowledge about the management of a residential service and how we could interact usefully with normal and disturbed adolescents. But I did not bring in preconceived ideas about the kind of treatment we should use. I had had a varied personal and clinical experience and an understanding that in working with disturbed adolescents one must use one's total life experience, and also that it required specialised skills, which only come from training and experience in the field as a learner.

THE MODUS OPERANDI AT BROOKSIDE

Having had a broad training and considerable experience and confidence in different kinds of treatment at the Northgate Clinic, and the different General Psychiatric hospitals I had worked in, I was comfortable in using any kind of treatment and in working with the most disturbed and difficult youngsters. There were some adolescent problems I felt we should not undertake, amongst them was the treatment of drug addiction. I had had ample experience of failure in this at enormous emotional expense. I was also determined that at Brookside we should not attempt to simply follow the practice at the Northgate Clinic, though we should use the valuable experience I had gained there. The Northgate Clinic dealt with mid/late adolescents between the ages of sixteen and twenty-one and there were some over twenty-one in the early stages. Brookside had to deal with early and mid adolescents – a very different proposition; and the staff structure in the two places were very different. *'Play it by ear, and adjust to the needs of the service'* was the motto in those early stages. The Northgate Clinic, under the directorship of Dr Brian O'Connell, which I regard as the cradle of my development of adolescent treatment skills, did it par excellence. They changed from a research unit into a treatment unit in order to meet the needs of the youngsters, and again changed to admitting girls to meet the regional need.

The idea of not having a preconceived idea of the kind of treatment we would use fitted in well with my wish to do research into the cause of adolescent disturbance and delinquency, for which we could not have a biased sample. I asked the Region for a specialist research post to be established, but this was refused. So I decided to do the research myself with the help of the senior registrar and the Department of Psychology of the London Hospital. We made no announcements about the type of treatment we were using and were open to referrals of any kind, literally from anyone – general practitioners, psychiatrists, specialists of any kind, Social Services, Probation departments, schools, Child Guidance Clinics, Children's Homes, etc. I wanted a *random sample*. Having collected and analysed an acceptable sample of referrals, I did in fact publish the research results. (*The British Medical Journal*, 1978, 1, 424–425.)

While the referrals were random, the youngsters we chose to take on for residential work were carefully chosen, for their ability to recognise that they had a difficulty, for their wish to change, their ability and wish to make relationships with adults/parents/staff. We looked at factors that were beyond their own control, which would interfere with their ability to take responsibility for their behaviour. Psychotics were given the appropriate medication, which invariably brought their symptoms under control. I was wary of taking in adolescents who had crossed the natural familial and social boundaries and had *enjoyed* the experience – such as physical assaults or abuse of parents or parental figures, and taking and driving. We were very careful of attempting residential treatment with youngsters charged with 'Taking and Driving', an offence in which they had crossed that all-important boundary between child and adult, which went together with a fantasy of omnipotence in controlling a source of such power (the adult world), and an exhilarating feeling of triumph over authority, when driving at high speed.

Sometimes we had to do some work with the referred youngsters in order to draw out their wish for help and their wish to make relationships with staff which lay just below the surface. We did not simply accept what the youngsters said as a true statement of their intentions. We recognised that there were unconscious motivations and a variety of factors that would lead them to cover up their real motivation. For instance, youngsters on a charge and awaiting sentencing are likely to say anything to get out of the difficult situation they are in and actually mean it at the time. Likewise, a youngster who badly needs and wants help may refuse to express the wish because they fear coming into the unit because of some previous experience or fear of being bullied by some other youngsters they had noticed in the unit.

The nurses too were carefully chosen for their ability to relate to the youngsters and their capacity to contain stressful material and to recognise and acknowledge weaknesses in themselves.

Most of the unqualified nursing assistants were graduates – intelligent young men and women who were keen to work with adolescents and learn, who thought the lowly job and low pay were not obstacles. I found that the unqualified nurses who came directly into psychodynamic work learned how to interact psychodynamically with adolescents more easily than the qualified nurses who had to unlearn much of the practice they had developed in Psychiatric hospitals, where medication was the major mode of treatment. At Brookside treatment was based on the interactions between patient and staff, where the staff had to cope with the full impact of the pathology of the patients.

In Practice

We worked with the adolescents first as day-patients. They attended school and then stayed on for discussions in groups. There was a morning meeting with all the youngsters and staff, a combined school assembly and a community meeting, for discussion of problems and difficulties the adolescents had in school and with the NHS staff. When the youngsters were able to talk openly about their troubles at home, we made links between their difficulties with the staff and their troubles at home. This outpatient work went on while the practical arrangements for residential work progressed. It was in February 1976 that we had the first admission of residential patients. It worked out fairly well because a point had been reached at which the youngsters were refusing to go home when the time came for the inpatient part to be opened.

We started the residential unit with six youngsters. The youngsters enjoyed being in Brookside and talking with staff. I recently came across a report written by an ex-resident at about that time, in which she has given an uninvited description of Brookside in a report she had written for a formal enquiry in which she was involved. Her description was:

> I am a married woman with four children, a son of twenty-one and triplets, two boys and a girl who are seven years old. My date of birth is …May 1961. I have worked for the Inland Revenue for fifteen years… Because my school education had previously been interrupted, between 1981 and 1984, I attended college and

obtained O levels and A levels... I took advantage of a career break to undertake a degree and graduated in 1998 with a BA in Social and Employment Studies. I also hold a certificate in counselling and do voluntary work for the Citizens Advice Bureau. ...My father was an alcoholic and a gambler and was violent towards my mother, who in turn was violent towards us, her children... From 1972 until 1973 I went to school in Basildon. Eventually my mother decided I was too much trouble and she could not cope with me... and I was sent to a boarding school for maladjusted children. I was the victim of bullying when I was there. When I left the school I spent the summer with my father in a caravan on a campsite, when he sexually abused me... My mother was hostile to me and did not want me back... In February 1975 or 1976 I was admitted to a residential unit for emotionally disturbed adolescents, which I believe was called Brookside Adolescent Unit. It was a brand new unit built on the grounds of Goodmayes Hospital. I recall I was only the seventh person to be admitted and was able to choose which bed I wanted in the four-bedded room... Brookside had a real community feeling. I loved it while I was there. I felt as if I belonged there and regarded it as my home. There was a school attached which I attended. I was able to be myself and have fun. There was always somebody to talk to and all the staff were very kind. Until then I had not met many kind people. We had regular group meetings with three or four residents and a nurse when we talked about our problems. I do not recall having one-to-one discussions with anybody...

While the experience of the patients as described by her was a positive one, the aim of the staff, as we discussed in our daily staff meetings, was to recognise and deal with their anxieties and to keep them safe and support their healthy development.

We did not start individual therapy with any of the youngsters because there did not seem any need for it at that time. The staff met daily for discussion about the group meetings we had with the youngsters and our daily interactions with them in the community. The staff and patients seemed to be gaining a lot from these. (More about individual therapy later on.)

STAFF CULTURE

When speaking to and about the residents collectively we

addressed them by different names – 'residents', 'youngsters', 'patients', 'adolescents', depending on the demands of the situation. They were in fact all of these. Never did we address them as 'children' or 'kids' nor treat them as such. We did not want to foster and promote the childish aspects of the youngsters, though we recognised that all of them were children in many ways. A universal quality in adolescents is their hatred of being *addressed* as children, while at the same time many of them demand being *treated* like children.

The aims of staff were to keep the patients safe, to listen to them and to discover the causes of their anxiety and distress, to observe peculiarities or abnormal behaviour and to prevent them from destructive means of defending against their fears or pain. All or as many as possible of the interactions of the staff with the youngsters was looked at and examined in our daily staff meetings. We took detailed histories of every youngster, from the time of their birth, and saw that they all had damaged and disturbed relationships with significant adults, especially their parents. The recognition that each of them had much to be angry about and serious discussion of these issues did much to alleviate the pain they felt and to prevent expression of their anger in action.

In our daily staff meetings I emphasised that it is the bad feelings within the patients that we should seek out and address, not the good ones; it is those which cause them trouble. We paid particular attention to their angry feelings about staff and we found that these were often feelings transferred from their experiences with parents – sometimes the youngsters were not aware of their anger with parents.

The transference of angry feelings from the past onto staff is one of the most important ways in which the unconscious feelings of a youngster (or an adult) can be understood. But I had observed that all too often, staff and qualified therapists alike tend to dismiss the patient's angry feelings about them as 'transference' without adequate examination of themselves and recognising the possibility that the anger of the patient may be legitimate in terms of the real relationship. So I made it a rule in our examination of the staff-patient interactions to first examine what actually transpired between staff and patient (the real relationship), and whether in fact the staff had done something to incur the patient's anger, before beginning to even consider it as transference.

I emphasised that the youngsters will feel safe in the unit and be contented only if they know that we the staff are truly interested in them and are working for their benefit, even if the necessary restrictions and deprivations imposed on them are disliked by them. One of the things we discovered, with some surprise, is that many adolescents truly believe that their parents and adults in authority enjoy depriving them of enjoyable things. This led us to examine our own motivations, and we discussed and looked within ourselves for characteristics like an enjoyable feeling of power over the youngsters which can lead us to exercise the power simply for its own sake (which I believe does happen widely in the bureaucratic world); staff envy of youth which has been lost to us forever; and other such motivations which would lead the youngsters to feel and believe what they did.

In our daily community meetings, attended by all the patients and staff including the teachers, I always found a slot to seek out anything that the patients felt was bad which was happening in the unit, and any dissatisfactions or anger they had with staff, and strove to understand their feelings.

It was the least experienced staff and the lowest in the hierarchy, the nursing assistants, who bore the brunt of the anger and attacks of the youngsters. Even though I interacted directly with the disturbed adolescents, as the Consultant I often received their anger at third hand, as it were. I never failed to appreciate this, and to note that their salaries were much less than mine, and my concern went some way towards mitigating the distress felt by them.

The daily staff meetings were used as training experiences for staff through discussion of the difficulties staff were having with the youngsters. The community meetings were discussed and the staff were encouraged to question me and each other about what we did and said, which I believed would lead to mutual learning and kept me on my toes. I had learnt well through the sensitivity meetings at the Northgate Clinic and my personal training psychoanalysis to cope with the discomfort of being questioned and criticised.

The staff meetings were not only used as clinical learning opportunities, but also for discussions about staff discontent and disagreements. I made it a point to continuously invite staff to bring into open discussion any discontent about the work of the unit whenever I saw the slightest evidence for it, and with it, any anger or dissatisfaction with me, as the head of the unit. I had a firm belief, which I expressed many a time, that if things were not working well in the unit it is the head of the unit who should be looked at. In a good organisation, all types of responsibility are passed up the hierarchy and support is passed downward. We reserved one staff meeting a week for discussion of staff discontent, which we called 'The Sensitivity Meeting'. Even though this once a week meeting with a special remit of talking about the disturbing feelings of staff was necessary, I emphasised to staff that all staff meetings were sensitivity meetings; that discontent should be brought up whenever staff felt the need to do so.

Even though I had overall responsibility, I was clear about the Nursing Officer's role and responsibility as far as the nursing structure was concerned. I did not want to interfere with her work unless there was clear evidence of something going wrong. My relationship with her was continuously looked at and brought into discussion.

The culture in the unit was all about relationships and roles. Relationships between patients, between patients and their families, between patients and staff, and between staff and staff, were constantly discussed. The importance of staff maintaining their adult, caring, therapeutic role with patients was emphasised.

Special relationships between the youngsters and staff, whether the staff were specially trained in psychotherapy or not, were supported and special relationships of youngsters with each other were discouraged (but not friendships). Special relationships between adolescents could result in the youngsters misleading each other and becoming locked-in in ill-judged relationships which went beyond their control. We had a clear unambiguous policy of 'no sexual relationships within the unit'. (See the section on Adolescent Sexuality).

One of the things that held us strongly together was my own genuine interest in the work of the unit, which I think was clearly evident. I was clearly 'in charge' and the patients regarded me as the feared authority as well as the safe benign carer. I was easily available on the telephone twenty-four hours a day to the nurses on duty and to the Senior Registrar. I never hesitated to come into the unit whenever it was necessary – a policy which I learned well from Dr Brian O'Connell at the Northgate Clinic. I was aware that they were trying very hard to work with the youngsters correctly, which was not at all easy. They were in the front line as it were, and absorbed the worst of the pathology of the patients.

A useful practical notion I brought in for the comfort of staff, especially the younger ones, was that every staff member should regard themselves as forty years old, irrespective of their age; and every patient should be regarded as a growing child, irrespective of theirs. There were three qualities one should strive for in staff relationships with patients – 1. Genuine interest in the patient; 2. Non-possessive warmth; 3. Empathy. These qualities of a therapist were first talked of by Carl Rogers, I believe.

THE WORK OF THE UNIT

It was only after we had gathered an adequate random sample of referrals for the research I had planned and analysed them that we decided to make a statement about the kind of treatment we were using.

While the majority of referrals for admission had Conduct and Emotional Disorders (87.9%), I also admitted those relatively few youngsters who had formal psychiatric illnesses – the psychotics and phobias who respond to medication and behaviour therapy.

The Psychotics

The psychotics were at first feared by the nursing assistants and some qualified non-medical staff. They were not welcomed by the other adolescents, who would at times demand that they be removed from the unit in which 'normal' people live. We discussed this fear often when we had a psychotic patient.

With patients – We put them in touch with their own feelings of madness - all adolescents, at some point in their development, feel mad or wonder if they are mad because of their intense and conflicting feelings about parents. We discussed this with them and helped them to recognise these feelings of 'madness' in themselves. This led to great gains in the youngsters' thoughtfulness and in the acceptance of the psychotics.

With staff – Having been in analysis myself and discovered psychotic aspects to my personality, I was not afraid to talk to staff of the fear of the psychotic aspects within ourselves being touched, and becoming psychotic ourselves.

All this led to much greater comfort in dealing with the psychotics we admitted.

Medication

I prescribed medication for those patients who were clearly psychotic, which, except in rare exceptions, led to perfectly normal behaviour, if the medication was carefully monitored and the side effects were dealt with effectively.

When I took in an adolescent who needed medication or when I talked of giving medication, to one who was already resident, I always met with a barely concealed resistance from all but the psychiatrically trained staff. I thought the resistance was because the use of medication was not fully understood by the non-medical staff, and unlike any other form of treatment it was the sole prerogative of those who were medically trained, the only area in which the others could not feel equal to the doctors. I often discussed this question when medication was used.

It turned out that the psychotics were in fact easier to manage and treat than the youngsters with conduct and emotional disorders. The psychotics were obviously ill. The boundary between them and the staff was clear. The staff could easily separate themselves from the psychotics and treat them as needing help, and feel safe and comfortable in their own sanity. The psychotics too felt ill, and they were grateful for the feelings of normality on the medication. The situation between the emotional and conduct disorders and staff was very different. Here the patients do not look ill and often do not feel ill. They experience the same emotions as staff who are often emotionally touched by the feelings of the adolescents. This often leads to anxiety in staff and danger of collusion with them or harsh rejection. Examination and understanding of staff feelings became of prime importance in the unit, which sometimes led to staff distress but overall to staff development.

We also recognised that psychosis did not necessarily obviate the manipulative behaviour of non-psychotic adolescents.

Mixed Treatment

Even though we eventually called ourselves psychodynamically orientated, we were constantly aware that we lived the Behavioural philosophy. Many of the staff had experience in it and I had a particular belief in its value (see Chapter II, 'Both… are Needed'). We used it freely in a natural way reinforcing good behaviour and discouraging bad behaviour.

The palpable relief and pleasure of staff when a particularly inhibited, soft-spoken, youngster, who we knew had much fear of his own hidden anger, burst forth in anger at one of the staff, acted as a huge natural behavioural reinforcement for losing his fear of his own anger. This then led to further psychodynamic discussion about his anger, which he could not now deny, and associated hidden feelings. All this made him a more confident and effective youngster.

We also used it more formally in order to enhance our efforts to bring out the suppressed and hidden 'bad' feelings of the youngsters.

Example:

> Alan had been brought up from an early age by his stepdad and very dominating mother, who insisted on his good behaviour, which included the non-use of slang words or the expression of anger in any form, either by him or his stepdad. When we found that he could not shake off the embargo placed on him even in the unit, which constantly interfered with his free expression of underlying 'bad' feelings which were causing him trouble, we organised a behavioural programme for him in which he was rewarded for expression of genuine angry feelings towards staff. The feelings had to be genuine. He very soon learned to accept his legitimate anger, which helped him greatly in his further exploration of his inner world.

Adolescents who had phobias of different types such as agoraphobia, or phobias for travelling by bus or train, were always given classical behavioural desensitisation, as well as the psychotherapeutic discussions in order to deal with the underlying cause.

These are examples of behavioural work, which are not in conflict with our primary aim of searching for underlying causes. The only kind of behaviour therapies we did not use were those that led to suppression of feelings, which involved punishment of the youngsters, even if they were token punishments.

Whatever the kind of treatment we used, it became clear that resolving the problem involved seeking and dealing with the cause. This was often far removed from the way they presented and lay deeply hidden from the conscious mind. It required a degree of training and knowledge of psychodynamics. We therefore decided to use the term 'Psychodynamically Orientated' to describe the work of the unit.

The term 'psychodynamic' had different derivations, which were applicable to the work we did. There was the contrast with a 'psychostatic' condition (if such a term exists), which deals with disease entities that affect the mind, which do not depend on or change with interactions, and need to be treated with drugs, as in General Psychiatric hospitals. In our conduct and emotionally disordered patients there was a perpetual movement of emotions between staff and patients and changes in the reactions of each. The interactions with the patients were alive; we could catch it in the air, as it were, and change its course by a judicious sentence. We defined psychodynamics as that method which recognises the importance of relationships with significant people, events and things, conscious and unconscious, in the causation, the perpetuation and resolution of disturbed behaviour. In fact our practice was *truly eclectic* in that we used the psychodynamic method as well as all other known methods in such a way that they would not contradict each other.

RESIDENTIAL COMMUNITY WORK (ON THE FLOOR)

While we used small group therapy, large group therapy, (and later on, Individual psychotherapy), it was the COMMUNITY THERAPY, (On-the-Floor) where the staff and youngsters interacted during all aspects of the daily living of the patients from the time they awoke or were woken from bed, through the events of the day, and evening activities, which formed the essential core of the treatment and were the most effective. It was treatment in which all staff participated, for which all the staff had intensive in-service training in daily staff meetings, as well as external psychodynamic training.

The late evening and night interactions with staff who were departing home after their evening shift was of particular importance. It was the time the youngster would imagine that the staff would be leaving them and be going to their own families. It was a time when the adolescents would be in touch with all the disturbing feelings of hurt, anger, sadness, depression and jealousy involved with the deprivations in their own family relationships. Much thinking and work went into devising programmes that would take into account the severely distressing feelings of the patents during this period – the aim being to put staff in touch with the sad feelings of the youngsters and the youngsters to know that the staff were in touch and understood. If the night staff had a bad night dealing with the disturbing behaviour of the youngsters, it was the work of the evening staff and how they left the unit which would be examined first.

We observed that if the psychodynamic philosophy of the unit was being followed by the staff, the adolescents would reproduce all the problems they manifested in their lives at home and in the wider community, through their interactions in the residential community. Their disturbed behaviour (Pathological), would occur together with the ordinary, natural, adolescent behaviour. Distinguishing between pathological and normal adolescent behaviour and the reaction/response of the staff, was an essential part of the therapy done in the unit. Here we made an important difference between responding and reacting to the behaviour of the youngsters.

Reactions and Responses

Reactions are important: adolescents want and need spontaneous reactions from adults in order to learn about themselves. As they reach puberty and adolescence they experience the most powerful biological, hormonal and emotional changes within themselves, which makes them unfamiliar and uncomfortable with what is going on in and around them. One of the most important ways they learn about themselves and their newly developing abilities and the world around them is through the reactions of others, especially of the adults and authority figures they come into contact with. So spontaneous reactions from staff to the behaviour of the youngsters is important. It is demanded by them. While these reactions form an important part of their healthy development, care must be taken that the reactions are couched in terms that do not destroy the youngster's confidence and his freedom to experiment and make mistakes.

Example:

> A new staff member who had learned how important reactions were to youngsters and who was given to expressing herself just as she felt, reacted to a fourteen-year-old who made a rude face and noise at her by reacting with an even ruder expression and said, 'You are disgusting, you are worse than an animal.' I was there at the time and I came in immediately to protect the youngster and try to mitigate the damage that statement would have done.
>
> It was difficult for me to the explain to the new staff that there are different kinds of spontaneous reactions and that we staff as trained professionals should have such an understanding of the struggles of adolescents, that our spontaneous, natural reactions to them would be one of understanding.

In contrast:

> Another youngster of fourteen who had had a very emotionally deprived life started secondary school for the first time. He had been in the unit for sometime and had been on home tuition. He was a timid, gentle boy who had made himself endearing to the staff. He was a slow learner. After a few weeks in school he returned one evening, joined the house meeting and within a short time uttered some foul abuse at one of the staff. Another staff reacted immediately and said, 'Mark, I am surprised at that. You are not like this usually. Is this what you learn in school? You may not realise that what you have said is very rude and hurtful.' Mark apologised immediately, but he seemed proud of what he had done. All the staff felt proud and pleased that he was developing.

Reactions can be harmful.

Invariably adolescents recreate, in the residential unit, the unhappy situations they have had at home with their parents. Parents generally react to the youngster's disturbing behaviour, to which in turn the youngsters react and parents react again and so on creating a vicious cycle which perpetuates the problem. Freud has suggested, I believe, that this recreation of bad experiences is a function of the death instinct – something that is self-destructive. In our experience at Brookside we found that while such recreation of bad experiences can be self-destructive if the staff, like parents, simply react to their disturbing behaviour; but it could be turned into something very constructive and rewarding for the youngster if the staff *responded* in a thoughtful, therapeutic way instead of *reacting* in the invited way – that is, to observe and take in and contain the behaviour of the youngster, try to understand why, and where that behaviour comes from, and respond in a thoughtful way.

Example:

> It became clear after a while that Doreen, an intelligent fifteen-year-old girl, was in continual difficulty with staff in violent arguments about one trivial thing or another. Careful consideration and discussion about these quarrels with staff showed that the arguments were about entirely unimportant matters created by Doreen; and that she would finally subside into a satisfied calm after the argument went on for a while and she was firmly told off by staff. The calm would last for a while after which the arguments would start again.

I was reminded of one of the papers by Freud, described by Dr A.H.Williams, which had impressed me in my student days – 'Criminal from a sense of Guilt' (Freud, S., *Complete Psychological Works*, Vol. XIX, p.49, The Hogarth Press, London, 1965). Dr Williams, who had himself treated innumerable offenders and recidivists at Wormwood Scrubs, described how recidivists repeatedly commit offences in order to satisfy an urge to be punished for some feeling of guilt, deep within them – about something in their unconscious minds. Punishing them, as they demanded by imprisonment, i.e. by simply reacting to their behaviour, merely allayed an uncomfortable feeling temporarily, after which the disturbing feeling of guilt recurred and the pattern is repeated.

Bearing this in mind after full discussion of Freud's paper, we decided that staff should not engage in the 'battle' with Doreen by reacting to her invitation; and instead should respond thoughtfully saying something like, 'Doreen, you are trying to make me argue with you, I do not want to do that, I want to talk with you. We can talk about so many interesting things.' I emphasised that each staff person should understand what we were trying to do and use his or her own language.

> After a while Doreen stopped her arguments and her underlying guilt emerged. She confessed with great shame that she had hit her mother on her large, pregnant, abdomen, because of the intensely disturbing feelings she had about the impending birth of the new baby. This amongst other things she had said indicated that she was deeply distressed about her feelings of jealousy about the other girls in the unit. This feeling affected her in all areas of her life and made her miserable.

This reproduction of disturbing feelings and behaviour they have had at home occurs in every aspect of the adolescent's life – sibling rivalry, wish to be the only child, stealing when they feel unloved, feeling of being disfavoured by a parent, bullying and being bullied, refusal to engage in studies for many reasons. These apparently simple problems, when left unrecognised and unresolved, can be unknowingly perpetuated or if suppressed by punishments, be left to ferment within and lead to quite seriously disturbed behaviour far removed from the original problem.

Example from Whitefriars:

> The Police wanted John, an intelligent, good-looking boy of sixteen, to be charged with Attempted Murder, but he was eventually charged with Grievous Bodily Harm. He had made a planned attack on another boy who had sustained a fractured arm and leg and several fractured ribs. That boy had evidently attacked and been sexually abusive to a girl he knew.
>
> His story unfolded through his behaviour and the one-to-one discussions he had in the unit. John's father was seriously physically abusive to his mother. He had witnessed quite brutal physical assaults on her when he was a little boy of four and five.

He was the elder of two boys and felt that as the elder of the two he should stop his father from attacking his mum. He felt immensely guilty and ashamed that he did not. He did nothing to protect his mother because he was frightened of his father. He was so frightened of him that he sometimes felt all he could do was to join him and be as violent as he was. He also felt that he was his mother's special person, because she clung to him in her misery, which he felt proud about.

At the age of six his dream of someday making up to his mum was rudely shattered. His mum left his dad to live with, and later marry, his stepdad. John was taken by his mum to live with them and an older step-sibling, a boy. He immediately lost everything he valued – his position of being the eldest and mum's special person; and his father, for whom he felt a degree of love and admiration. Even though his stepdad was an extraordinarily good and caring man, who disciplined him when he expressed any bad feelings verbally or through his behaviour, John grew up feeling angry and resentful, with all his child feelings of anger, shame, and guilt, not only unresolved but pushed into the deeper recesses of his mind and festering into a state where he nearly killed a boy who unknowingly recreated a most humiliating experience for him, an experience which he was now big enough to redress.

His feelings for his mother swung between intense love as the most precious thing in his life and being totally uncaring and dismissive of her.

John worked through all his disturbing feelings in the unit mainly through acting them out in the unit community and discussion (sometimes, his refusal to discuss) with staff 'on the floor'. He smashed all the pictures in the house on two occasions, and some windows on another, for which he was not punished; it was discussed and interpreted. He made reparation for the damage he had done. I thought his behaviour was a transference and a token of his feelings of wanting to smash and destroy his parents and his home. In his individual psychotherapy with me he worked through fantasies of destroying the unit, and all the houses down the road, about which he had dreams. He worked through fantasies of becoming the worlds most efficient and ruthless drug baron and gangster.

Some months before he left he was apprehended and charged with Taking and Driving Away. In view of his previous offence and the judicial climate at the time there was a danger that he would be sent to prison. I wrote a report to the courts giving

> clinical evidence to show that it was not an act of delinquency but a simple adolescent act of showing off to his friends, one of who owned a car and had given him a lift many times. John had just begun to come into his own as an adolescent with his own identity. It could be regarded as about the first normal thing he did. The judge acceded to my request that he be placed on probation. John lost his fantasy identity of a 'tough' criminal.

It is two years since he left, at the time of writing this. He has not got into any trouble and from all accounts is doing well.

No Individual Psychotherapy for Two Years

Even though my previous experience at the Northgate Clinic had been to combine individual psychotherapy with small and large group therapy, and other forms of treatment, we did not use individual therapy at Brookside, at the outset. We started the unit with group work and there was no reason to change this for about two years. The staff were outstanding in their keenness and enthusiasm to learn and to make the new unit work. The nursing officer was a charismatic personality on whom authority sat comfortably. She was respected by all the nurses and an was an excellent leader of the nursing staff. Having worked for something like five years as a Charge Nurse at the Northgate Clinic Adolescent Unit, she had developed much confidence in her knowledge and ability in community work with adolescents. She held the nursing staff together. Under her leadership of the nurses we had clinical meetings everyday together with the clinical staff, (The Senior Registrar, the psychologist, the social worker, and the art therapist), during which time the youngsters attended the unit school. The staff learnt fast and learnt well. I taught them practical psychodynamics using the difficulties they were having with the youngsters in the unit as material for discussion. Having taught in the Introductory Psychotherapy Course for Doctors at the Tavistock Clinic, and having taught and interacted with nurses at the Northgate Clinic, I loved teaching psychodynamics to beginners. Being a relative beginner myself, I had not forgotten the difficulties of the beginner in understanding.

The result of all this was that we found ourselves working well with the youngsters in the unit. The daily community meetings which I attended, with all the staff and teachers, was a multi-purpose meeting, in which we gave all the youngsters and staff an experience of the philosophy of the unit – listening to the youngsters, discussion, interest in the patients, looking at underlying meanings – all this with unambiguous standards of what is right and wrong, and good and bad for adolescents. I took the opportunity of making comments and interpretations and transference links in the community meetings. I also invited the staff to make comments they thought were useful, emphasising that any observation sincerely felt by staff within the context of their role as therapeutic staff was of value. I had learnt how to disagree while supporting staff at the same time, and to receive criticism from staff graciously, both of which I was able to do effectively most of the time. I made it clear that disagreements between staff in the presence of the youngsters was entirely appropriate, as long as we were all working together in the interests of the youngsters and we were able to disagree with respect to each other. Any distress or confusion caused to patients could be taken up in the small group meeting which followed, and later on in the community interactions (on the floor). Distress caused to staff was taken up in staff meetings.

Thus it seemed that the pathology of the youngsters was being dealt with in a satisfactory way. It seemed that many or all of the staff interacting with the patients therapeutically, in depth, on the floor, was more effective than one single therapist doing it, while the larger group neglected or unwittingly contradicted his/her therapeutic interactions.

Individual Psychotherapy Started

After two years two, of our original clinical staff – the Senior Registrar and the psychologist – and some enthusiastic nursing assistants left. They were replaced with staff unfamiliar with the patients and the philosophy of the unit. At about the same time the charismatic leadership of the Nursing Officer started wearing thin. The insecurity among the staff was accurately reflected by insecurity in the adolescents. It was my fear of the youngsters feeling progressively more insecure through the loss of their safe relationships with staff that spurred me on to talk with staff about starting individual psychotherapy for the youngsters. Whatever the value of individual psychotherapy, it always provides the youngsters with a special relationship with which they can feel safe. I felt the youngsters would be in safe hands. We started it with total agreement from all the disciplines of staff. The psychotherapy was conducted by the clinical staff – Senior Registrar, social worker, psychologist and art therapist under my supervision. I took on those cases that were left over.

While this introduction of individual psychotherapy had its advantages, it also brought in a new source of tension for staff. The staff now felt there were two grades of staff – the elite who did this mysterious, secretive thing called psychotherapy and the others who did the 'dirty work' of dealing with the patients' misbehaviour. I removed the mysterious secretive quality of psychotherapy and did much to eliminate the type of difference based on the discipline to which a person belonged, by bringing psychotherapy into open discussion and encouraging outpatient psychotherapy by selected nursing staff, under my supervision.

I was able to justify this, in spite of the what I had gathered from the Tavistock Clinic practice, where only those in formal training and personal psychotherapy were permitted to undertake psychotherapy. I was acutely aware of the close relationship and discussions some youngsters were having with their social workers, who were completely untrained and unsupervised. Our staff, though untrained, were closely supervised and were having constant in-service training. Further, responsible staff who were untrained and aware of the importance of understanding the unconscious in psychotherapy were particularly careful about their interactions with youngsters and brought them into discussion continuously. There was plenty of time for these discussions, apart from daily staff meetings, and small-group supervision, and nursing meetings and nursing supervision. I made myself easily available to all staff for discussion of anything they wanted to talk about pertaining to the work.

FAMILY WORK

We discovered that adolescents are strongly affected by their relationship with their families. In every case, even in those relatively few who were diagnosed as schizophrenic, there were problems in the relationships within the family. Work with families was essential if the problems of the youngsters were to be addressed.

Having actively participated in the original Family Therapy Workshops between the department of Children and Parents and the Adolescent Department, at the Tavistock Clinic, I had learned much about family therapy, which I unstintingly shared with the staff, as my own Consultants and Supervisors had done with me. I had had the privilege of participating in teaching groups conducted by Roger Shapiro and Salvador Minuchin from the United States – Shapiro in Psychodynamic Family Therapy and Minuchin in Structural Family Therapy. In the Tavistock Clinic I learned how to conduct the 'ideal' family therapy session, in which the parents were sophisticated enough to recognise that there was a family problem and were consciously prepared to look at themselves and the whole family. We learned about and practised very interesting methods such as 'Role Playing' and 'Family Sculpting' and other techniques. The families we worked with were from Hampstead.

The most needy families in the North East Thames Region, extending from Tower Hamlets to Colchester in Essex, were however of an entirely different nature to the sophisticated parents from Hampstead. They would go to any lengths to defend themselves as good parents, particularly if they felt accusations were being made about their parenting, or they would attribute the cause of the problem to anything outside the family.

I used some simple principles of family therapy I had learned at the Tavistock Clinic to suit the families we had to deal with and we called it *Family Work*, not Family Therapy, so that we did not tread on the corns of the formal Family Therapy Training Institutions, which were just beginning to be established.

In many cases the family work has been the first opportunity that the adolescent has had to be heard and be taken seriously by the parents. This can make a huge difference to the family dynamics. I have had a few cases in outpatient family work where meeting as a family alone has solved the problem for the youngster and the family and further treatment was not needed.

In some cases a member of the family, usually one or other

parent, while being genuinely interested in the family, are so defensive that they are unable to have any insight into their own behaviour, which is a source of great distress to the family. In such cases we have found that methods such as role playing or family sculpting can be a powerful and effective method. Great care was taken in such cases, as the revelation may have been too shocking for the particular family member.

In some cases the system of operation within the family was entrenched leading to a homeostatic resistance, which could seem impossible to shift. In such cases we have found that if the therapist has worked sensitively with the family, he/she easily becomes a part of the family system. From this position 'within the family' the therapist or therapists can do much to change the system so that the different members of the family acquire different and more constructive roles. Getting out of the family system can be much easier than one would imagine if it is done through discussion.

I sometimes came across social workers who said that it was useless to try to engage the parents in family work because they had tried ever so hard and had failed to get the parents interested in their child. In such cases I had to devise ways to visit the parents myself, without offending the social worker, and find out for myself how such an unlikely thing was happening. I thought it was unlikely because I believed that without exception every mother loved her offspring – a law of nature. Unlike man-made laws, laws of nature are not broken by human beings who are but creatures of nature. In fact, in every such case I found that the mother and almost invariably both parents did in fact show great willingness to engage in family work in order to help their child. Much depended on the approach to the parents and the convictions of the worker.

Some principles we became aware of were:

- The parents are the two who started the family and brought up the children, which makes them feel responsible if their child becomes disturbed. They become extremely defensive.
- Concentrate on listening to the children.
- Do not meet the parents by themselves until the children

have had a full hearing.
- Do not ever make any statement which indicates that the parents had not done a good job of parenting their child. They should discover it themselves through discussions with us.
- Look carefully at the relationship of the parents who do not quarrel openly – that is where the problem often lies.
- Every family is different. Let the family session be a means of finding out about the family, which can lead to mutual learning.
- Join the family. Feel free to get into the family system. You can always come out of it at the right time.
- If you get the parents to become interested in and concentrate on their problems with each other, you have often solved the family problem.
- Getting together with the family and talking about parents and the extended family gives adolescents a sense of their identity, which helps them to feel they belong and safer with their feelings.

GROUP CULTURE

There is a strong tendency for individuals to lose their individual identity and acquire a group identity when they become members of a group. In so doing they often become the victims of the projections of others with which they are likely to identify. The ideal situation is to be an active member of the group, while yet retaining one's own individual identity. Our task in our small and large group meetings was to ensure that individual youngsters do not identify with the projections of the others, while they share in the common feelings of dependency, frustration, anger and love of parents.

Small Group Therapy With Adolescents

Training in small group therapy was very confusing. Observation of the process through a one-way screen, the chief feature of which was the silence of the therapist, was awesome – for me. I observed the silence of the therapist. It took me quite some time to realise that I was expected to observe the behaviour of the group and not the therapist. Then, after weeks of observation of a group trying to engage a silent therapist, I observed the changes in the group's behaviour after the therapist uttered one of his short indecipherable gems – it was the silence of the therapist, which gave him an aura of immense power, and the manner of the delivery, which gave the impression that something very valuable was being said; and it was utterly incomprehensible to me, as I thought it must have been for the members of the group. It was the perfect caricature of 'pearls being cast before swine'. These were adult groups.

I understood subsequently that the Consultant's role was to be non-interfering and allow the group to have the experience of making their own changes, without being dependent on the therapist to lead them, without 'running away' from (avoiding facing) the problems they bring up and create, or getting into wishful thinking and fantasies that someone or something else will make the changes for them. This would give each of them more confidence in themselves and a higher self-esteem.

The basis of adolescent group therapy is very different. Adolescents demand much more from their group therapists. Unlike adults, they are in a phase of development in which they are in truth dependent on adults, and need information and guidance.

We started the unit with one small therapy group which increased to three small groups of four to seven youngsters in each group, each run by two of the more experienced selected nursing staff of different gender. By 'experienced' I mean those who had attended the staff discussions keenly, asked questions and had been keen on bringing up their interactions with the youngsters for discussion. It must be understood that by the time the residential part of the unit had started, about six months of these daily discussions had gone on. There was regular supervision of these groups, initially by me and later by a senior psychologist as well who shared in the supervision of staff.

The small groups were meant to give the youngsters the opportunity to talk more intimately about their feelings, to be unafraid to share their thoughts with each other and gain help from each other with the support of staff. The influence that adolescents have on each other is generally greater than the influence adults have on them. If left alone, adolescents invariably get together and engage in ventures they do not have the courage to engage in by themselves – in those things that are forbidden by the adults or something against the adults, who have unwittingly incurred their anger. It is not considered prestigious by adolescents to listen to sensible advice from an adult, though listening to the same thing from another youngster is quite acceptable. We were amazed at how much the youngsters had in common underneath widely varying superficial expressions of the problem.

While the group phenomena in an adolescent group did have the features of adult groups – the three Basic Assumptions of a non-working group, Dependency, Fight or flight, and Pairing, as described by Bion – the commonest non-working phenomena in our adolescent groups were, the challenge to the authority of the staff (Rebellion), rivalry for the favour of staff (Rivalry), and seeking approval of the peer group (Approval). These were expressed in different ways, and sometimes by non-attendance. By the very nature of adolescence, a good working group seemed to belong to the 'dependency' basic assumption group, as judged by the standards of an adult group. We felt that a degree of dependence was appropriate as long as it did not acquire unrealistic proportions.

Each small group needed to make their own set of rules, led by the staff, such as: all members must arrive in time for the groups; no one is allowed to leave the group while it is in operation; members must listen to each other with respect; no one is to laugh or make fun of each other's problems or each other's parents. Adolescents have a great sense of honour about sticking to their commitments to each other.

The chief problem in small groups was the maintenance of the authority of staff. The staff were required to enable the youngsters to express themselves freely and fearlessly, and yet respect the authority of staff – a task which may be considered impossible by some. Unlike in a school, the staff were not there as didactic teachers; they were there essentially to enable the adolescents to learn from experience about their own and each other's difficulties, and how they can best be dealt with. Staff also had the task of imparting knowledge to the youngsters, which was necessary for their healthy development.

The staff learned to be wary of a youngster who controlled the others in the group, 'so that the group could function properly', thus doing a job for staff in a way that could be a relief for staff, who may at times feel helpless trying to control the youngsters. It is done in a way that staff would not have done, by intimidating the others. The question we asked was what was he doing with his own problems with authority, when he takes on an authority role? Even when the patients genuinely became interested in another's problem and were trying to be helpful, we looked upon it as avoidance of dealing with their own problems, which are often projected and seen by them in another. While not discouraging them from caring for each other, we made it clear *that the best way to help each other was for each youngster to concentrate on their own problems.*

One of the most useful maxims for staff was, 'You cannot control an adolescent, you should not even try. You can control yourself and become in charge of both yourself and the adolescent.'

A good working group was not often achieved. The value of the groups however was in the process of trying to achieve a good working group, through which much of the pathology of the patients is highlighted and thought about. There were periods when the combination of patients in the groups was fortuitous and the staff worked well with each other, when the groups did in fact function as working groups. The gain made by the youngsters at such times in their understanding and acceptance of their own relationships with staff, their families and with each other was great.

One of the chief things looked at during supervision was how the two staff were working with each other. The greatest efforts were made in trying to achieve a good working relationship between the two, as good parents in a family. A significant observation we made was that if the staff worked well with each other, then, as in a family with parents who loved each other, the group functioned effectively.

ART THERAPY

We were fortunate in having an art therapist who had a natural aptitude for understanding aspects of the unconscious mind through drawings, paintings, shapes and colour. The adolescents found that expressing themselves through art was more enjoyable, and far less threatening than 'going for therapy'. We found ourselves gaining much by listening to the art therapist's descriptions and interpretations, in our staff meetings. Once-weekly staff meetings were soon set aside for discussions around art therapy. The information we gained about patient pathology through art therapy was great, and eagerly grasped and used in their group and individual psychotherapy.

Art therapy soon became one of the major modes of 'therapy' in the unit. It was done in groups where the youngsters worked individually and in groups where they worked together on the same project under the supervision of the art therapist.

Keeping any group of adolescents out of mischief is a difficult task. To do so with fifteen to sixteen youngsters at a time was even more difficult. There is nothing so unpleasant for both, adolescent and adult, as for the adult to continuously and repeatedly restrict the youngsters. We had to devise programmes that were constructive and beneficial to the adolescents, so that all hours of the day were organised for them. The programmes we organised had to be genuinely beneficial to the adolescents rather than activities 'to keep them occupied' and out of trouble. We found that when the staff took the trouble to organise programmes that were designed for the benefit of the youngsters, they attended the event, while those that were done for the benefit of staff, or for staff comfort, often went unattended. Art therapy, which was regarded more or less synonymously with teaching art, came in very usefully here.

A unit journal, with art work and writings – poetry and prose by the adolescents and staff – was established, with the art therapist as the leader.

A big group art project was just started as an evening activity, when the unit was closed.

Management Committee formed

After about five years, when I found that the unit was depending too much on the leadership of the Medical Director and the Nursing Officer, we agreed that a management committee should be formed whose task would be to devise policies and decide on all management issues (non-therapy matters) in the unit. The art therapist was elected as chairman of the committee. As the Medical Director, I kept out of the committee, but I reserved the right veto and to intervene in exceptional situations.

DANGERS AND DIFFICULTIES OF THE NON-PUNITIVE PSYCHODYNAMIC APPROACH IN A RESIDENTIAL SETTING

Covert Dangers

There is a universal human tendency to 'get rid of' unpleasant experiences that have invaded one and as it were threatened to take root within. These unpleasant experiences are most frequently got rid of by retaliatory reaction, often seen in its simplest form by the offended person shouting back in anger, when the unpleasantness is evacuated into the perpetrator – it is returned. One of the more sophisticated forms of this mechanism is seen in the sexual abuse of children by one who has himself been sexually abused as a child – if it was an unpleasant experience – when the unpleasant experience is evacuated into a likely recipient. (This can happen even if the child abuser was not literally sexually abused but has had the psychic experience.)

In all adolescent units there are no built-in mechanisms designed to protect staff from anxiety and stress, as there are in Psychiatric Hospitals which emphasise the difference between staff and patients and depersonalise both, with staff in uniforms, bedhead ticket numbers, and splitting up of duties related to each patient. The staff interact with the whole patient and absorb the full unmitigated pathology of the patients, particularly in those that do not use punishments to control the misbehaviour of youngsters. The disturbed and disturbing behaviour of the patients is unleashed in its full force into staff.

The difference in a non-punitive psychodynamic unit

It is in the experience of staff who have to confront and face the disturbed adolescent that the difference between a 'Reward and Punishment' behavioural unit and a non-punitive psychodynamic unit is most acutely felt. In the former, the mere fact that punishments in some form are incorporated into the legitimised treatment programme affords the offended and distressed staff member, whose equanimity has been invaded by the disturbance of a disturbed youngster, a means of evacuating the 'offence' into the punishment part of the behavioural programme without internalising it. *It allows retaliation and evacuation of the disturbance created within them.* In a psychodynamic unit, however, in which thoughtful responses are more valued than simple reactions, evacuation of unpleasant experiences is not legitimised. The staff are expected ideally to take in what the patient does or says, try to understand it and give it back in a more understandable form. It often happens that they do not understand it and do not *give it back* in any form. They simply suppress their reaction and internalise the 'bad' experience. The continuous internalisation of minor bits of patient pathology can lead to an accumulation which eventually causes great distress.

If projective-identification occurs (explained in other chapters), between the unwanted pathology of the patient and a staff who is unsure of his/her own identity, it can cause serious distress and lead to staff wanting to leave if it is not identified and dealt with properly.

In good psychodynamic units there is another opportunity to unload the bad experiences – in staff sensitivity meetings. In good sensitivity meetings the other staff listen and take in the distressing experience of an 'offended' staff person and share the distress carried by them.

This kind of difficulty is not observed by an onlooker. It can only be understood by one experienced in the process. It is covert.

Overt Dangers

In addition to the covert dangers, there are the more obvious dangers caused by the defiant and uncontrolled behaviour of the youngsters, which may include damage to property, and behavioural, verbal and physical attacks of staff. While this can happen at any time in a youngster's stay in the unit it is particularly unbridled at the beginning of their stay in a non-punitive environment. Most adolescents whose behaviour has been controlled all their lives through punishments and fear of punishments, go wild with their new-found liberation when they first come to a non-punitive unit, where they imagine they can do anything they want without having to face the consequences they fear. It takes them varying periods of being in the unit, together with appropriate staff and patient interactions, to recognise that there are consequences – the consequence of thinking about and discussing their behaviour, and coping with their feelings about what they did, which are often more painful to them than 'mere' punishment.

In considering admission of youngsters to an open non-punitive psychodynamic unit great care should be taken about the combination of the different types of patients in the unit at any one time. Youngsters have great influence on each other, and too many conduct-disordered adolescents or juvenile delinquents can influence each other more powerfully than staff, to their mutual detriment. On the other hand, one delinquent youngster who has been in the unit long enough to consciously feel the benefit he has gained can be a more powerful source of beneficial influence than staff.

Limit Setting

It is imperative therefore that a non-punitive unit should have a well thought out set of rules for the youngsters; rules designed for the benefit of the youngsters – not for the convenience of staff – and which are eminently reasonable. And there should be a low threshold for misbehaviour. Many a youngster has grumbled at me saying, 'You can't expect me to behave perfectly,' when my response has always been, 'I'm sorry, I do expect you to behave perfectly, why can't you?'

The slightest infringement should be noticed and picked up by the staff in one form or another and discussed. Otherwise the behaviour will escalate into proportions that may become extremely distressing for staff. Adolescents go on increasing their disturbing behaviour until they are sure that staff recognise their badness, and are capable of containing it.

The therapeutic discharge

One of the greatest obstacles to therapeutic progress in a non-punitive, non-secure treatment unit for adolescents, is the development of a *false sense of omnipotence* in the adolescent. This fantasy of omnipotence which is there in its rudimentary form can develop rapidly in the unit when the youngster sees that there are no apparent consequences to his 'bad' and destructive conduct. Understanding is often mistaken for weakness. The fantasised weakness of the authority in the unit feeds their own fantasies of omnipotence.

We found that a few of the deprived adolescents we worked with reached a point when they were unable to work usefully anymore even though they clearly had the ability to do so. They would engage in intractable disruptive behaviour even though the therapeutic interventions of the staff were good and right and they could clearly see their behaviour to be destructive and intolerable. Some would verbally express their wish to be discharged and demanded it, accompanying the demand by smashing a few windows or threatening staff with violence. Others said they did not want to leave but would contradict this by escalating their disturbing behaviour. It was a form of negative-therapeutic reaction, underlying which, we found, was a sense of omnipotence. They felt the staff were impotent to do anything about their behaviour. The exhilarating feeling of triumphing over authority seemed too good to give up voluntarily – a situation which often frightens adolescents; their escalation of the behaviour could be seen as a plea for some action to stop them and demonstrate that the authorities over them are indeed powerful enough to deal with their disturbance and violence, so that they could feel safe in the unit.

We did not want to discharge such youngsters and forever lose the chance of helping them to deal with the problem which seemed to be lurking just behind and just out of reach. Yet some action needed to be taken for the survival of the unit and the staff. Trying to be more powerful than the youngsters and using some 'powerful' method of controlling them we found was a bad idea. It would only lead to a competition in which the youngsters had the advantage because they were not bound by regulations and standards of behaviour, which staff had to maintain. We found that the safest and most realistic way of dealing with the false sense of omnipotence was to present them with reality, while continuing with the non-punitive psychodynamic discussions we were having with them.

The method consisted essentially of discharging them because we could not cope with their behaviour – we were not omnipotent. But the discharge was to some place where we (the same staff) could continue therapeutic work with them. The aim was to readmit them to the unit when the staff who worked with them had dealt with all the underlying factors that led to their intolerable behaviour and felt that they could truly cope.

These youngsters who had worked well with us, up to a point, had made good relationships with staff. Once discharged they developed an abiding desire to get back into the unit, which provided them with a powerful motive to deal with the problem. The relief from the intensive interactions and pressure in the unit helped them to think more clearly and also gave staff who worked with them a fresh view of the problem.

The therapeutic discharge was successfully used with several recalcitrant youngsters in Brookside YPU and Whitefriars Children's Home with varying overt behaviour, but the underlying theme in all of them was the fantasy of omnipotence.

Some of them were overtly *Omnipotent and Manipulative*, who had thus far had considerable success in manipulating parents and teachers from an early age, and felt they had succeeded in manipulating some staff in the unit. Others were youngsters who had been *so emotionally deprived* that their very survival depended on their fantasies of omnipotence. The latter would present with varying types of overt behaviour.

The therapeutic discharge, in its description, is often confused with a *suspension* or *Time-out*. The difference is significant. A suspension or time-out is a punishment for bad or unacceptable behaviour, it is for a specified period, and return to the unit is promised anyway – there is no motivation to change. It would only feed the fantasy of omnipotence in the youngster. A therapeutic discharge is not a punishment. It is aimed at emphasising a reality to the youngster and at creating a better situation for him/her to work effectively in the unit. Even though experienced staff would have a good realistic idea that the youngster has shown the ability to work through the fantasy of omnipotence and return to the unit in due course, it is stated clearly and loud and seriously that he will not be readmitted if he does not make the required changes, which will be judged not by promises he makes, but by the experience of the same staff who have worked with him and know him well, seeing the relevant changes in him.

A case which illustrates the therapeutic discharge is the story of Jack, whom we were loath to discharge from Brookside as a failure in treatment because apart from being a very needy youngster he had shown ample evidence of being able to value and make good relationships. He had been admitted as an emergency and did not go through the usual assessment procedure.

Jack:

> Jack was a very sad, depressed seventeen-year-old. He had become uncontainable in a children's home (one of many he had been in) and the social services were stuck with no place for him. He was one of the few cases who was assessed as an emergency and found to possess characteristics we thought we could work with. He was brought up by adoptive parents from the age of three. When he was admitted and I wanted to have meetings with his adoptive parents, the social worker informed me that there was no point because she had tried to have discussions with them and had failed to invite their interest in him, 'They have given up on him,' she said.
>
> My experience of his parents was the exact opposite of what the social worker described. Mother and father were desperate about Jack – they clearly loved Jack. They had adopted him because they loved to have children but had been unable to have any. They had tried very hard with him following the advice of the Social Services on how to manage the child, and felt that they had failed to provide Jack with his needs, about which they felt guilty. They were very willing to try again in the regional unit. We started family work which both parents attended willingly.
>
> Jack's story was not unfamiliar. He had been troublesome from an early age. When adoptive parents found that Jack was exhibiting disturbing behaviour they did not understand, which included masturbating in front of his mother, they asked for Social Services intervention and he was soon taken into care; he had several placements in children's homes and had been found to be uncontainable in each. *It was stated by the social worker that Brookside YPU was the last resort.* Jack was confused about why he was admitted to Brookside and from time to time convinced himself that Brookside was forced to take him in because nobody

else wanted him. He had good reason to feel that he was incurably bad and unwanted, which he believed was also the reason why he was rejected by his natural parents. He retained this feeling despite being told by us that we admitted him because we believed he had a curable problem and because we wanted to work with him. He did not believe our words – a common problem with deprived adolescents, many of who have had the most appalling experiences of being let down by the words used by the different authorities in their lives.

In Jack's case the Social Services did not find any other place for him and give him a choice. He knew that we did not know him well enough to say that he was not incurably bad. He had agreed to come to Brookside because he had been told by the Social Services that the alternative was a secure unit.

Jack let the staff know that he could be very endearing, but also let us know how bad he was. He abused and threatened staff sometimes, sniffed glue, and smashed windows periodically. When he found that we were dealing with these problems, not by threatening to discharge him, but through understanding, he felt safe, but became confused.

He developed good relationships with the staff, most of whom had a great empathy for the very emotionally deprived life he had led – being abandoned by his own parents, rejected by his adoptive parents and being in so many different children's homes within a relatively short space of time. He clearly demonstrated his need for care and love from staff. He had bad dreams that frightened him and had taken to placing his mattress just by the nursing station door, on the floor, at night, where he fell soundly and safely asleep. But periodically he became defiant and demanded that he be sent to another place, and emphasised the demand by engaging in another bout of destruction. He seemed to be unsure that he was wanted by the staff in Brookside, and had developed a fantasy of omnipotence as a survival mechanism.

We invited his social worker to remove him from the unit, for a therapeutic discharge, being convinced that he would want to return very soon. The Social Services said no one would admit a boy who had created so much trouble as Jack and did not even try seriously. Jack kept escalating his behaviour and brought us to a helpless situation.

Finally we ourselves contacted a children's home near us, explained the idea of the therapeutic discharge and made arrangements with them for his admission in case it was needed. Then, when Jack was on one of his destructive rampages, he climbed the roof and started throwing slates from the roof at staff standing below trying to persuade him to come down. At this point we invited police action. The police removed Jack to the police station to be charged. We told the police that we would not take him back and that they should inform the Social Services to take charge of him. This led to some unpleasantness between the Social Service department and ourselves, but they had no alternative but to take charge of him. They placed him in the unit we had arranged.

We then saw Jack regularly as an outpatient. He created no trouble in the other children's home. He had all the opportunity to see that we were quite capable of dealing with his destructive behaviour and were under no obligation to readmit him. He felt he wanted to return. *We felt we had dealt with two of the problems that had led to his intractable behaviour* – his belief that we merely said we wanted him because there was no other unit that would take him, and his fantasy of omnipotence that he could do anything he wanted with no consequences. He was readmitted in three weeks and left the unit in a further three months without causing any further trouble.

When he left he told us that he was going to become a social worker because he had learnt how to deal with adolescents in trouble.

SOME THINGS WE LEARNED ABOUT GROUP AND INDIVIDUAL BEHAVIOUR THROUGH OUR COMMUNITY INTERACTIONS.

Acting out.

Acting out is behaviour that is compulsively embarked upon under the threat of an emerging unconscious experience. It could be described as 'instead-of behaviour' – that is, instead of experiencing the conflict, painful feeling or fantasy, which is threatening to emerge from the unconscious mind, some activity is substituted which dissipates or by passes the internal experience. A careful examination of the nature of the acting out will give clues about the nature of the unconscious internal conflict.

Example:

At a time when we had about fourteen residents we found that many of the youngsters were visiting the pub down the road, against the rules of the unit, and coming out apparently in a state of inebriation. Many of them were underage. We did our best to argue the youngsters into stopping what they were doing: 'What waste of time.' 'There are programmes arranged for you in the unit which were much better.' 'Drinking is bad for you.' 'This is not social drinking.' etc. They had answers for all these. Informing the manager of the pub that underage youngster were drinking in the pub was of no avail. They said they only drank soft drinks and they were not drunk.

Then a staff member informed us that one of the neighbours who had witnessed the behaviour of the youngsters after they had visited the pub, had commented that they did not think much of the staff's ability to look after the youngsters if this sort of thing goes on in the unit. This led to our recognition of what we had learned about acting out: that acting out was an external expression of an internal feeling or event in the unconscious mind. That examination of the behaviour and its results would give a clue to its underlying meaning.

In the next staff meeting we had a discussion about whether we were acting in an uncaring way with the youngsters, and how difficult it would be for them to confront us with this. Amongst other things it would bring back painful memories of their experience of parental neglect. Following a useful discussion about this in the staff meeting in which we looked at ourselves as honestly as we could, we dealt with the problem in the next community meeting. We brought up the idea that some of the youngsters were finding it difficult to say that they had feelings of being uncared for by staff. The staff in the community meeting were in the mood to listen and find out, and we had a most useful meeting about the feelings the youngsters were having about being uncared for, which was taken very seriously by the staff. No mention of their visits to the pub was made by anyone. They ceased.

The interactions of the youngsters in the unit were full of acting out. We learned that if we found ways of preventing acting out by the youngsters, then there was a better chance of their unconscious disturbing feelings emerging for discussion.

Acting out need not be antisocial or unlawful. Much normal adolescent behaviour in schools, in groups, and on the playing field is true acting out, which is acceptable in their particular social setting. If such behaviour represents unconscious adolescent conflicts, which are dissipated, then the youngsters would grow into healthy adults without having experienced much of the confusions and conflicts of growing up.

Similarly, much adult activity may be seen as socially or politically acceptable acting out through which disturbing impulses emanating from their early relationships are dissipated or bypassed.

Learning comes from emotional experience

That people do not learn from understanding something intellectually or change from being determined to change, is something that we had plenty of opportunity to learn from our experience.

Everyone who has done work with families over a period of time will have come across several instances where one or other of the parents has said, 'I see how much of what is happening to "Cliff or Sara"' is just the same as what happened to me when I was their age. I was determined when we have children, that we will not do with them what my parents did with us, and I find that I have done exactly the same.'

I observed then, that, that parent had lived on with the emotional experience they had had with their own parents, and had not had the opportunity of having a mitigating emotional experience either in their life events or in the form of psychoanalytical psychotherapy.

In our work in the unit, one of the most memorable experiences I had of the importance of learning from experience is the episode with Bill, a charge nurse for whom I had the highest regard, who had great empathy with the youngsters. It was one of the rare occasions in which I exercised my authority as Medical Director with a staff member.

The teachers in the unit school often grumbled about the adolescents not being interested in their studies and never doing the homework given to them. They complained about the nurses and the NHS part of the unit not sharing in the support of the education of the youngsters. I brought this up for discussion in our staff meetings, explored all angles of the problem and pointed out the amount of time there was in the evenings which was often wasted by the youngsters, and I suggested a period to be set aside specifically for homework, to be supervised by the nurses. This was discussed thoroughly at several staff meetings. No one could give any valid reasons for not having a time allocated for homework, when the youngsters would be expected to be seated in a specified area in the unit, quiet and engaged in the studies given to them by the teachers. Many staff welcomed the idea, because finding gainful activities for the youngsters which they all would attend every evening was not easy. It was an eminently reasonable idea. But there was one important staff member who opposed it – Bill – and he was a senior charge nurse, without whose agreement it was impossible to implement it. Bill finally came out with the reason why he felt unable to agree with the idea – he believed that the adolescents would not like the idea of sitting quietly and studying in the evenings and he felt he could not compel them to do what they did not want to do. All discussion and arguments failed to persuade Bill, and the new Nursing Officer did or said nothing.

I telephoned the head of nursing services, who was located at the main hospital, discussed the situation with her, and got her agreement for me to instruct Bill to do what was needed to start the homework period. The next day in the staff meeting the topic came up again, and I said we had had enough discussion about the homework period and it was clear that there was no valid reason to stop us from implementing it. I then instructed Bill, who happened to be the charge nurse for the evening, to start the homework period that same evening. He said he could not. I then told the Nursing Officer that I would expect him to take action against Bill if he did not. There were protests and loud noises in the meeting but I knew I had the support of the head of nursing. It was an important and memorable event in the unit because my 'authoritarian' attitude was quite out of character.

The community meeting in which we had discussed homework many times followed the staff meeting. I announced that the homework period would start that evening. Bill started the homework period as instructed and it worked extremely well. He came to me about a week later and said what happened was about the best learning experience he had had in the unit. He said he was forced to do what he did not want to do, and when he found that he could indeed do this thing he did not like so much, he was able to help the adolescents to do what they did not like. He was a sincere and honest man.

Homework went on smoothly for many months till the teachers protested about something, which led to it being stopped.

Equilibrium of inner and outer worlds

One of the striking observations we made concerned the impossibility of persuading some youngsters to keep their rooms tidy, and how this was related to the confusion and mess within their inner worlds. The staff were not obsessive about the standards of cleanliness and neatness, yet some youngsters found it impossible to maintain a basic level of tidiness.

> John, the same boy I have referred to elsewhere, was a very polite gentlemanly lad of sixteen. He tried hard to please staff in every way and complied with all the rules of the house. But his room was inordinately untidy and messy. He could not keep his room tidy for more than a few days, even though every effort was made by staff to help him with this.
>
> He had been taken into care because he had become uncontrollable in his home with his mother and stepdad, who by all accounts had been extremely caring parents to him. He had truanted from school and had kept late nights in the company of delinquent mates who were in constant trouble with the police. His rebellious behaviour culminated in him being charged for Grievous Bodily Harm when he attacked another boy causing fractures of an arm and leg and several ribs.
>
> His own parents parted when he was six years of age after a disastrous marriage, in which his mother was constantly beaten and battered by John's father. John being the eldest of two boys enjoyed a special relationship with his mother and felt enormous guilt that he did not intervene to help his mother. He recalled that he was too frightened of his father.
>
> Then mother left home, taking Alan and his younger brother with her, to live with stepdad and his children, amongst whom was a boy older than John.
>
> John had lost everything he had valued in one blow, as it were. He lost his father, for whom he had a deep affection; his special relationship with mother, which was taken by his stepdad; his position as the eldest in the family; and his love for his

mother. He did not know what he felt about her who had done all this to him.

As John talked to me about his feelings for his mother, about which he was very confused, loving her intensely at times and despising her at others, he gradually found himself able keep his room tidy. It was as if his mind was the room which became tidier and tidier as he worked through and clarified his feelings about the most important things within.

Similarly, as shown in Chapter II – 'Both… are Needed' – changes in the external representation of an internal conflict can lead to striking changes in the internal world and consequently, far-reaching and widespread changes in many related areas in behaviour.

The equilibrium between the two worlds demanded by the human condition is a most powerful unconscious mechanism and affects almost every aspect of one's life.

The most unbelievably powerful effect is seen in *projective-identification*, when *admired qualities* of one person are taken in (Introjected) by another, or unwanted qualities in one are pushed into (Projected) a vulnerable recipient. This intrapsychic interaction can lead to the most powerful physical experience of *wanting to get into each other in a love relationship* in the first case, and into *sado-masochistic sex* in the latter.

Changes in Authority lead to Changes in Adolescents

We found Kurt Lewin's Field theory[1], which represents relationships between human beings by different positions in a magnetic field, to be of the greatest practical value in understanding and working with our relationship with adolescents in particular and with all relationships in general. As staff, caring for all aspects of the developing multifaceted personalities of adolescents, we sometimes had to make decisions, caring decisions though they were, that were not liked by them. At such times, the youngsters who were strongly influenced by their past experience of authority (the Transference), would place us in different positions, as authority figures they have disliked – parents who do not love them, teachers who punish them, or the police who frighten them. According to Kurt Lewin's theory, they placed us in a different spot on the magnetic field than we were in. We were in fact in the 'caring spot'. At such times, if we try to adjust our position in the field in order that we may be seen as we were, in the right position, the dynamic forces at play would place us in an alternative position, again giving the adolescent (or viewer) a distorted position. Then attempts to further correct positions would lead to further distortions and to profound confusion in the viewer.

We learned that the thing to do was to first ensure that what we were doing was indeed caring, and then to remain in the position we were in irrespective of the position we were placed in, in the mind of the viewer. The adolescent or the viewer would soon find that the position they placed us in was not right and they would replace us in a position nearer where we really were and keep repeating the process till eventually we would be placed in the right position. This eventual correction can occur only if we remain in the position we originally took up. It is beholden on us to ensure that it is indeed the caring position we intend it to be.

A vital corollary to this is that if we are in the wrong position we should change it soon and then remain in it. This corollary is of great importance because it became clear to us that invariably the adolescents' behaviour depended on how we as their authority behaved with them – they were dependant on us. They reacted to us. (Except in the beginning when they were strongly influenced by their past experience – the Transference.)

This fact when translated into general terms is relevant in diverse situations in life. It places those in authority, and those who have power, in positions of the gravest responsibility with regard to the way they behave in relation to those dependent on them. It is relevant in all areas where there are people in different hierarchical roles, to the activities of the establishment, in the political arena, and in international affairs. If change is to be brought about, it is those in authority who have the ability to change their position, who should first make the change, when those dependent on them will have to change their position.

REFERENCES

[1] '*The Life and Work of Kurt Lewin*', *The Psychoanalysis of Organisations* by Robert De Board, Routledge, 11 New Fetter Lane, London EC4P 4EE, pp. 49 –64.

Chapter II
BOTH PSYCHODYNAMICS AND BEHAVIOUR THERAPY ARE NEEDED

Behaviour therapy and Psychodynamics are generally regarded as antagonistic forms of treatment. In truth, these two very different methods tackle different aspects of the same problem. Behaviour therapy acts at the symptomatic level, at the surface, at the level where the problem is seen and experienced. Psychodynamics acts at a deeper causal level, which is often not seen. If the cause of the problem is unconscious, it may not be recognised by the patient or offender.

If they are properly regarded and used, they should give something akin to binocular vision of the problem and complement each other to form a whole.

In medical terminology, the behavioural approach is similar to aspirin and cold sponges for the fever, while psychodynamics is like the antibiotic that deals with the underlying infecting agent.

Ever since the acceptance of the HAS document *Bridges Over Troubled Waters*, Psychodynamics in the Adolescent Services has been marginalised, leaving a form of behaviour therapy – the Reward and Punishment type – as the only approach to managing disturbed adolescents; a form of treatment which does not do justice either to the complexities of the adolescent's mind nor to the philosophy of behaviour therapy.

In this chapter I shall show that Behaviour therapy, as advocated by default by the HAS report, and practised by a large proportion of those in the service, needs psychodynamics to give it wholeness. I will show that psychodynamics values and incorporates the kind of Behaviour therapy which does not dehumanise the adolescent, into its own philosophy and practice.

BEHAVIOUR THERAPY

The theory and practice of Behaviour therapy is derived from experimental psychology. The extrapolation of this to human behaviour gave rise to Social Learning theory, which states:

Behaviour is socially learned; maladaptive or 'bad' behaviour which has been learned, can also be unlearned, and new, good or normal behaviour relearned to take its place.[1]

Were one to acknowledge that the learning referred to, is done principally through relationships with significant people, and occurs at both conscious and unconscious levels, there will be no difference between this statement and the understanding in psychodynamics.

Broadly speaking, there are two kinds of Behaviour therapy. One that treats the recipient as simply a bundle of nerves and muscles – *Operant Conditioning* (Skinner), and others that treat him as also having a mind – *Reciprocal Inhibition* (Wolpe), and *Cognitive Behaviour Therapy*. Operant conditioning has its value in training a child, because even though behavioural theory does not recognise it, the experience is taken into the mind and has its effect on the entire personality, which can be positive or negative in terms of the development of the youngster's personality.

THE NEED FOR BOTH APPROACHES

The Normal Adolescent

Adolescents are in their formative years. They are in the process of leaving the *child world* behind and entering into a *new world of adults*. Having lived in a secure child world they feel very insecure in the new world where everything seems to have changed – feelings about their parents and family and their knowledge of themselves. They must find out about themselves by testing themselves out with the new world around them and most importantly, with Authority. They are very ashamed of their feelings of inadequacy, and of how much they want to feel safe as little children again, and they exaggerate the 'grown-up' parts of themselves and put on 'super-adult' behaviour. However much they challenge and defy authority, they are aware at a deeper level that they are still learning from adults, authority figures in particular, about what is good, bad and acceptable in the wider world. Underneath the veneer of 'superior knowledge' and defiance, there is a growing insecure child who wants to know about himself/herself and learn how to live in the adult world. They would welcome guidance and criticism of their conduct, if they can get it without being humiliated or 'losing face'. Approval and disapproval of their conduct, a kind of behavioural retraining is necessary in this new phase of their lives, in which they have begun to discover unfamiliar feelings and abilities. This is normal adolescence.

The Disturbed Adolescent

With the disturbed youngster however, the need for understanding the underlying cause of their disturbed behaviour becomes pre-eminent. To imagine that a disturbed youngster who has already been trained in what is good and bad, and right and wrong, can be dealt with effectively purely through behavioural retraining, would clearly be unrealistic. The underlying disturbed behaviour needs to be looked at and understood, if the cause is to be dealt with. But these youngsters also need the behavioural approach, for they too have normal adolescent confusions and developmental needs which must be met; however, it is imperative that the kind of Behavioural approach should not lead to suppression of their disturbed and disturbing impulses, neither should it be the kind of Behaviour therapy that reduces them to unthinking masses of nerves and muscles.

I think every experienced clinician in the speciality will recognise that disturbed adolescents can be truly helped only by a judicious combination of dealing directly with the disturbed and disturbing behaviour (the Behavioural approach), as well as with the underlying feelings and impulses which are often unknown to the youngster (the psychodynamic approach). Care must be taken to ensure that the two approaches are not in conflict, in each individual case.

It will be seen that much of this behavioural influence occurs in a natural and meaningful way during the process of psychodynamic therapy, though in some cases separate, complementary formal Behavioural treatment can be of value and may be necessary.

BEHAVIOUR THERAPY IN PSYCHODYNAMICS

All kinds of behaviour therapy which do not dehumanise the patient form an integral part of psychodynamics. It is my experience that there is little difference between good psychoanalytical psychotherapy and sensitive behaviour therapy which treats the patient as a thoughtful sensitive human being. Much depends on the therapeutic relationship between the patient and the therapist and the sensitivity of the therapist.

I think that it is not commonly known that Melanie Klein, who is regarded widely as the most rigid and uncompromising advocate of the psychoanalytical (psychodynamic) method, has herself categorically recognised the value and importance of dealing directly with (external) reality – i.e. behaviour:

> If the unconscious fantasy is constantly influencing and altering the perception or interpretation of reality, the converse also holds true: reality impinges on unconscious fantasy itself. It is experienced, incorporated and exerts a very strong influence on the unconscious mind. Take, for instance, the infant who is beginning to get hungry and who overcomes hunger by an omnipotent hallucination of having a good feeding breast: his situation will be radically different if he is soon fed, from what it will be if he is allowed to remain hungry for a long time. In the first situation the real breast that is offered by the mother will, in the infant's experience, merge with the breast that has been fantasised, and the infants feeling will be that his own goodness and that of the good object are strong and lasting. In the second case the infant will be overcome by hunger and anger and, in his fantasy, the experience of a bad and persecuting object will become stronger with its implication that his own anger is more powerful than his love and the bad object stronger than the good one.[2]

Wolpe's Reciprocal Inhibition has been used with great success for phobias of different kinds. Sometimes the deeper underlying cause has been resolved by attention to the symptom, which happened in one of my own cases. I think the matter is important enough for me to reproduce the short paper that was published by the British Journal of Psychiatry: Perinpanayagam, *British Journal of Psychiatry*, Vol 119, No. 550, September 1971.

A Monosymptomatic Phobia Treated by a Single Session of Behaviour Therapy
by K.S. PERINPANAYAGAM[3]

This is a case in which it seems reasonable to assume that a patient developed a maladaptive conditioned response, which was symbolic of an underlying conflict. She was treated successfully by a single session of Behaviour therapy. Not only did the symptom disappear, but there seems to be an improvement in the underlying unconscious conflict.

Case History
Mrs Joy S, was about 30 years of age when she was referred for psychiatric opinion by her general practitioner. She had been suffering from symptoms of moderate depression for the previous few months. Prominent among her symptoms was guilt about being unable to satisfy her husband's sexual needs. She had always been disappointed by her sexual experience and had never enjoyed it, though her marriage was in general a happy one. She was an intelligent, well-spoken woman of previously good personality.

She had been terrified of snakes from an early age. She could not recall any encounter with a real snake, nor could she explain how this fear arose. She first realised her revulsion for snakes at about 10 years of age, when she visited the London Zoo. She could not stay in the same room if there was a picture of a snake in it, nor could she watch television if there was any likelihood of a snake appearing on the screen. This phobia for snakes had recently begun to cause problems at home because her two children had realised their mother's fear and had begun using it to control her.

Mrs Joy S was an only child. Her father died suddenly when she was 26 years of age. She described him as an affectionate and sensible man whom she respected and loved deeply. She was less enthusiastic about her mother, who was alive, though on the whole she got on well with her. Nudity had always been a practice within the family, and as far back as she could remember all the family would walk in and out of the bathroom in the nude, and would sunbathe or lie around in bed in the nude. Sex *per se* was never discussed in the family, though she felt she had been brought up to be unafraid of sex.

Treatment

She was treated with Concordin 5 mgs tds for one month, during which her depressive symptoms disappeared completely, but her phobia for snakes remained unchanged.

One session of systematic desensitisation was carried out by the technique described by Freidman (1966), using an intravenous injection of a 2½ per cent solution of methohexitone sodium. A very lifelike toy rubber snake was used to build up a hierarchical system. Within 45 minutes she was able to play with the toy snake without anxiety. Three days later she arrived for continuation of the treatment; she said she did not experience any anxiety at the thought of a snake, and was actually able to play with the snake without any anxiety. She was asked to come again three days later; as before, she experienced no anxiety and played with the snake.

Progress

She was not seen again for two years, at the end of which period I made enquiries about her health and the snake phobia. She wrote saying that she was very well indeed. Some extracts from her letter: *…I have had no recurrences of the depression and I am coping with all my day-to-day problems with little trouble … I have seen a grass snake in a glass case … pictures of snakes no longer bother me … I read an article on the adder … It is a welcome relief to have no fears when at the cinema that a snake might appear on the screen.* I got in touch with her again and had a final interview with her. She was indeed extremely well and happy, her sex life had improved and she was able to enjoy sex for the first time.

Discussion

One could conjecture that Mrs S's phobia for snakes was symbolic of her wish for her father's penis and at the same time a fear and guilt arising from this wish, creating conflict and anxiety. This conflict had been constantly kept alive by the nudity within the family. Failure to discuss sex in the family had denied her the opportunity to work through this conflict, and at the same time had prevented the conflict from becoming either deeply ingrained or becoming attached on to any other aspects of her personality. It remained, as it were, free-floating in her unconscious mind in an unsophisticated primitive form and was expressed in her conscious mind as a snake phobia. I did not make any interpretations to her and did not even discuss the sexual aspects of her phobia. She has evidently been completely cured of the phobia as well as the original conflict from which it arose – enjoyment of sex being the criterion – with a single session of desensitisation. It has not been replaced by any other neurotic symptoms and indeed she seems to be a much happier person and is leading a richer and fuller life.

Acknowledgement
The author is grateful to Dr T.M. Moylett, Consultant Psychiatrist, Fairfield Hospital, for his co-operation and permission to publish this case.

Reference
Friedman, D.E., (1966), 'A new technique for the systematic desensitization of phobic symptoms'. *Behaviour Research and Therapy,* 4, 139–40.[4]

Having engaged in Behaviour therapy as well as in psychoanalytical Psychotherapy extensively, I can safely say that a better result, with resolution of the underlying problem, could not have been achieved by Psychoanalytical psychotherapy. My understanding of what happened to engender such a quick and complete resolution of the problem is that it was the relationship with Mrs S that had the greatest influence on the outcome. The relationship consisted of two elements, the real relationship and the transference relationship. There was a real relationship between Mrs S and me in which there was mutual respect. I treated her as a whole person. She formed a transference relationship with me in which I took on characteristics of father. This time she could not have anxiety-making, guilty, sexual fantasies, which mitigated the wish-guilt she had about the relationship with father, and therefore permitted a guilt-free sexuality and better sex with her husband.

PSYCHODYNAMICS AND BEHAVIOUR THERAPY

Both are Needed

There is nothing called pure psychodynamic therapy. Behavioural principles of conditioning and deconditioning, and desensitisation are always used in a natural way in the course of psychodynamic work.

The psychodynamic approach embraces the basic tenet of

Social Learning theory that behaviour is learned. But unlike Social Learning theory, it recognises that the learning is done through both the conscious and the unconscious mind. It recognises the importance of relationships with significant people, including the therapist, in the genesis, the perpetuation and the resolution of disturbance. It also recognises that painful experiences, which may include learned experiences and reactions to them, or painful fantasies are often pushed into the unconscious mind from where they influence feelings and behaviour.

It does not deny the value and importance of the behavioural approach.

The psychotherapist forms a relationship with the patient/offender and creates a climate of safety between them which is akin to relaxation under light hypnosis used in Behaviour therapy when helping the patient/offender to think and talk about distressing events during the session. The patient/offender may even regress back to his childhood under the impact of the *transference* relationship (see below), and recall forgotten distressing events in full consciousness – something that is done under hypnosis in Behaviour therapy, when recollection is not a fully conscious experience and therefore less effective; it may even be denied in the conscious state.

When a patient/offender achieves something worthwhile in his therapy or in his social life, the natural feeling of pleasure and happiness in the therapist and the staff around him acts as a reward and encouragement to the patient.

If the patient confesses to a misdemeanour, and is distressed by what he has done, the seriousness with which the therapist and staff treat the issue acts as a painful confirmation of his own disapproval. If he is flippant or uncaring after a misdemeanour, the therapist's spontaneous remark and the natural responses of staff act as a behavioural deterrent.

These spontaneous natural responses of staff are much more effective than the 'contrived' responses of Behaviour therapy, arranged by the behaviour therapist which may come to be regarded as a game by the offenders and indeed by some staff.

Behaviour Therapy, as practised with disturbed adolescents, on the other hand, limits its useful application to a small minority of youngsters, and totally denies the relevance of psychodynamics.

Behavioural theory states: 'Therapy is based on learning theory. Other Behaviour therapy assumptions include: (1) Concepts like the unconscious, id, ego, superego, insight, and self are not necessary in, and usually hinder, the understanding and treatment of deviant behaviour. (2) The symptoms are the deviant behaviour. Remove the symptoms and you remove the behaviour Disorder.'[5] (*Four Psychotherapies* by Leonard Hersher, Cautela – *Behaviour Therapy*, Dr Joseph Cautela, pp.85–111. Appleton-Century-Crofts, New York.)

There is no argument beyond that point if one accepts the philosophy of behaviour therapy as stated above. One may want to prove the theory to be wrong, which I think will be futile because it is indeed true for some cases. I have found that the most useful way of choosing one of the innumerable number of theories that abound is to use one's common sense and simple rational thinking to judge the value of each.

Let us compare the treatment plans for a young rapist using Behaviour therapy and using psychodynamics:

Treatment of Sex Offenders – a rapist and a child-abuser

A Rapist

The Behavioural Approach:
He would be in a secure setting – prison or a Youth Treatment centre. All efforts are concentrated on ways of discouraging such impulses and thoughts through planned management and treatment manoeuvres.

The aim of treatment is to remove an exciting and pleasurable experience he has of raping a girl or changing it to a painful one. It is often done by delivering electric shocks of increasing pain while the offender re-experiences the rape scene, in the form of pictures, films and/or imagination. This process without doubt results in the subject finding the rape scene to be unpleasurable and painful. However, Whether or not there have been any real changes in the offender's attitudes and impulses as a result of treatment will always remain in doubt, because they have been suppressed by the painful experience. Further, behaviour therapists have not had training in methods of recognising and understanding underlying feelings by observing external behaviour and therefore are in no position to make critical evaluation of the success of their treatment.

The Psychodynamic Approach:
It will be seen in the psychodynamic approach that it encompasses all the beneficial effects of the behavioural approach, and in addition offers more effective deterrents.

The offender in psychodynamic treatment would also be in a secure setting – treatment prison or a Youth Treatment centre. Here too the conduct is discouraged – explicitly through the very fact of his incarceration and through all the practical manoeuvres taken to prevent him from re-offending whilst he is in treatment, and implicitly through the natural abhorrence that the staff have for his offence. All this is experienced by the offender in behavioural treatment.

In addition there will be discussion and support of the part of the offender which has a distaste for what he has done.

In the psychodynamic approach the offender is also helped to get in touch with the cause of the problem, which inevitably involves a token attack on some loved person – say, a dominant, seductive and tyrannical mother. For an adolescent, and for any human being, such an attack on mother (a loved person), is perhaps one of the most reprehensible of acts. Recognition that it is his own mother on whom he has made an attack – a token attack though it may be – is far more painful than any physical pain the behaviourist may deliver. It is a deterrent that he will carry with him all his life.

Through discussion with the therapist of the events and feelings surrounding the attack, the offender would hopefully understand the reason for his impulse to attack his mother, which can lead on to further useful discussion which may change his feelings from anger to understanding, when the need for a deterrent will be obviated.

I think it will be readily seen that the psychodynamic approach which combines the behavioural is far more effective and quick in creating a change of lasting effect. It is important to ensure that the offender is genuinely helped to reach his own particular, unconscious motivation, rather than it being merely an intellectual exercise, learned from a text book and concocted out of the therapist's head. This is something that all those well trained in psychodynamics will know about. The speed and effectiveness is particularly evident in adolescents, in whom the unconscious conflicts are very near the surface and reached more easily then in an adult. Further there is a greater chance of detecting real change as opposed to pseudo-change, in a youngster who has opened himself to examination of his deeper problems, by staff who have had the specialised training. There will be a change in the feelings he has nurtured for his mother, which will be reflected in his attitude to older female staff.

A child-abuser

It has often been found in child sexual offenders that they themselves have been the passive victims of sexual abuse as children. The behavioural understanding of this is that he has learned to abuse children through being abused himself as a child. Therefore unlearning this behaviour by relearning through painful experiences, as described above for a rapist, is necessary.

The psychodynamic understanding of this is that the child who has had an unpleasant experience and has not had the opportunity to talk and think about it, discuss it, work through it and be relieved of the unpleasant experience, will, under stress, find himself trying to get rid of the experience in a concrete way by ejecting it (re-enacting the abuse) into an available accepting/vulnerable child.

In fact, not every child-sex-abuser has been sexually abused himself. Psychodynamic understanding would show that any kind of abuse – emotional or physical, at certain stages of the sexual development of a child – can become confused with sexual abuse in the psyche. This was discovered by Sigmund Freud through one of the best known mistakes in the history of psychoanalysis, made by Freud himself, when he believed that many parents had sexually abused there little children. He himself recognised that he had mistaken psychic reality for factual events, and he corrected this mistake (at great expense to his personal prestige, it must be said).[6] (Jones Ernest, *Sigmund Freud, Life and Work*, Vol.1. pp.292–294, Hogarth Press, London, 1953.)

However, it is always true that an abusive sex-offender has had unpleasant abusive personal experiences as a child.

This has two serious implications for those who undertake treatment of sexual offenders without training in psychodynamics:

1. Attempting the usual 'reward and punishment' Behaviour therapy would inevitably lead to the offender to link the punishments used in the behavioural system with the unpleasant abuse he suffered in his early life, with reinforcement and exacerbation of the problem, together with more effective suppression of the impulse to express it.

2. Those behaviour therapists not trained in psychodynamics and who therefore do not recognise the existence of psychic reality, have been known to try to persuade or coerce offenders to confess to having been sexually abused as children – the father or a close relative is chosen as the suspect. The offender is thus subjected to enormous pressure to 'confess' and to further psychological abuse, with reinforcement of the problem.

The general natural attitude to child-abusers and rapists is one of aversion to what they have done, which often is expressed in abusive treatment they receive within and outside institutions. This abuse of the offender, even if it is not expressed in physical exhibitions, is often expressed in attitudes, all of which repeat the childhood abusive experience of the offender. There is thus a built-in natural vicious cycle which causes the problem within the offender to be perpetuated.

In good psychodynamic therapy it behoves the therapist to always be aware of the whole of the patient – the abused child as well as the adult or adolescent abuser, and to bring these split-off (separated) parts together; and to always be a whole person themselves with the patient.

The Recidivist

One of the effects of the relationship between the offender and the psychodynamic therapist who deals with the offender in an entirely non-punitive manner, concerns its mellowing influence on the harsh and cruel superego (conscience) of the offender. Delinquents often have extremely punitive superegos, which have developed partly through punitive treatment from their parents and carers and partly through projections onto carers of their own aggressive impulses. This punitive authority, which is partly created by the infant, is absorbed (introjected) from babyhood, and then through a series of real or imagined reactions and counter-reactions, it becomes excessively punitive towards the offender's own conduct. Such offenders are sometimes so terrified by their own conscience that they refuse to acknowledge feelings of guilt and come over as people without a conscience. It has been shown by Freud, in his paper 'Criminals out of a sense of guilt',[7] that it is this excessively punitive, harsh superego, which, paradoxically, drives the recidivist to repeated offences. The offences are committed in order to obtain punishment and allay deep unconscious guilt which is not allowed into the conscious mind, i.e. the feelings of guilt precede the commitment of the offence. In most cases this guilt can be reached and worked through if it is not repeatedly allayed, albeit temporarily, through the punishment he seeks. The author has had several experiences of the effective use of this principle with offenders who have come under treatment with him The story of Jim in Chapter X, 'The Mellowing of a Cruel and Punitive Superego', would serve as a good example.

One would expect that those who practice the behavioural approach, are as honest, compassionate, empathetic and caring, as the psychodynamist, but their ability to influence the cruel and punitive superego of an offender is jeopardised because of the method of Behaviour therapy – which includes punishment; as soon as the offender experiences punishment in whatever form, it links with the punitive superego, and mellowing of the superego to an understanding and kindly authority, becomes impossible. Those who offend out of a sense of guilt, will continue to do so.

The Relationship Between Staff and Patient/Offender in Psychodynamic Therapy

In psychodynamic therapy it is *the nature of the relationships between the therapist/staff and the patient/client*, which becomes of crucial importance. The relationship has two elements to it, the real relationship and the transference relationship.

The real relationship

It is essential in good psychodynamic therapy with adolescents that the patients/offender knows that the therapist is a caring, reliable, trustworthy person in his/her real life and will use these qualities in his/her interest.

Examples:

1. Jacky, a sad, disturbed sixteen-year-old, came to my room one day and said, 'Dr Perin, I don't want to be in Alan's group anymore.' When I asked the reason for this, she told me she had overheard Alan, one of the co-therapists in her 'small group therapy' group talking on the telephone to make a secret appointment to meet a girl. It was well known in the unit that Alan had a steady girlfriend.

2. Michael, a boy of seventeen who was in my small group when I was a junior doctor, held me in high esteem. He found it impossible to attend my groups until it was ensured to his satisfaction that the tablets seen in my car were for medicinal purposes and not for drug abuse, which was rampant and in the news at that time.

In both these cases the adolescents could not form a trusting real relationship with the therapist.

The transference

This is an unconscious phenomenon during which forgotten and partially forgotten experiences are constantly re-experienced in the current relationships or situations, when there is something in the situation which bears any kind of resemblance to significant events in the past. Most of these have occurred many years previously and have been pushed into the deeper recesses of the mind. It is used to help the youngsters to recall these relationships of the past, to re-examine them and to understand them in terms of their current experience with the therapist/staff and therefore gain a renewed experience of the original relationship. This renewed experience of the past relationship can change the entire life of the patient.

Two of the commonly occurring transference situations with adolescents are:

1. Anger with the therapist for simply being an authority figure, even though the therapist does not merit the anger through his/her behaviour with the youngster.
2. The fantasy of sexual love with the therapist, transferred from childhood feelings of affection for the parents.

The transference relationship occurs anyway, with any person or situation that reminds one of the past; it does not depend on the kind of therapy used. (Though the psychodynamic therapist is trained to behave with the patient in such a way as not to jeopardise the transference.) It is only through training in psychodynamic therapy that one learns how to recognise the transference and to deal with it in such a way as to avoid pitfalls and disasters and to benefit the patient.

It is in adolescence, when the instinctual drives and feelings of conflict receive an added momentum because of the massive hormonal, physical and intellectual changes, that these unconscious and partially conscious disturbing experiences and feelings become easily accessible. They are often transferred onto therapists. If these troublesome feelings are not recognised, brought out, and dealt with adequately at this stage of their lives, they can become pushed underneath the surface, and deeper into the unconscious mind (repressed), under the influence of behavioural manoeuvres, and can cause serious trouble in later life.

The anger with parents can develop into pathological proportions where there have been traumatic relationships between parents and between parents and children – the majority of disturbed and delinquent youngsters. The pathological rebellious feelings will inevitably be expressed in the transference relationship with therapists or staff of a unit, as described above.

Simple behavioural ways of trying to deal with these feelings, without recognising the transference, can lead their repression and the creation of criminals and potential terrorists.

Example:

In Chapter X, 'Some Interesting Cases' is the story of Jim – 'The Mellowing of a Cruel and Punitive Superego'. Jim had a strong transference relationship to me and saw me as a cruel, punitive authority – based on his relationship with his parents and the police. After each staff meeting we had, following some incident in which Jim was involved, he attacked me verbally and threatened me, for being against him and wanting him put away. It was very interesting to us, because amongst all the staff it was I who had been the most eloquent and unambiguous about the need to be non-punitive and treat him as our patient, rather than as a criminal who needed punishment.

My non-threatening responses to Jim's attacks were puzzling to him initially, till he had good evidence to realise that the real relationship (feelings), I, the authority figure, had with him was very different from the one he had imagined (transferred). The repeated experiences of non-threatening responses he had had from staff formed a supportive background. This was the beginning of a radical change for the better in Jim. He stopped all rude and delinquent behaviour and became much more thoughtful and pleasant to be with. We were sure that whatever experiences he had in the future, the experiences he had had with us in the unit would stay with him and influence him towards thoughtful creative responses.

While we did not try to alter Jim's behaviour through directly tackling his rude, threatening behaviour, either by simply reacting to it or by using 'Reward and Punishment' programmes, it should be recognised that a part of the techniques we used were Behavioural – Wolpe's Reciprocal Inhibition. We recognised that his fierce attacks on me, the authority figure, and the other staff when they took on the role, were really expressions of his abject terror of the punishments he expected, and we repeatedly allowed him to experience staff's non-punitive response and attempt to understand, which in principle is no different from Wolpe's desensitisation and deconditioning under relaxation.

CONCLUSION

Psychodynamics acknowledges its need of the Behavioural philosophy to make its treatment method whole. It incorporates Behavioural principles into its own philosophy.

Behaviour therapy unfortunately makes claims of being entirely self sufficient.

> Concepts like the unconscious, id, ego, superego, insight, and self, are not necessary in, and usually hinder, the understanding and treatment of deviant behaviour. The symptoms are the

deviant behaviour. Remove the symptoms and you remove the behaviour disorder.

Written by Dr Joseph Cautela about Behaviour therapy: '*The Theory and Practice of Behaviour Therapy* (Cautela, 1970[5]). What is more and of the greatest relevance to the practice in the UK is that it is this theory and practice which has been aggressively followed after the HAS document, *Bridges Over Troubled Waters.*

In truth, attempting Behaviour therapy with adolescents without psychodynamic understanding does them more harm than it does good.

The Nature of Adolescence

The very nature of adolescence, which is characterised by an inherent urge to develop one's own identity, makes an *exclusively* behavioural approach invalid.

All adolescents are driven by an instinctual urge to break away from their childhood authority and to develop their own authority. The way in which each youngster expresses and achieves this varies, depending on his/her inheritance, and the environmental influence. In adolescents who have had a bad experience of authority, such as deprivation of normal parenting, cruel or bad parenting – the commonest type of youngster who requires admission to an institution – this normal instinctual drive becomes an urgent pathological need. As they develop physically and intellectually and sense, more and more, the possibility that they are indeed capable of exerting their own authority, the urge to try it out becomes paramount.

They often get into a phase of 'pseudo-adulthood' in which there is a powerful urge to equalise themselves with adults; most do it in their fantasy lives. In a residential setting however, in the safety of the company of other youngsters, they literally try it with the staff in the cleverest ways. If they cannot elevate themselves to pseudo-adulthood, they often manage to bring adult staff down to the adolescent level, by touching off the adolescent feelings that lurk beneath the surface in most normal adults. If the adult workers are not sophisticated (psychodynamically trained) in recognising what goes on within themselves, and in dealing with them effectively, they may repeatedly fall prey to these adolescent manoeuvres, which could result in massive staff stress and irresponsible adolescent behaviour by staff. It is only training and experience in psychodynamics and good psychodynamic supervision of staff that can help staff to recognise these phenomena and prevent escalation into uncontrollable proportions in a residential setting.

When these challenges to authority are looked at and dealt with behaviourally, without psychodynamic understanding of the underlying motivation, the relationship between the treaters/staff and the youngster inevitably degenerates into a battle of wills and struggles to control each other. *Attempts to control adolescents almost invariably lead to further rebellion, and escalating attempts to control.* The more spirited and inventive the youngster, the greater is the need for stronger methods of control. In such a contest the adolescent has the advantage; unlike the staff, he is not constrained by his role, the law nor by a sense of responsibility.

Behaviour therapy programmes which require close co-operation with a well motivated patient, carefully graded hierarchical targets, and close monitoring, go overboard, and are replaced by activities which are glorified by the term 'behaviour modification techniques'. These may include any available way of controlling the youngsters – forcing them into 'Time Out' rooms, for instance, is a common practice. As long as the practice, however horrendous, is couched in technical terminology, it becomes acceptable to the perpetrator; it becomes part of his professional duty. He has to control the youngster – he/she has no other option; *'Pin Down', becomes a natural progression*.

It must be understood that in Social Service institutions, where adolescents and children are placed together, it is the adolescents who will take the lead and set the culture; the children merely follow. If the approach is purely behavioural, and only the behaviour is looked at they will both be treated in the same way.

Many youngsters in fact are not old enough or spirited enough to fight on. They are successfully trained to behave well, for a while. The question then is what has happened within the mind of the youngster during this process?

Psychodynamists believe that the disturbance which is

suppressed, becomes walled off and isolated from the total personality. It becomes worse as a result of the isolation, and is then liable to erupt under stress and break through the defensive wall, into action, possibly of a worse type than before.

I would like to suggest that the validity of the Behaviourism is far too obvious to be neglected or ignored; it pervades all areas of human life. Similarly, underlying, unconscious (psychodynamic) influences are ever present and influence all aspects of human behaviour.

But the psychodynamic effects are not obvious; they are difficult to recognise, understand, and work with; they can easily be ignored, at great cost to offenders, to the victims and to society. Unawareness or suppression of phenomena that lie below the surface, as proposed by certain forms of Behaviourism and widely used in the service, can at best lead to ineffective treatment; at worst, it can lead to reinforcement and exacerbation of the problem and to serious disasters.

The General Method of Psychodynamics with Offenders

Pain is well recognised as the most effective, (if not the only), deterrent. Behaviour therapy incorporates the use of pain, which is delivered externally through its well-known reward and punishment programmes.

Those who are not trained and experienced in the psychotherapy of adolescents, and imagine it to be a gentle, non-punitive method, which overflows with kindness and understanding, would naturally be sceptical about its effectiveness in the treatment of offenders. 'How', one may ask, 'is it possible to engender change and prevent further offending, if some sort of pain [punishment], perhaps the only known deterrent, is not used?'

The psychodynamic method is in fact not gentle. It is realistic and non-punitive. It seeks out the natural feelings of the offender and uses these creatively in order to achieve the desired effect. In Behaviour therapy, a painful experience is dispensed for 'bad' behaviour; in psychodynamic treatment, the painful experience within the offender is uncovered.

Staff strive, through caring discussion, to enable the youngster to recognise the internal pain and unhappiness he creates for himself and for those he loves, by his offending activities. He is helped to get in touch with his own deeper awareness and feelings about himself and his conduct. These are invariably linked to deeper feelings of guilt and pain associated with relationships with parents; the sensitivity of the offender is enhanced and refined.

In my own experience of over twenty-five years in psychodynamic work with disturbed adolescents, amongst whom several have been offenders, there has not been a single offender who has remained in treatment for more than a few months, who has not explicitly stated a preference for ordinary punishment, to the pain of thinking about his offences and experiencing the guilt about the damage he has done.

REFERENCES

[1] Policy Document of Glenthorne, Youth Treatment Centre. DOH unit.

[2] Segal, Hanna, *Introduction to the Work of Melanie Klein*, p.15, The Hogarth Press and The Institute of Psychoanalysis.

[3] Perinpanayagam, K. S., 'A Monosymptomatic Phobia Treated by a Single Session of Behaviour Therapy', in *The British Journal of Psychiatry*, Vol. 119, No. 55, September 1971.

[4] Friedman, D.E., 'A new technique for the systematic desensitization of phobic symptoms', *Behaviour Research and Therapy*, 4, pp.139–40, 1966.

[5] Cautela, Dr Joseph, *Behaviour Therapy, Theory and Practice*, in *Four Psychotherapies*, Leonard Hersher, Appleton-Century- Crofts, New York, 1970, p.86.

[6] Jones, Ernest, *Sigmund Freud, Life and Work*, Vol.1, pp.292–294, London, The Hogarth Press, 1953.

[7] Freud, S, *Complete Psychological Works*, Vol. X1X, p.49, London, The Hogarth Press, 1965.

Chapter III
A SHORT HISTORY OF THE ADOLESCENT SERVICES FROM 1965

This chapter gives a short history of the Adolescent Services starting in 1965, when the government White Paper 'The Child, the Family and the Young Offender' was published and the Approved Schools system was abolished. It was the birth of psychodynamics in the service for adolescents – treatment was being designed to deal with the cause. This progressive move did not last long. Restriction of punishment in schools followed by an upsurge of indiscipline, misunderstandings about psychodynamics and the socio-political mood of the time led to a demand for harsh treatments. This was eventually given clinical validation by the report of the Health Advisory Service of 1986. This report discarded psychodynamics as of no importance, leaving 'Reward and Punishment' Behaviour therapy as the only alternative. The chapter ends with an evaluation of the kind of reward and punishment Behaviour therapy used for adolescents – operant conditioning.

The need for something new and different in the adolescent service, a method that seeks and deals with the cause, began to be recognised by the government in the mid-sixties when the success rates of the Approved Schools had fallen to 38%, from 85–90% in the early twentieth century ([1]Mays, 1975). The government of the day investigated the nature of this apparently inexplicable phenomenon and in August 1965 published a White Paper, 'The Child, the Family and the Young Offender'. The White Paper stated:

> The government attaches great importance to further development of the service concerned with the prevention and treatment

of juvenile delinquency and with other similar problems affecting children and their families... juvenile delinquency has no single cause, manifestation or cure. Its origins are many and the range of behaviour which it covers is equally wide. At some points it merges almost imperceptibly with behaviour which does not contravene the law. A child's behaviour is influenced by genetic, emotional and intellectual factors, his maturity and his family, school, neighbourhood and wider social setting. It is only a minority of children who grow up without ever misbehaving in ways which maybe contrary to the law.(²HMSO, Command 1968.)

The importance of the relationship between the offender, the offence, and the cause was being recognised. The idea of *clinical treatment* for delinquency and adolescent disturbance on a wide scale was brought in for the first time.

Together with the publication of the White Paper the Approved Schools were abolished. The emphasis was shifted from training-out or suppression of the delinquency, as in the Approved School System – a Behavioural method – to recognising and dealing with the cause – a psychodynamic method. This was the beginning of formal recognition of the concept of psychodynamic treatment for disturbed youngsters.

There was a new-found freedom in the clinical field for responsible experimentation and research in the treatment of delinquency and adolescent conduct disorders. The causes and rational treatment was being sought. I was the Registrar at the Northgate Clinic in NW9, at the time. Under the leadership of Dr Brian O'Connell, Medical Director, the staff had the freedom to use a variety of methods of investigation and treatment – Behaviour therapy of different types, psychodynamic methods of different kinds, and medication, with non-dogmatic, open-minded discussions of the highest calibre. Every youngster in treatment was thoroughly investigated, including electroencephalograms – brain-wave tests. It seemed as if a certain philosophy of treatment with an emphasis on meaningful relationships with the offender and a breadth of view – *Psychodynamics* – was beginning to be recognised all over the country, in the NHS and the Social Services, as the most enlightened and effective. The interest in psychodynamics was such that a long paper on the *Psychodynamic Approach* was broken up into six parts and published at weekly intervals in the *British Medical Journal* in 1978.[3]

It was a golden era for psychodynamics. But it did not last long.

Together with the White Paper and the abolishment of the Approved School system, harsh treatment of adolescents became unpopular. There was a softer mood in the country which extended to all adolescents. The authorities made a clean sweep of it, and corporal punishments in schools were also restricted by law. This was a triumph for those adolescents who were delinquently inclined as well as for the ordinary robust, exuberant, youngsters who were in the natural adolescent state of rebellion against authority, who had been controlled by the stringent discipline in schools, and there was an explosion of adolescent indiscipline and hooliganism.

The psychodynamic approach to adolescence in its search for underlying causes, and therefore disinterest in punishment, was wrongly associated with this failed 'soft approach'. In truth, psychodynamics suggests *replacement of punishment* with a thoughtful, unambiguous firm authority, and honest discussion with youngsters. Mere removal of punishment indeed would lead to rampant expression of an adolescent's fantasy life.

In the midst of this adolescent indiscipline and increasing delinquency, there was an election promise by the Conservative Party that the prevailing delinquency and crime would be dealt with effectively. The shrill cry, 'A crime is a crime is a crime!' reverberated throughout the country and there was a change of government in 1979. Simply stopping the delinquency in any available way seemed the thing to do. In this socio-political mood, Behaviour therapy was seen as the solution. The term itself appeared to hit right at the heart of the matter; it was the behaviour of the youngsters, after all, which caused the trouble; it was that surely, which needed to be dealt with. Behaviour therapy seemed to be the answer. The Reward and Punishment type of Behaviour therapy was easy to understand. It promised quick, effective results. The psychodynamic approach was marginalised.

The term itself was not understood; it seemed far too complicated.

HARSH TREATMENT REINTRODUCED

The 'short sharp shock' and tough measures for dealing with adolescent disturbance and delinquency were introduced no sooner the new government came into power. However, in the Conservative Party manifesto of 1979 was the promise, 'in certain detention centres we will experiment with tougher regimes…', and research was organised by the government.

This research was not necessary, neither to discover the value of 'tougher regimes' nor to give guidelines to the government. Mays had shown convincingly that in the nineteenth century, when harsh and punitive methods for dealing with young offenders were replaced with humane forms of training, there was a huge increase in the success rates as judged by a three year follow up of offending behaviour. The norm for that period was something like 75%. After the First World War the certified schools, 'notched up the greatest success rates of between 85% to 90%.' ([1]Mays, 1975.)

The findings of the research conducted in two centres emerged many years later. The conclusions after the experiment stated:

> The introduction of the pilot project regimes had no discernible effect on the rate at which trainees were reconvicted. A number of ways in which effects on reconviction might have been masked were considered and discounted.
>
> These findings are fully in accordance with previous research which showed there is little relationship between crime rates and the average severity of custodial sentences. ([4]Thornton, Bayfield, 1978, p.230.)

Then even though there was formal recognition and acknowledgement once again that punishments and harsh treatment of adolescent disturbance did not bring any useful result, there was no change of policy.

It is in this climate that the psychodynamic approach to adolescence was rejected by the psychiatric establishment, (*Bridges*

Over Troubled Waters, Horrocks, 1986) giving clinical authenticity to the socio-political momentum of the time.

The only kind of behaviour therapy which could be used *en masse* – the *Reward and Punishment* type, *Operant Conditioning*, came in once again, and this time *in opposition to, and with the exclusion of the psychodynamic approach*.

It is in this climate that 'Pin Down' occurred in the early nineties, in which conscientious senior staff used the most draconian methods to control youngsters in children's homes. They thought they were doing their duty, in accordance with the higher authority. In the event they were dismissed from the service, even though the fault was not theirs (see Chapter II – 'Systems Theory').

PSYCHODYNAMICS

The history and fate of 'Psychodynamics', 'Psychotherapy' and 'Psychoanalysis' (terms which are loosely used interchangeably) have been greatly influenced by the reactions and attitudes of professionals, most of whom do not work in the field and have only a theoretical understanding of psychoanalysis as it was practised in the time of Freud.

Some Misapprehensions about Psychodynamics

Psychodynamics and Pain

Psychodynamics is thought of as 'the Soft Approach'. One of the common misunderstandings about psychodynamics is caused by too much attention being focused on its *non-punitive* aspect. It is very difficult to get away from this as a central issue, because psychodynamic treatment is indeed not concerned with inflicting pain in any form, even to an offender. Though, in truth, it does something more effective for offenders.

In a good psychodynamically orientated unit, the painful experience for misdemeanours forms an integral part of the psychodynamic process. In the usual 'Punishment systems' or the behavioural 'Reward and Punishment systems', an *externally* painful experience is *dispensed* for bad behaviour. In the psychodynamic process an *internally* painful experience *within the patient is uncovered*. Staff strive, through discussions, to enable the patient to recognise and experience the internal pain he creates for himself through his actions, in terms of his relationship with significant people in the community and in his life. This internal pain, usually accompanied by guilt, is far more troublesome to him than any form of external physical punishment. These feelings are invariably linked to deeper feelings related to the primary source of the problem – *the relationship with parents and the family*. (Freud, 1961; Winnicot, 1965.) It leads to a natural urge on their part to make amends. Invariably recipients of the psychodynamic approach make every effort to resist the process. I have had many conduct-disordered adolescents and delinquents, say, during a group discussion with them, 'I'd rather be punished than get go through this.' When they do go through it they are often very grateful because it relieves them of disturbing, unhappy feelings they have lived with for years, which are intimately related to feelings of inferiority and inadequacy, badness, ugliness, and a host of related unpleasant experiences of themselves, which adolescents often cover up by acts of bravado, including delinquency.

The ultimate aim of psychodynamic treatment is to help the patient/client to face his/her own reality about themselves, some of which may be painful initially, and thereby come into possession of the whole of themselves. Patients/clients are helped to recognise aspects of themselves that they do not like and to change those that can be changed, and to accept those that cannot be changed. It leads to a miscreant or an offender to use his own understanding, his own controls and his own authority to change himself and put things right. It increases the self-esteem of the adolescent in a real way.

There are instances where a period in prison is consistent with the psychodynamic philosophy.

In contrast, each time an adolescent is punished in order to control his behaviour, his immature, diffident mind receives a message. The message is that he is no good, that he does not have much of a mind to be able to think and change his own behaviour, and his self-esteem drops a notch lower. He becomes more resentful.

Punishments indeed are not the answer. *Equally, mere removal of punishments are as inappropriate*, because youngsters would simply go wild with triumph and, paradoxically, panic at being suddenly left to get on with their own controls. Their misbehaviour is likely to become as gross and as dangerous or frightening as the feelings within them. Their misbehaviour is often an attempt to invite controls and punishments which make them feel safe. *It is the psychodynamic interactive process, which takes in the frightening, dangerous feeling and gives back safe understanding of the adolescent's feelings that is important.*

The psychodynamic approach deals with the realities of the youngster. It can be used as effectively in a secure setting as in an open one, if 'security' is recognised as necessary for whatever reason (to protect society and the youngster himself, from his own uncontrolled and dangerous impulses). *Psychodynamics recognises that there are some types of serious offences where punishment serves as a necessary prerequisite for the offender to be able to use his abilities in his own favour.*

REACTIONS TO PSYCHODYNAMICS

Broadly speaking, there are four reactions to psychodynamics amongst those in the service who are not trained in the speciality which comprise a large group – many Consultant Psychiatrists working in the speciality of adolescence, most psychologists, and social work professionals, managers and policy-makers.

1. The Envious
Psychodynamics requires a training over and above the basic training for specialists. It has an elitist, esoteric quality which can make it the focus of envy amongst some professionals who desire to have it but have not obtained the training for some reason. Envy is a secretive quality, well recognised in all societies, which is closely allied to the wish to destroy. In some Eastern countries newly born babies, whose parents think they are particularly beautiful, are painted on the forehead with a black mark, it is said, to ward off the 'evil eye'. In Western psychodynamic philosophy it would mean making the baby look ugly to ward off envious attacks.

Those who possess the quality of envy may suffer too much from the pain of not ever being able to have (the ability in) what seems so attractive. They would strive to diminish the envied thing or dispel it from existence or from their vision, in order to rid themselves of pain.

The story we heard when learning about envy, which describes it in simple terms, was the story of the 'Sour Grapes' from Aesop's fables. It is the story of the fox who spied an extraordinarily delicious looking bunch of grapes in the orchard across the fence. He tried his best to reach for it for many hours, and when he could not, he finally gave up, saying, 'It is only a bunch of sour grapes.'

If people in authority possess this quality of envy about psychodynamics they can be devastatingly destructive to institutions and individuals who practice it keenly.

In the document *Bridges Over Troubled Waters, A National Survey of the Services for Disturbed Adolescents, (HAS, 1986)*, the term Psychotherapy was not mentioned even once in its 77 pages. This strange absence of the word, even to criticise the practice, could be seen as a function of envy where even the sight of the word causes pain. (Steiner,1986.) The document proved to be the 'death blow' to psychodynamics in the service for adolescence.

In the clinical field, psychiatrists who have this envious quality can be dangerous in their practice, as they would see medical psychiatric conditions where a psychodynamic one exists. They will not be able to differentially diagnose psychodynamic conditions which mimic a formal psychiatric illness; and they may prescribe medications which can be damaging to the personality.

2. The non-envious worker who recognises that learning it is a long and arduous process which they should have undertaken when they were younger.

They may go fully into the practice of behaviour therapy, which is far easier to understand and learn. If they are medically trained (psychiatrists), they may choose to engage with only those 12% of adolescent problems which require psychiatric expertise. Or they may try engaging in psychodynamic treatment under supervision. Some of this group, who value the psychodynamic approach, may encourage and support subordinates and younger colleagues to learn and practise what they themselves have missed.

3. Those who are clever enough to pick up and use the phraseology may seem to be knowledgeable. They may use the language lavishly and inappropriately in situations where they themselves do not have to face the consequences, such as in secure units or outpatients' clinics.

They could engage in unsupervised individual psychotherapy where the client is always blamed for the mishaps and failure, or operate in secure units where disruption caused by misinterpretation and mishandling of a situation by the staff leads to the residents being locked up and penalised.

This group can do as much lasting damage to clients and indeed to the concept of psychodynamics than the envious group mentioned above, for they often profess a diehard loyalty to psychodynamics, while continually giving evidence of how ineffective their own practice is. They thus give truth to the envious attacks on psychodynamics in full view of the executive administrators, managers and policy-makers.

4. A well respected common misunderstanding amongst professionals who are not involved in the psychodynamic treatment of adolescence, is expressed in the following description from Cautela. ([8]1970.)

> According to this model, therapy consists of the removal of basic underlying unconscious conflicts. This involves much exploration and time. Also under the medical model, ward personnel such as attendants, nurses and volunteers play a very minor role in the alleviation and remission of the maladaptive behaviour of institutionalised individuals. In this model the ward personnel act more or less as custodians until the 'real' therapy can be administered by the psychologist or the psychiatrist in individual or group situations.

This description is accurate for the attempt at the practice of psychodynamic therapy in an inpatient setting perhaps some three or four decades ago. The practice is lengthy, invidious, expensive in time and money and impractical.

As in all branches of medicine there has been much progress in the psychodynamic treatment of adolescents over the last few decades.

Today, in a good psychodynamically orientated unit, all staff participate in the treatment. There is constant in-service training of staff through regular staff discussion about all aspects of work. Treatment occurs with the youngsters throughout the day through psychodynamic interactions in the day-to-day living. The effect of all the staff interacting with the adolescent with an understanding of his underlying problem, and affecting it in a therapeutic manner, is far greater than the effect of a single trained therapist seeing the youngster once or twice a week for therapy. Serious problems are resolved in a relatively short while. One single well-trained consultant in psychodynamics is all that is necessary for the most effective work, if the rest of the staff are well chosen. The consultant works mainly with the staff, not with the patients. Whitefriars Children's Home for Adolescents, which operates in this manner, provides a good example. An excerpt from its Statement of Purpose and Function should be self-explanatory:

> The attitudes and behaviour of the staff with the young people is crucial to the good work of the unit. Therefore, an ongoing critical examination of the feelings, attitudes and behaviour of staff, including the house manager and the consultant psychiatrist, in relation to the work of the unit, forms an integral part of the philosophy.
>
> The essential treatment of the youngsters is done by the staff. For this purpose, the interactions of the staff with the youngsters in their daily activities, and in the daily house meetings are examined together with the consultant psychiatrist, in hand-over meetings four times a week.
>
> Staff sensitivity meetings are held once a week. The chief purpose of the sensitivity meetings is to encourage staff criticism of each other; it requires the attendance of all staff.

Thus a constant drive towards good practice is built into the system, and will be built into any well-run Psychodynamic system.

BRIDGES OVER TROUBLED WATERS –
THE NATIONAL SURVEY OF SERVICES FOR ADOLESCENTS

Psychodynamics, which was progressively marginalised from 1979, was swept away from the adolescent services in 1986. The Health Advisory Service Report *Bridges Over troubled Waters – A*

National Survey of the Services for Disturbed Adolescents, delivered with much pomp and splendour, did not give 'Psychodynamics' or its twin, 'Psychotherapy', even a small space in its 77 pages. ([7]Steiner, 1986.) *The term was not mentioned even once.*

The Royal College of Psychiatrists gave its support to the document and it became the 'bible' of the service, whose guidelines were to be followed by all health authorities. Social Service departments felt it was safe to follow that lead.

Several letters were written to the Bulletin of the Royal College at the time, notably one by the Chairman of the Association of Psychoanalytical Psychiatry ([7]Steiner, 1986), and one by the author of this book, ([9]Perinpanayagam, 1987), pointing out the serious omission and bias in the document and its likely deleterious effect on the service. Two hundred years of progress, it seemed, were being wiped out in a stroke.

However, the support for its proposals went on unabated, although in effect 88% of disturbed adolescents ([10]Perinpanayagam, 1978) were losing their means of gaining treatment, and professionals were being deprived of the means of managing them.

During the following years, the number of institutions and organisations that were actively involved in psychodynamic practice and training, gradually dwindled. Financial and other ways of support were gradually withdrawn. Some were forcibly closed using the most ethically and morally dubious methods ([11]Perinpanayagam, 1986).

The adolescent services were then left only with *Behaviour Therapy* and its extension *Behaviour Modification* as the method of managing and treating disturbed adolescents.

BEHAVIOUR THERAPY

Behaviour therapy is often spoken of as if it were a single entity; a form of treatment, which is corrective of the misbehaviour of youngsters. In the sociopolitical climate of any developed free society, where adolescent idealism and exuberance is rampant and sometimes reaches dangerous proportions, it would seem to be the heaven-sent answer – a form of treatment that is corrective of the behaviour of youngsters.

In fact there are different kinds of Behaviour therapy. The well-recognised varieties are *Operant Conditioning* (Skinner), *Reciprocal Inhibition* (Wolpe), and *Cognitive Behaviour Therapy*, each of which are different in their theoretical stance and in their practice. I shall be dealing here, with the behaviourism widely used in adolescence – the Reward and Punishment type called operant conditioning.

Operant conditioning denies the relevance or even the existence of the unconscious mind or anything called a mind. An authoritative statement about it is:

> Concepts like the unconscious, id, ego, superego, insight, and self, are not necessary in, and usually hinder, the understanding and treatment of deviant behaviour. The symptoms are the deviant behaviour. Remove the symptoms and you remove the behaviour disorder. ([8]Cautela, 1970.)

It postulates that the treatment of youthful misbehaviour can very easily be eradicated by simply finding ways of removing the misbehaviour, without any consideration of the existence in him/her of a mind. It is the easy way of looking at the problem – the lazy way. It does not need the assiduous training that those undertaking the work seriously would have to do. It is easier to take a monistic view and devise programmes of 'treatment' which take into account only one aspect of behaviour and to totally disregard what is known by any thinking person, that the human is a complex, intelligent being with many different aspects. Thinking then becomes unnecessary and the difficult specialist training for dealing with the unconscious is thus irrelevant.

The other two kinds of behaviour therapy recognise underlying feelings and the unconscious mind. Reciprocal Inhibition deals directly with maladaptive feelings, which are not in the control of the patient, and uses different manoeuvres to change them to more adaptive and desirable ones. Cognitive behaviour therapy works on the basis that appropriate conscious thinking is stronger than the maladaptive unconscious forces and uses intellectual work to overcome the disordered feelings.

In this chapter I will deal only with the Behaviour therapy commonly used with conduct disordered adolescents – operant conditioning. The usefulness and importance of the kind of Behaviour therapy which recognises the mind is dealt with in Chapter III – 'Both… are Needed'.

OPERANT CONDITIONING

Operant conditioning (Skinner), is the 'Reward and Punishment' type of behaviour therapy whose theoretical stance is described above.

While certain aspects of the behavioural philosophy are indeed valid and necessary in dealing with adolescents (see Chapter II), who are in a stage at which they want to learn about themselves and the world around them, *it is the attempt to deal with them as mindless individuals which causes the problems*.

The method proposed by this kind of behaviour therapy is simple, easy to understand and seems logical. Good behaviour is promoted by giving rewards and bad behaviour is discouraged by punishments. This is the method used in most children's homes and adolescent units which contain disturbed adolescents. Parents are frequently advised by professionals that similar methods be used with their teenage children.

Common sense seems to dictate that punishments would have an inhibitory effect on bad behaviour; and that the reward and punishment method would be eminently suited to deal with the problem.

In practice however, this method has very limited usefulness. It is of value only for those very few (or non-existent) adolescents who have had *no* 'upbringing or training', and cannot distinguish between right and wrong. This is the method which is successfully used for training little children of four and five, who are meeting the social environment for the first time in their lives. The kind of adolescent and juvenile delinquent who it is deemed require treatment are not growing children who are meeting the socialised world for the first time. They are youngsters who invariably have already had training, discipline, and punishments throughout their childhood and early adolescence, in their homes or their schools. The method does not work with them.

There are no rewards that can be given to youngsters today that they value, unless they are already leading unusually restrictive lives, and there are no punishments you could give them which they fear, unless you break the rules laid down by the Children Act. (See 'Pin Down' in the early 1990s, and the resulting disciplinary action against conscientious staff who thought they were doing their duty extraordinarily well.)

Delinquent adolescents laugh within themselves at the efforts of staff trying to teach them something they already know, through reward and punishment programmes. The more intelligent ones will feel insulted and develop contempt for authority. Every delinquent knows exactly what good behaviour is. For some reason, often unknown to themselves, they do not behave well or are compulsively drawn or driven to delinquency, often against their better judgements. They have no respect for any treatment that does not recognise that they have minds and reasons for behaving the way they do. They have no respect for the punishments they receive and for those who mete them out. They spend their time finding ways of avoiding the programmes by manipulating and tricking the staff. Reward and Punishment Behaviour therapy for youngsters with conduct disorders and delinquents could be regarded as the training ground for youngsters to learn how to outwit and outmanoeuvre authority and become even cleverer delinquents.

I think it will be relevant and useful to hear opinions of operant conditioning from two authoritative sources – the *Encyclopaedia of Mental Health*, and Sir Karl Popper, arguably the greatest philosopher of science the world has known, and then put it away.

From the *Encyclopaedia of Mental Health*:

Operant conditioning was popularised by Burrhus. F. Skinner's experiments with rats and pigeons. Skinner's experiments led him to believe that emotions had no part to play in behaviour. He believed that the claim that emotions are an important factor in behaviour was a 'mental fiction'. His assertion was that 'people are sorry because they cry', or that 'people are afraid because they tremble'.

However we shall see below, Mowrer's research revealed that Skinner's ideas about emotion do not make logical sense even for non human animals. That fact is all the more interesting because

Skinner's research subjects were almost all non-human animals – usually rats and pigeons. However to Skinner's credit, he never advised the extrapolation of his animal research findings to human beings. As late as 1960, he warned that whether or not extrapolation of his research discoveries to people is justified cannot yet be decided. The behaviouristic psychologists who introduced operant conditioning into behaviour therapy… either did not know or ignored that non-human brains cannot and therefore do not process sensory input in the way that human brains process it. …The behaviourist's model for behaviour is: 'People are what they do'. In reality, though, only by magic can making a stupid mistake convert a human being into a stupid person or swimming like a fish convert one into a fish. That is not just a matter of semantics; …When scientists ignore that fact, they sometimes use unsuspected magical thinking to describe empirically valid research findings. As a result they misinterpret their data and FORMULATE USELESS TREATMENT PROCEDURES. ([12]*The Encyclopaedia of Mental Health*.)

From Sir Karl Popper:
Popper's thoughts about denial of the existence of the mental and emotional world are woven into his view of human existence. As expressed in his book *Knowledge and the Body-mind problem,* human activities belong to three different worlds which have a relationship with each other. He describes the three worlds as – world one, or the world of physical or material things; world two, or the world of mental and psychological phenomena; and world three, as containing the products of the interaction between the two – creations of human endeavour which encompass a whole range of things from scientific discoveries, works of art, music and human behaviour of all sorts, good and bad. He recognises the error in philosophies and philosophers who deny the existence of one or other of the worlds, or reduce one into the other, giving rise to philosophies such as idealism, materialism, etc. In Popper's words:

> The prevailing fashion in philosophy is decidedly monistic, and it has been so for a long time. There have been quite different kinds of monism. Until not very long ago a school was fashionable,

which tried to interpret physical things as bundles of phenomena, or as observational possibilities, or as constructs of observation, or sense data. That is to say it was fashionable to try to reduce the first world into the second. This type of monism was called by various names, by 'phenomenalism' for example. At the present time another form of monism is more fashionable. It is called 'physicalism' or sometimes 'behaviourism' or 'materialism'. And it says that to accept what I call world 2 is to introduce unnecessary complications, since it is simpler and more convenient to say that only physical things and physical states exist... but it is held to be quite unnecessary to assume that you or I, are doing anything like paying attention or thinking... I admit that denial of mental states simplifies matters. For example, the difficult body-mind problem disappears, which no doubt is convenient: it saves us the trouble of solving it. ([13]Popper, 1994.)

Further comment about the treatment for disturbed adolescents we have been left with by the HAS report and the psychiatric services seems unnecessary.

REFERENCES

[1] Mays, J.B., (1975) *The Social Treatment of Young Offenders,* Longman, London and New York, pp.2–3.

[2] H.M.S.O. Command, April 1968, London, *Children in Trouble*, p.3, presented to Parliament by the Secretary of State for the Home Department by command of Her Majesty.

[3] Perinpanayagam, K.S., Feb–March 1978, *British Medical Journal* Vol.1.

[4] Thornton, David, 'Tougher Regimes in Detention Centres', 1983, para 8.21. Report of an evaluation by the Young Offenders Psychology Unit by David Thornton, Len Curran, David Grayson, Vernon Holloway Directorate of Psychology Services, Prison Department, London, H.M.S.O.

[5] Freud, S., *Complete Psychological Works*, Vol. XIX, p.49, London, The Hogarth Press: and Winnicot, D.W., *In the Maturational Processes*, London, The Hogarth Press, 1965.

[6] Horrocks, Dr P., *Bridges Over Troubled Waters*, A Report from the NHS, Health Advisory Services for Disturbed Adolescents, March 1986, ISBN 85197 053 3, p.9, para 3.1.1.

[7] Steiner, John, Bulletin of the Royal College of Psychiatrists, Correspondence, September, 1986.

[8] Cautela, Dr Joseph, '*Four Psychotherapies*', 1970, p.85, Ed. Leonard Hersher, Ph.D.

Appleton-Century-Crofts, New York.
[9] Perinpanayagam, K.S., Bulletin of the Royal College of Psychiatrists, Correspondence, February, 1987.
[10] Perinpanayagam, K.S., *British Medical Journal*, 1978, Vol.I pp.424–425.
[11] Perinpanayagam, K.S., *Response to the Review of Brookside*, 1986, written for the North East Thames Regional Health Authority.
[12] The *Encyclopaedia of Mental Health*, Vol.1, p.226.
[13] Popper, Dr Karl, *Knowledge and the Body-mind problem*, Ed.Notturno, Routledge, London and New York, p.8, n.d.

Chapter IV
A VIEW OF THE SERVICES THROUGH SYSTEMS THEORY

This chapter describes the unavoidable situation that arises if one tries to deal with disturbed adolescents using only the Behavioural philosophy without attempting to understand the underlying problem, i.e. without the use of psychodynamics.

INTRODUCTION

The residential services were badly shaken in the nineteen nineties when it was discovered that *Pin Down* was being used to control adolescents in institutions run by Social Service departments. 'Pin Down' is a manoeuvre applied to youngsters in care who would persistently refuse to comply with the requirements of the institution. Typically, they were placed in locked rooms, in night clothes or underwear, and deprived of all social interaction and privileges until they complied. A significant feature of the practice was that it was done *openly*. The methods used were approved by *responsible, senior officers in the service*. They evidently believed that their actions were correct and would be approved of by the authorities. In the event, such 'abuse' of children became the subject of parliamentary comment, and the authorities used the ultimate solution – dismissal of the senior, responsible officers; a 'clean sweep of the service', it would appear.

Together with the Children Act, 1989, which emphasised the rights of children, the authorities became much more exacting about how youngsters were treated, and the pendulum swung the other way. Today, those who run children's homes are threatened both by the authorities and by the children themselves, who are well apprised of their rights. When there is a particularly difficult youngster in care, the tendency is to try to get them into a secure unit, a sector which has become overcrowded, or to get them out of care, which can be done legally if they are over sixteen years, or avoid taking them into care, if possible. Such 'difficult' youngsters are then back in the community where they were uncontainable in the first place, with no controls or help for them or their families. The general perception of the public today, that disturbed/delinquent youngsters are either allowed to run wild, or placated by expensive holidays and trips abroad, is indeed founded on a certain reality.

Such swings from one extreme to the other occur when the true cause of a problem has not been recognised. The action taken over 'Pin Down', was so drastic that it created an illusion of the problem having being dealt with radically, while the true causes remained unrecognised.

In fact, Pin Down and similar practises, are the natural result of the elimination of the *Psychodynamic* approach from the adolescent service, as proposed in the Health Advisory Service document (HAS), *Bridges Over Troubled Waters, a National Survey of the Services for Disturbed Adolescents* (Horrocks, 1986), and supported by the policy-makers of the establishment. Professionals had no means of dealing with the disturbing behaviour of the youngsters except by punishments – couched in clinical terminology – *Behaviour therapy* or *Behaviour modification techniques*. Pin Down is a behaviour modification technique and could easily be included in a Behaviour therapy programme. The true value of Behaviour therapy and its misapplication in adolescent disturbance are discussed elsewhere.

An objective view of the residential services for adolescents through Systems Theory, I think will show how the service operates today as a consequence of the of the HAS report.

THE ADOLESCENT RESIDENTIAL SERVICES AND SYSTEMS THEORY

Systems theory, which was first postulated in the early twentieth century, by Ludwig Von Bertalanffy, an anthropologist, is derived from an understanding of the relationship between the structure of physical matter and human activity. ([1]De Board, 1978.) It is widely accepted as providing a most effective way of looking at how organisations work. In clinical terminology a family may be regarded as a system. The relevant postulates of the theory are:

1. An organisation may consist of several smaller parts, all of which together form a system. The activity of one part of an organisation is affected by and related to the activity of each of the other parts. The whole organisation operates on a method or system of interaction with its parts. Its parts may be called subsystems, each of which uses their own system or method.

2. A 'closed system' is one that operates as if it were independent of its environment. Even if its own operational system or method is highly advanced, it reaches a steady state, when no further work can be done, e.g. a torch battery.

3. An 'open' system is one that has continual exchanges with the environment, which revitalises it. Even though this may also reach a steady state for a while, it is in dynamic equilibrium with the environment from which it continually gains replenishment; it is alive, and further development is possible. The human being, or a healthy family, can be considered to be the ideal open system. A car battery, which is continually being recharged by the dynamo, could be considered a partially open system.

4. The method of operation within a system could be 'creative', when work and progress is possible, or it could be 'self-defeating', when even a potentially open system will tend to destroy itself, e.g., a family in which the abnormal relationships are not recognised, when the most vulnerable of the children often becomes disturbed.

5. Systems aim at homeostasis, and external efforts to create change usually lead to homeostatic resistance.

The adolescent services may be regarded as a system which contains several subsystems within the residential part of the service.

1. CHILDREN'S HOMES, most of which are controlled by the Social Services. Some are privately run.

2. ADOLESCENT UNITS which are a part of the psychiatric establishment, controlled by NHS Health Authorities.

3. YOUTH TREATMENT CENTRES, controlled by the department of health.

All of them are influenced by policies of the government and are looked at critically by the media and the public. The British judiciary and the European Courts of Human Rights have judicial authority over all of them. Children's homes are the largest in number and Social Services departments in charge of them are the most vulnerable.

A TYPICAL CHILDREN'S HOME

The task (the product) of the children's home is 'care and control' of the resident children/adolescents. The system within the children's home consists of a set of rules and regulations with which the youngsters are expected to comply, so that the staff may be able to exercise care and control (manufacture the product). If the youngsters do not comply with the set rules, planned measures will be taken, in a well-run institution, to encourage them to comply. These measures will include persuasion of different kinds, as well as carefully thought out 'non-damaging' sanctions and punishments. These interactions, evidently, have been found to be effective in keeping the system working, at least for a short while.

HOW THE SUBSYSTEM GOES WRONG

A child, say John, deemed to be having a problem at home, has been placed in one of these Social Service institutions. Examination of John's family system will typically show that the problem he has presented with, is related to the interactions, conscious and unconscious, of other members of his family with each other and with John. These interactions within the family are designed to allow each of them to feel relatively well, and remain as a family. In other words the family, in order to survive as a family and as individuals, have unconsciously created a situation which makes

John 'the disturbed one', the carrier of the family problem.

The real problem in the family is Mother, who from her young days could not make satisfying relationships. Today, as before, she is unable to make a satisfying relationship with her husband and makes a special relationship with John which keeps her happy and satisfied. The whole family is glad of this because Mother's contentment is of primary importance. John becomes dissatisfied as he grows older. He does not know why, and he creates trouble. The family are happy to regard *him* as the troublemaker, rather than mother, and they unwittingly create situations which 'prove' this.

The removal of John from the family does not alter the family system in any real way, at least for some time, because the absent 'disturbed child' is still a member of the family and is expected to return home soon; he is still the carrier of the family problem, though he is situated in a different place. The rest of the family remains protected, and John produces the same problems in the institution.

John does not comply with the set rules and does not respond to the care and control measures in the children's home, because he has a sense that he would be letting down Mother and his family if he became better, especially when he is away from home. Indeed, if he did get better, he will stop being the carrier of the family problem; then, the family as a whole, or another member of the family – Mother in this case – may become and be seen as disturbed. John's loyalty to his mother and the family does not allow him to get better.

When John does not respond to the measures taken by staff in the children's home, the system in the children's home is threatened. Staff, in a well-run children's home, would then have a meeting and come to the reasonable conclusion, that the planned measures have not been effective and therefore more effective measures should be taken.

The only measures known to the children's home in which psychodynamics is not understood or recognised, are rewards, sanctions and punishments. Rewards for the youngster are limited and ineffective – chocolates and sweets, the pictures, a TV programme, etc. So sanctions and punishments of a 'more effective' kind are used; yet John does not respond. (John is a spirited youngster and he loves his family too much. As described previously, he senses danger to his family if he behaves well in the community home). Yet stronger measures are taken to no effect. Staff feel angry and frustrated. One of the most devastating experiences for professional staff is to be rendered ineffective by a mere child or adolescent. The system becomes jammed, and if it is a closed system, it may break down completely.

If the organisation has the mechanics of an open system, a specialist/expert may be called in for advice, or, the children's home may have a regular consultant, a psychiatrist or a psychologist. Psychiatrists (most are not trained in psychodynamics) often do no more than a clinical psychiatric examination of the youngster and declare him to be free from an identifiable psychiatric disorder. They are unable to give further advice; something that has little practical value in solving the problem of the children's home. In some cases it allows the non-psychiatric professionals in charge of the youngsters to throw caution to the winds and feel free to use harsher methods of control.

Psychologists, most of whom have not had specialist training in psychodynamics and experience in understanding adolescent problems, are equally ineffective. They may institute a formal behavioural programme, which in effect does not differ from the sanctions and punishment methods already in use. In practical terms, *'More effective measures to control the youngster'*, is indeed the only advice given implicitly or explicitly. In effect the system remains closed. The frustration of the staff reaches high levels. John, who initially simply felt unable to comply with the rules without knowing why, now feels triumphant over authority (the staff); the other youngsters share his triumph and join in defying staff, and the community home is soon in utter chaos. The enormous anger that has been generated in the staff, which is really against the psychiatrist or the psychologist or the system, is displaced onto the rebellious youngster.

In this situation, the statement, 'It is clear that the sanctions and punishments used do not hurt, sanctions that do not hurt are not sanctions,' comes to be regarded as the most welcome pearl of wisdom. 'Pin Down' can easily follow as a natural phenomenon;

it seems the only thing to do to prevent dangerous acting out. It resembles measures that have already been taken and accepted as the norm and it is seen as the thing to do; it is what has been implicitly advised by the specialists and supported by the other parts of the system.

THE OTHER PARTS OF THE ORGANISATION

OTHER SUBSYSTEMS:

THE PSYCHIATRIC ESTABLISHMENT

It is to psychiatry that the other parts of the system turn, for expertise, guidance and direction.

The psychiatric establishment however has neatly sidestepped the issue. In the Health Advisory Service (HAS) document, *Bridges over Troubled Waters*, mentioned above, the term PSYCHOTHERAPY or PSYCODYNAMICS was not mentioned even once in its 77 pages. ([2]Steiner, 1986.)

The document also made a definitive statement on the role of psychiatrists, exonerating psychiatry from responsibility for the management and treatment of the vast majority of disturbed adolescents and protecting psychiatrists from entering into the rough and tumble of real work with the majority of disturbed adolescents. It states:

> In addition to taking full clinical responsibility for the treatment of the small proportion of disturbed adolescents who suffer from identifiable psychiatric disorders, the psychiatrist has a consultative role in helping to define the needs of young people within the responsibility of other professional workers and offering help and support. ([3]Horrocks, 1986.)

Studies on the morbidity in adolescence, put the 'small proportion' of adolescents who suffer from an identifiable psychiatric disorder at around 12%. ([4]Perinpanayagam, 1978.)

Thus, 88% belong to the group of 'young people within the responsibility of other professionals' who were to be helped and supported by the psychiatric services. The recommendations however, did not encompass a structure or support for the provision of training that would equip the 'other professionals' to engage in psychodynamic methods, nor psychiatrists to offer the help and support they needed.

This leaves Behaviour therapy as the only acceptable method for dealing with adolescent disturbance, which in effect, is no different from the simple use of punishments for controlling behaviour. There were letters to the Bulletin of the Royal College of Psychiatrists pointing out the marked bias in the document and warning of the dangers to the service, notably from John Steiner, Chairman of the Association for Psychoanalytical Psychotherapy (September 1986), and from the author of this book. (°Perinpanayagam, 1987.)

In the case of John, the psychiatrist's role ends with his declaration that he is free from a formal psychiatric illness, and defining his needs as requiring some other form of treatment whose name was not mentioned in the report, which he is not trained to do and would not know how to support.

Till this report the various departments and authorities in the service chose their own policies of dealing with adolescent disturbance. The non-punitive, psychodynamic approach, which attempts to deal with the cause of the problem, was generally regarded as the most enlightened, and the one to aim for.

The psychiatric establishment, through its acceptance of the HAS report, has not merely deprived the workers and clients/patients of their most potent tool and ally – the ability to understand and deal with the underlying problems – it has made a definitive alteration to the system in the service, creating a homeostatic resistance to such understanding work.

THE SOCIAL SERVICES

The Social Services, who at one time showed great interest and aptitude in working psychodynamically with the underlying problems of youngsters and their families, have in recent years moved very distinctly into regarding their role as solely concerned with 'care and control', and the legal aspects of child care. This, I believe, is directly related to the stance taken by the psychiatric part of the establishment. The Social Services, who are far more vulnerable to attacks from the environment than the psychiatric establishment, cannot risk undertaking anything more than 'care and control', because they are aware that the help offered by psychiatry is no more than a gesture. The Social Services have turned away from psychiatry. Two major subsystems have stopped interacting effectively.

Using the analogy of the family and the family system, the two parents, Social Services and Psychiatry, have tacitly turned away from each other, instead of facing the problem and dealing with it, as any good family therapist will suggest; it is the child, the children's homes, and around 88% of disturbed adolescents who bear the result.

THE DEPARTMENT OF HEALTH

The Department of Health epitomises the contradictions in the system. It does not seem to know whether the youth under their care are there for 'care and control' or for 'treatment'. They are placed in 'Youth *Treatment* Centres' run by civil servants, while social workers who have not had specific training in treatment are responsible for supervising the work of the units. Psychiatrists appointed to work in the units have no executive role in the treatment of the youngsters.

THE ENVIRONMENT

The interactions of the adolescent service with the environment, consisting of the government, the public, the media and the European Courts of Human Rights, which could provide a basis for an effective open system, instead, has a negative effect. There are no 'life-giving' exchanges. The interactions are largely unidirectional, towards the adolescent services, critical and controlling. There is no response to the environment except defensive gestures and mutterings.

When one sets out to offer something that would appear to be so simple as 'care and control', and then fails, or does it the wrong way, what can one say? The establishment, principally the Department of Health and the Social Services, pass on the negative interaction to the subordinate YTCs and Children's Homes, sometimes with considerable violence. The negative communications eventually reach the youngsters. 'Pin Down' becomes a natural sequential event: Diagram 1 shows the closed system. Diagram 2 shows an open system.

The attitude of the government of the day, whether it be punitive or understanding, will naturally have a powerful effect on the approach and performance of the services, the punitive attitude giving an added momentum to 'Pin Down'.

Following the 'Pin Down' episode and the Children Act, 1989, which came into force in October 1991, difficult to manage youngsters are either sent to expensive privately run children's homes or simply discharged into the community, if they are over sixteen.

The diagrams show the services for disturbed adolescents as they are, Diagram 1; and as they could be with psychodynamics, Diagram 2.

CLOSED SYSTEM

COMMUNICATIONS UNIDIRECTIONAL NEGATIVE AND CONTROLLING INTO THE SYSTEM. THESES ARE PASSED ON TO YOUNG PEOPLE WHO REBEL - NO UNDERSTANDING BY STAFF IS POSSIBLE - CONTROLS INCREASE - REBELION INCREASES ⟶

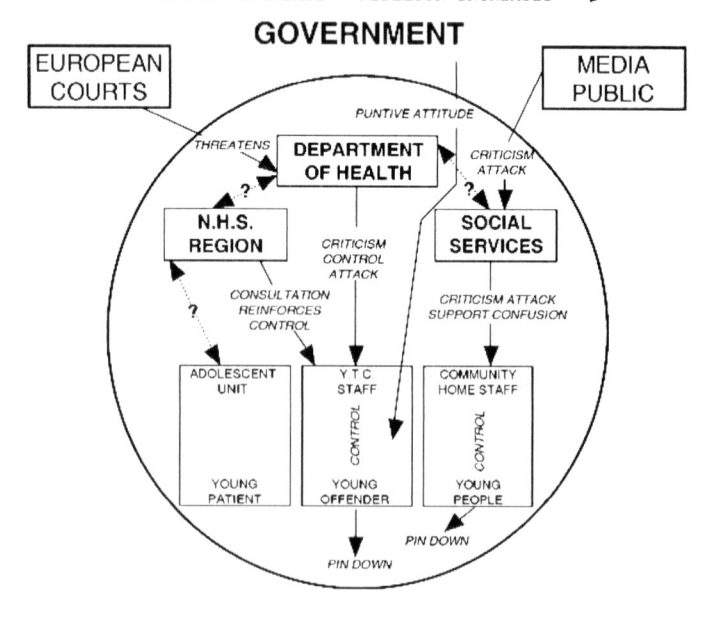

GOVERNMENT

- EUROPEAN COURTS
- MEDIA PUBLIC

PUNTIVE ATTITUDE

THREATENS — **DEPARTMENT OF HEALTH** — CRITICISM ATTACK

N.H.S. REGION — CRITICISM CONTROL ATTACK — **SOCIAL SERVICES**

CONSULTATION REINFORCES CONTROL

CRITICISM ATTACK SUPPORT CONFUSION

ADOLESCENT UNIT	Y T C STAFF	COMMUNITY HOME STAFF
YOUNG PATIENT	YOUNG OFFENDER	YOUNG PEOPLE

CONTROL — CONTROL

PIN DOWN — PIN DOWN

OPEN SYSTEM

THE KEY TO OPENING THE SYSTEM IS THE UNDERSTANDING PSYCHODYNAMIC APPROACH PROVIDED BY THE PSYCHIATRIC ESTABLISHMENT, WHICH IS NOT ONLY AVAILABLE IN THE PRESENT SCHEME

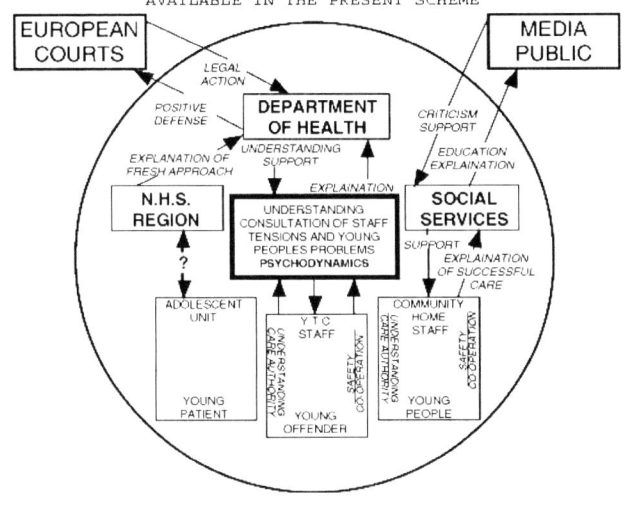

REFERENCES

[1] De Board, 1978, *The Psychoanalysis of Organisations*, Routledge, London, New York.
[2] Steiner, John, September, 1986, *Bulletin of the Royal College of Psychiatrists*, Correspondence.
[3] Horrocks, *Bridges Over Troubled Waters, A Report from the NHS Health Advisory Services for Disturbed Adolescents*, March 1986, ISBN 85197 053 3, p.9, para 3.1.1.
[4] Perinpanayagam, K.S., 1978 *British Medical Journal*, Vol. 1, pp.424–425.
[5] Perinpanayagam, K.S., February, 1987, *Bulletin of the Royal College of Psychiatrists*, Correspondence.

Chapter V
PSYCHIATRY AND PSYCHOANALYTICAL THERAPY – A SCIENTIFIC VIEW

'There is no more to science than its method…'
Sir Herman Bondi, FRS[1]

Psychoanalysis is conducted in strict privacy, and inevitably, has become invested with a mysterious quality, around which myths have arisen. Its abstract nature and subjective methodology have defied demonstrable validation of its efficacy; it has not been embraced wholeheartedly by the psychiatric establishment.

As the hope of categorising all psychiatric conditions as diseases progressively fades, together with the prospect of being able to treat them in a simple mechanistic manner, the need for psychoanalysis to give wholeness to psychiatry becomes more and more evident; it is the only discipline that attempts to understand the workings of the mind.

In the following pages I have commented on some of the best known criticisms of psychoanalysis. I have attempted to simplify and demystify the psychoanalytical process and show that it is an authentic method of solving problems of the mind, and I have shown that it merits the greatest respect for its stringent methodology. Contrary to popular opinion, it is not in conflict with formal psychiatry. It seems to straddle the abstract world as science does the material world, contributing to the formation of a consistent whole.

It subscribes closely to Sir Karl Popper's formula for development – p1---->TS---->EE---->p2. As with medicine and science in general, so with psychoanalysis: theories are inevitable and they will come and go; it is the methodology that is of lasting value.

I have not attempted to elaborate on the many different ways in which psychoanalysis effects its beneficial changes in this chapter.

PSYCHIATRY
FORMAL PSYCHIATRY – PSYCHOANALYSIS

INTRODUCTION

Psychiatry has, for too long, been riding on an impression and a hope. A surprisingly large proportion of people, even amongst the sophisticated, believe that it is concerned with the study of the human mind. They go to a psychiatrist when they are troubled, in the hope that they would be helped to understand their experience, and instead, in the majority of cases, find that they are simply given a pill. Some feel better, often no one actually knows why or how; others are angry.

Psychoanalysis, the only discipline which purports to study the human mind, is viewed with suspicion and is poorly supported by the psychiatric establishment.

The view that disturbances of the mind are diseases caused by some, as yet undetected, organic lesion, is the favoured one. A pattern in some psychiatric conditions, that seems observable at times by some, gives hope to this view; its resemblance to the medical model gives it respectability. However, attempts to discover the organic, biochemical or genetic causes of such 'diseases' have been woefully unproductive for decades. Yet the favoured view remains.

In formal psychiatry (sometimes regarded as being synonymous with psychiatry) drugs are given for conditions whose aetiology is unknown; often good results are achieved. Whilst this practice can be philosophically justified in our present state of knowledge, it cannot be credited for its methodology nor its scientific status; it does not conform to the medical model of matching the treatment to the cause.

Even though the very core of psychiatry is concerned with the recognition of intangible, abstract phenomena and their effects upon the mind and body, the fact that sometimes the abstract pain is relieved by something so tangible as a pill, invites one to neglect the importance of understanding these abstract causes, or to even dismiss them as unreal; they are difficult to deal with. The remark to patients from doctors and even some psychiatrists, 'Oh, it is only in the mind, forget about it,' is frequently reported. There is failure to recognise that often the pain is not relieved by a pill, neither are the many unhappy problems we see in society today, which are caused by disturbances of the mind – violence in a marriage between two perfectly nice intelligent people; delinquency and recidivism amongst those who clearly go against their natural wishes and their environmental conditioning; alcoholism, drug addiction and so on.

There have been attempts to narrow and confine the limits of psychiatry to 'formal psychiatric conditions', those few conditions that respond to drug therapy, and to formalise their separation from 'disturbed and disturbing behaviour', as the concern of non-medical treatments allied with psychoanalysis. This is more a clumsy political manoeuvre to avoid embarrassment, rather than a useful practical or a clinical differentiation; the two are not mutually exclusive and in any case, an understanding of both is necessary to make a differential diagnosis.

More recently there has been a minor capitulation, and there seems to have been a variable, tentative acceptance of psychoanalysis as a relevant part of psychiatry; the appointment of a few psychotherapists is the NHS has been permitted, but the mix is far from adequate, both in the training aspects and in the service to patients.

Training for the membership in psychiatry does not include training in psychoanalytically based therapy. Any psychiatrist who has had such training has done so at his own expense and in his own time and had to be fortunate enough to be working in an environment which supported his or her ambitions. Even the department of inland revenue seems to have joined this 'conspiracy'; tax relief on the expenses of the training is not permitted. As a result, by far the majority of psychiatrists are untrained in this speciality and are unable to engage in the appropriate kind of psychoanalytically based treatment when it is needed; they are not in any position to support or supervise the work of paramedical staff who purport to do psychotherapy, and they cannot even protect their own patients from the claims of charlatan practice.

This issue is of particular relevance to the treatment of criminals and abnormal offenders, being treated in special hospitals and penal institutions. Are they 'mentally ill' requiring formal psychiatric treatment, or are they 'disturbed' requiring psychoanalytically based treatment, or do they suffer from a combination of the two requiring both? Are the responsible services geared to offer them what is necessary?

CRITICISMS OF PSYCHOANALYSIS

Psychoanalysis, and with it the many forms of treatment derived from it – interpretive psychotherapy, group therapy and others, broadly called psychodynamic psychiatry – have come in for heavy criticism from the scientific world. Sir Peter Medawar, Nobel laureate in medicine, has decried 'the Olympian glibness of psychoanalytical thought'.[2] Sir Karl Popper, who has been described as 'incomparably the greatest philosopher of science that has ever been'[1], has shown that it does not conform to the criteria of a science; its theories 'had the unfalsifiability of a religious faith'.[3]

Many of the general criticisms of psychoanalysis can be easily refuted because they have not been about the process of psychoanalysis itself, but about a theory or some aspect of its practice or malpractice. Its conduct in privacy/secrecy, by an 'exclusive' group of people, has not only made it susceptible to much mythologising, but also sometimes to quite devastatingly destructive envious attacks. However, the criticisms of Medawar and Popper do, I think, require special attention.

Sir Peter Medawar's Criticism:

In his essay on psychoanalysis,[2] Sir Peter Medawar makes a clear distinction between psychiatry and psychoanalysis. He gives a lucid description of the polarity that exists between nature and nurture, as causative factors in psychiatric disorders, and comments on the differing treatment methodologies in each case, psychiatry (formal psychiatry) being associated with the nature aetiology and psychoanalysis with nurture. He states that it is a mistake to trace disorders wholly to one or the other and suggests that both nature and nurture contribute to psychiatric problems, though sometimes in very unequal degrees. He recognises that nature and nurture do not operate independently in a simple relationship and is duly emphatic about one being a function of the other.

However he does not treat the overall approach to each of these causative agents in the same manner. He goes on to favour the nature aetiology, and with it the formal psychiatric approach, as being the more rational, using two inherited conditions, the XYY syndrome and phenylketonuria, to illustrate his point. In each of these conditions, the chromosomal genetic constitution, it has been discovered, predicts the pathology, and treatment, therefore, can be rationally directed to well anticipated corrective measures.

Indeed, I think it will be impossible to refute the logic of matching the treatment to the cause, as illustrated in these two conditions, and I believe that any psychiatrist or psychoanalyst of experience will be hard put to deny the contributions made by both nature and nurture to the aetiology of psychiatric problems, albeit in differing degrees. But equally I think there will be universal agreement that in the vast majority of psychiatric disorders, the nature causes are nowhere near as clearly recognised as in the examples he has chosen.

While Medawar has been strictly accurate in the qualitative sense in his statement regarding contributions made by both nature and nurture and their functional relationship to each other, he seems to have given an importance to the contribution made by nature without the evidence needed to do so. While being emphatic about the functional relationship between the nature and nurture aetiologies, he has not considered the possibility that dealing with the known nurture factors could decrease or even completely eliminate the detrimental effect of the nature causes.

In the same essay he makes sweeping criticisms of all aspects of psychoanalysis. In order to support his arguments, apart from the comments referred to above, he has essentially used Popper's work on the definition of scientific theories (on which I comment below) and has referred to some presentations in a psychoanalytical congress. Apropos the conference, he quotes:

> The snake representing the powerful and dangerous (strangling), poisonous (impregnating) penis of his father and his own (in its anal-sadistic aspects). At the same time, it represented the destructive devouring vagina… The snake also represented the patient himself in both aspects as the male and female and served as a substitute for people of both sexes. On the oral and anal levels the snake represented the patient as a digesting (pregnant) gut with a devouring mouth and expelling anus…

Two others are of a similar nature.

Having assured the readers that he did not select the quotations for the purpose of poking fun at psychoanalysis, he goes on to describe the absence of hesitancy, humility and doubt in the minds of the analysts and speaks of:

> …the Olympian glibness of psychoanalytical thought … where shall we find evidence of hesitancy … the sense of groping …A lava-flow of ad hoc explanation pours over and around all difficulties…

Indeed, to those untrained in psychoanalysis, the examples he has quoted I think will probably be entirely unintelligible and perhaps alarming. However, even if it were the case that untrained laymen should be able to comprehend communications between specialists, Medawar's criticisms seem to have some relevance to the way psychoanalysts communicate with each other in a congress, rather than to any aspect of psychoanalysis itself.

In order to put Medawar's comments on psychoanalytical thought into the appropriate context, I think I could do no better than reproduce a very small piece from Freud's own writings of more than thirty years earlier, and invite readers to dip into the work of Strachey, Ezreil, Malan and many others who have striven painstakingly to seek better and better methods of achieving accuracy of understanding and interpretation. From Freud:[4]

> What we are in search of is a picture of the patient's forgotten years that shall be alike trustworthy and in all essential respects

complete ... and here at the very start, the question arises of what guarantee we have while we are working on these constructions that we are not making mistakes and risking the success of the treatment by putting forward some construction that is incorrect... In reality things are not so simple and we do not make it easy for ourselves to come to a conclusion.

Sir Karl Popper's Criticism:

Sir Karl Popper's criticism is of a different nature. It entirely concerns psychoanalytical theories and the demarcation between science and non-science.[5] Having first defined the essential criterion of the scientific status of a theory as being its falsifiability, or refutability, or testability, he then goes on to illustrate why the theories of Adler and Freud could not be considered scientific. Magee describes Popper's view of these theories thus:[3]

> ...and Popper saw that their [the theories'] ability to explain everything, which so convinced and excited their adherents, was precisely what was most wrong with them... their ideas had the unfalsifiability of a religious faith.

Popper's comments on the scientific status of psychoanalysis have been misunderstood and misquoted. It is important to recognise that they concerned the demarcation between science and non-science, and not between sense and nonsense, as Magee has emphatically pointed out.[6] The implication of this is that Popper's own view was that even though psychoanalysis did not conform to the criteria for a science, yet it is possible that it could be a valuable and authentic treatment method. I believe also, that Popper confined his comments to psychoanalytical theories and certain attitudes he observed in the Vienna of his youth; he did not comment on the psychoanalytical method of discovering and dealing with problems of the mind.

THE REAL PROBLEMS WITH PSYCHOANALYSIS

Whichever way one looks at the criticisms and defences of psychoanalysis, the unbiased thoughtful observer must, I think, remain seriously doubtful about its authenticity as a valid method of treatment; Popper has shown that it does not subscribe to the criteria of a science, and he has likened it to astrology and Marxism.

There are two major problems with psychoanalysis:

1. It is an entirely subjective, abstract and rational process (the term 'rational' is being used in its philosophical sense, as opposed to 'empirical'), and therefore cannot subscribe to the criteria for the empirical validation demanded by the scientific tradition.

2. The majority of the communications are subjective in both the therapist and the patient and therefore are likely to be considered unreliable as accurate observations. This question, subjectivism in psychoanalytical therapy, is dealt with in the next chapter – Objective Subjectivism.

RATIONALISM – EMPIRICISM

Popper has shown entirely convincingly, I believe, that the polarisation between the empiricists, who argued that the only reality is that which can be tested by our five senses, and the rationalists, who believed that truth and reality can be reached only through pure thinking, is not based on any real foundation. He has shown that pure empiricism does not exist. I think just one example from his seminal work, *Conjectures and Refutations*, would serve to illustrate the point; commenting on Newton's theories, which were reputed to be the ultimate in science and arrived at through empirical observation, he has referred to Kant as saying:

> Newton's dynamics goes essentially beyond all observation. It is universal, exact and abstract... and we can show by purely logical means that it is not derivable from observation statements.[7]

Einstein, I think, nailed the coffin of any further argument when he described in his autobiography the joy and wonderment he felt when he discovered that it was possible 'to get certain knowledge of the objects of experience by means of pure thinking'.[8] Further, in a letter to Popper, Einstein has stated his explicit agreement 'that theory cannot be fabricated out of the results of observation, but that it can only be invented'.[9]

Einstein's theory of relativity, arrived at rationally, subscribes to Popper's criteria for a science because it exposed itself to refutation by predicting observable effects. Its validity was demonstrable.

What if his theory, arrived at entirely through the rational process, concerned matters that were entirely abstract and therefore could not be subjected to the observation required to demonstrate its scientific status?

Psychoanalysis is in this unenviable position. The process is rational and it concerns phenomena which are entirely abstract. The changes in psychoanalysis are felt by patients and reflected in the quality of their lives; observation of these phenomena by the five senses is not possible; clearly it is not possible to demonstrate its validity by the accepted empirical criteria used for a science.

Abstract Phenomena: it must be remembered that philosophy has recognised and endorsed our everyday common-sense experience of the real existence of abstract phenomena which are experienced but cannot be observed by our five senses. (Professor Whitehead's third existent,[10] and Popper's world two and part of three.[11])

THE SCIENTIFIC TRADITION – METHODOLOGY

Freud basically did two things:

1. He devised a systematic way of discovering things that go on in the conscious and unconscious minds of individuals, which has been continually developed and improved on since his time – psychoanalysis.

2. He postulated theories of human behaviour and showed how these could be used beneficially, in the method of psychoanalysis.

Freud believed in his theories; he argued about them and tried to prove them, as do many others with his and their own. Indeed it is right that anyone who has a theory or believes in one, should endeavour to prove its validity. Ironically, however, proving the correctness of a theory scientifically or otherwise is of little lasting value.

Of science, Magee has said, in agreement with the views of

Popper and several other philosophers of science before him:[12]

> That the whole of science, of all things, should rest on foundations whose validity it is impossible to demonstrate has been found uniquely embarrassing... Virtually all have felt bound to say, in effect: 'We have to admit that, strictly speaking, scientific laws cannot be proved and are therefore not certain'. (It was said with specific reference to the traditional scientific method of induction.)

Popper himself devised a better theory of how scientific discoveries are made and proposed a method for verification of a scientific theory, based on its falsifiability. However, he was satisfied that even this did not demonstrate evidence of lasting value and he concludes:

> So it is a profound mistake to try to do what scientists and philosophers have always tried to do, namely prove the truth of a theory, or justify our belief in a theory, since this is to attempt the logically impossible.[13]

He comes to this conclusion because he saw that what we call our knowledge is of its nature provisional. The history of mankind has shown that what has been 'known' and 'proven' at one time or another, has eventually turned out to be untrue; Newton's laws provide a good example.

Popper showed that the only real basis on which progress is made is through tentative solutions, examination of these for errors, elimination of errors, formulation of better tentative solutions and so on, without at any point claiming a final solution or final knowledge, but rather, continually looking for further errors and better solutions. He applies this concept to progress in science, as well as in intellectual and artistic activities of all kinds, thus making a distinction between 'dogmatic man', who perishes with his dogma, and theories and 'thinking man', who is enlivened by the discovery that some theory or solution is wrong or inadequate, even his own. What we are left with, then, as the only really worthwhile thing, is a certain attitude or an approach or a method, which is applicable to all kinds of human endeavour.

Popper has summarised this process in the formula:

p1---->TS---->EE----p2

where p1 is the initial problem, TS the trial solution proposed, EE the process of error elimination applied to the trial solution and p2, the resulting situation with new problems. It is essentially a feedback process. It is not cyclic, for p2 is always different from p1: (and an advance on it): even complete failure to solve a problem teaches us something new about where its difficulties lie... This formula incorporates some of the most important of Popper's ideas. He himself has put a good strong saddle on it and ridden it into many fields of human enquiry; and where he has not been, some follower of his often has... 'A task does not begin with the attempt to solve a problem. It begins with the problem itself, and the reasons for its being a problem.'[1]

A close look at the psychoanalytical method I think, will show how closely it subscribes to Popper's formula.

THE PSYCHOANALYTICAL METHOD

In describing the psychoanalytical method I will not elaborate on phenomena such as transference, resistance and dreams. Their use is essential for recognising and dealing with the unconscious mind; they do not in any way interfere with or change the methodology which I shall describe.

1. Psychoanalytical therapy is a process in which an attempt is made to solve problems by the co-operation of two people, the therapist and the patient. There may be times during the therapy when the patient may not want to be understood and may not want to co-operate.

2. Much effort is put into discovering the true nature of the problem presented by the patient, often the real problem in the patient's mind is hidden.

For example:
M had a session with me, during which he was very troubled and anxious about a decision he had to make. He had telephoned and made an urgent appointment. His problem as described by him concerned his accommodation; he was 'squatting' in his girlfriend's

home, where he was welcome, though it was clearly a temporary arrangement, which he felt had gone on for too long. He had recently been invited by a good friend of his to stay with him. This too would have been a temporary arrangement. He had been advised by his girlfriend to move into digs by himself as this would be a more permanent arrangement; he also felt he should do this. He was in a panic, he felt he must make a decision soon – urgently. He did not know what to do. The result of a discussion was that M realised that there was no hurry about making this decision. He felt that his friend has no reason to withdraw his offer. There was no danger of him being thrown out of his girlfriend's home. He did not have any digs in mind which he would lose if he did not decide quickly. M left relieved and feeling greatly helped, though neither of us knew what the problem was or had been.

The problem which had caused him the panic emerged only in the next session, i.e., after the 'red herring' had been cleared away – he feared a homosexual attraction to his friend, which he had been harbouring at only a partially conscious level and which had been exacerbated by the thought of staying with him.

The process of discovery of the problem and its solution is essentially one of trial and error through the exchanges between the two. Suggestions are made by both. Those made by the patient are often in the form of expressions of anxiety, distress, disagreements, anger, missing sessions and other expressions of emotion; those made by the therapist may take the form of actual suggestions, tentative interpretations, interpretations and ordinary human reactions.

3. The raw material (data) used by the therapist in this process comes from the direct communications of the patient, the attempt to discover and differentiate between conscious and unconscious elements in them are through different techniques, such as recognition of the transference, free associations and unconscious accidental communications and from further enquiries and clarification of these.

4. The attempted, tentative understanding and interpretation of the data come from the recognition of certain laws of human nature and known distorted expressions of them, from the body

of theoretical knowledge which has been built up over years, from the understanding of dreams and the transference, from the therapist's total life experience, from intuitive inspiration and from knowledge of the patient gained through continuing repeated interactions with the patient.

> Laws of Human Nature: just as science is derived from an understanding of the laws of nature – gravity and electricity for instance – so psychoanalysis is derived from an understanding of what may be called 'laws of human nature', which are universal to all human beings; some of them are self-evident and others can be arrived at a priori. For example, all normal human beings feel like crying when they are sad, want to smile and laugh when they are happy, fear punishment, feel guilt when they do something they think is bad, are distressed when they are parted from a loved one, have unconscious minds which are subject to phenomena such as transference, resistance, etc.

Interpretations are of two types:

a) Exploratory, tentative ones which are used for the purpose of gaining further understanding through error elimination. These may or may not be articulated by the therapist.
b) Those which are certain and therefore problem-solving, for the particular situation in question.

Interpretations which are certain. In a field in which the entire process is rational and subjective, where no observation is possible, the notion of certainty of an understanding and interpretation may seem contradictory. In fact this is not the case. As every well-trained and experienced analyst will know, the use of the 'transference', together with an examination of the 'problem question' in terms of the current situation and the history of the patient, as experienced by the patient, (James Strachey[14]) provides a three-dimensionally determined focal point of understanding, which gives as much certainty to an interpretation as one can achieve in the context of a scientific experiment. The details of how exactly this is done are described in the next chapter

'Objective-Subjectivism'.

5. The solution of a problem is not indicated by the acquiescence of the patient, but by different expressions of freedom, loosening up, greater communicative ability, all of which lead to the presentation of other problems which are a consequence of the solution of the former.

Comparing this process with Popper's formula, using the example quoted above:

M's homosexual anxiety (Popper's p1) was resolved with the discovery that as a boy, he had had sexual fantasies about his Mother. He had been unable to tolerate this idea; they were intimately involved with feelings of loneliness and his childish wish for the comfort of being close to mother, when his sexual feelings were aroused. Whenever he felt lonely and depressed he had preferred (unconsciously) to divert any sexual feelings towards males rather than allow them their natural course towards females and risk a drift towards mother – an area of taboo with serious emotional consequences.

This was discovered only after he and the therapist had explored a variety of different areas into which M appeared to lead the therapist (Popper's TS and EE). Once he remembered his childhood fantasies and found that he could tolerate the idea, there was no more need for him to avoid heterosexual fantasies when he was lonely and depressed. He had completely forgotten about his homosexual feelings (this was solved) and he had progressed into dreaded territory (Popper's p2) he had never dared to explore before – his fear of relationships with girls, with the presentation of fresh problems for himself and the therapist.

Each session in authentic psychoanalytical therapy, and each problem within each session, is approached as a mini-scientific discovery, the methodology is the same. The difference is that one belongs to the abstract world and the other, to the world of material things.

Of this method of progressing in the development of knowledge, embodied in Popper's formula, Magee has said, 'The point is that, whether they realise it or not, this is the rationale of what they [scientists] do, and accounts for the way knowledge develops.'[15]

It can be seen then, that the knowledge gained by the therapist about the patient in an authentic analysis, occurs in the only real way that knowledge is gained in science or in any human endeavour.

Something that is pertinent to the human element in psychoanalysis, which is not operative in the scientific world, is that in progressively discovering more and more about the patient's inner world the therapist continuously relieves the patient of his/her anxieties by taking into him/herself the troubles of the patient, understanding or partially understanding them and returning the semi-digested material to the patient for further work. Thus the therapist and the patient share in the discoveries; and the patient's capacity for containing and dealing with problems is progressively developed.

The method of psychoanalysis has been described in simple mechanistic terms in order to illustrate the sequence of events. In practice, supervision and training and much understanding of one's self, is necessary to enable one to fulfil the task adequately. Today, a thorough personal psychoanalysis is considered to be an essential part of the training. A complex relationship develops between the therapist and the patient: first, the therapeutic alliance, which involves the real personality of the therapist; and then the transference, i.e., unconscious feelings of the patient related to significant figures and situations from the past which become attached to the therapist and the therapy situation. An appreciation of these two enables the analyst to understand the unconscious feelings of the patient which otherwise he probably would not have been able to do. A thorough understanding of how the transference works and how it is used to understand the unconscious mind is crucial for effective psychoanalytical therapy. Inability to recognise the transference or its mishandling can lead to serious consequences.

The process is further complicated because the patient unconsciously resists the discovery of his inner world, using a variety of defences, which invariably become the real problems he presents to the therapist.

In the understanding and interpretation of the problems of the patient, the therapist will take into account the realities of the patient, whether they concern his mental, physical, material or social status. For instance, a patient who needs to be on medication for whatever reason, will continue on the medication as long as the reason for it remains. The therapist's interventions will help him to understand and cope with the psychological and concrete effects of being on the medication. Thus, even though psychoanalysis does not use concrete material, it can have a beneficial influence on the detrimental effects of organic disease and material realities.

Through this process, more and more of the underlying problems of the patient are progressively and sequentially revealed. Those that have a solution are solved, the patient develops capacities he never had before to contain and deal with those that cannot be solved. The patient imbibes a different way of looking at his difficulties and has adopted a different method of dealing with them than hitherto; harmful psychological defences have been replaced by less harmful or constructive mechanisms. The patient is then ready to stop the therapy. Periodically, the patient takes the analyst back to problems which were apparently solved earlier. This happens when the earlier resolution had only been partial, or the problem has recurred for some other reason. In essence, the therapy has not immunised the patient from experiencing difficulties or having problems. It has cured the resistance to seeing and has removed the obstructions to developing – or at least many of those blockages.

The value of a psychoanalytical theory of human behaviour is immense in terms of its contribution to the total pool of knowledge, providing opportunities for examination, comparison, error elimination, in the service of the growth of knowledge. Its practical value in the therapy of a patient however, is chiefly to offer to the therapist opportunities to avail of the body of collective psychoanalytical experience and to provide him (and sometimes a knowledgeable patient) with ready made material for exploration. He will therefore not simply apply onto the patient, as the truth, either a theoretical concept or any other experience from his past; these will be used by the therapist experimentally, in his own mind or in open discussion with the patient, for the purpose of arriving at the particular meaning appropriate to the particular patient in the particular situation under consideration.

THE ROLE OF THE THERAPIST

In order to fulfil his role effectively, the therapist must have the ability to receive and accept the communications of the patient in whatever form they are made, which may sometimes be very unpleasant and difficult for him – nasty and hurtful comments directly from the patient, and indirectly through the emotional pain of the patient, which the therapist experiences empathically; they may touch on and exacerbate the therapist's own similar personal pain. The therapist must be able to understand the feelings created within himself and know how to use them for the understanding of the patient's problems.

Even though all therapists are subject to the same laws of human nature as the patient, have grown up in the same world as the patient, and to some extent, have been subjected to similar conditioning influences, there may be cultural and individual differences. The therapist must therefore be aware that he may be making human errors in his interactions with the patient. Like the patient, he himself will tend to view the patient's communications in terms of his own past conscious and unconscious experiences – his own transference. He may experience counter-transference feelings for the patient, which may become confused with his natural real ones and interfere with true understanding of the patient. The therapist must constantly watch himself and correct the mistakes he makes.

Throughout the process, the therapist must have the ability of staying with the problem and not knowing the answer, which will only crystallise in due course through the continuing appropriate interaction with the patient.

It is clear that the therapist must know himself very well indeed. Apart from authentic training in the method of psychoanalytical therapy, the single most essential requirement in the therapist must be the ability to look at and recognise his own weaknesses and how this may be interfering with the process of therapy. This is where the personal psychoanalysis becomes invaluable.

The therapist's primary interest must be *the Process* that is being undertaken. This, at first glance, may seem to conflict with care for the patient, but some thinking on the matter will show that in practice, caring for the method being used is synonymous with caring for the patient. Paradoxically, 'caring' for the patient in the ordinary sense of the word can lead to a self-defeating process.

This idea that the method or the process is of more importance than anything else, I believe, is true of the entire range of human activity, whether it be in politics, economics, medicine, management, the repair of a motor car or the building of a house. Sports went very well when players followed the old adage – 'When the great scorer comes to write against your name, he writes not that you won or lost but how you played the game.'

THE RELATIONSHIP BETWEEN THE THERAPIST AND THE PATIENT

The relationship between the therapist and patient has been likened to that between a mother and her baby, where the mother acts as the container of the troubles of the baby, and alters these troubles to make them more acceptable.

Bion drew an analogy with the feeding process that may be observed between a mother and baby bird, where the mother bird takes any indigestible food out of the baby bird's mouth, chews on it herself for a while and then gives it back to the baby in a more digestible form. The baby bird then continues the chewing and is able to swallow and digest the food. It is the return and acceptance of the indigestible food or in the case of the baby, its troubles in a modified form, and their further elaboration within the baby's mind which leads to the emotional development of the baby as the digested food leads to the baby bird's physical growth.

An ordinary, normal mother would quite naturally listen and take into herself the baby's troubles, which it cannot cope with, communicated unintelligibly through noises, screams of pain and anger, crying, etc. She would try to understand the meaning of these communications intuitively and through a process of trial and error, give back to the baby understanding in the form of a variety of actions and communications such as feeding, burping, or cuddles and soothing noises, i.e., in a manner which the baby can understand and accept. Some of these troubles may actually be removed by mother, but some are not fully understood, and they remain, while baby is helped to cope with them by the love and concern and the attempts at understanding by mother; the latter is of particular value in helping baby to mature and grow emotionally.

This similarity to the most universal and natural process in the world, is I believe, one of the strongest validations of the psychoanalytical process.

It is worthy of note that both the natural process which occurs between a mother and a baby and the ideal psychoanalytical process can be seen as similar to the process, which is said to be occurring between Christ and man. Christ takes into himself the sins (troubles) of the world and gives back understanding, forgiveness and love. Yet man, like the baby and the psychoanalytical patient, is allowed to retain responsibility and to develop; all trouble is not removed from man. The phenomenon was first studied by Klein and she called it Projective Identification.

PSYCHOANALYSIS AND THE MATERIAL WORLD

Popper's formula for progress can be applied to the history of the development of science, as well as to the discovery of psychoanalysis. The great discoveries of the material world – gravity and electricity – were developed through successive steps over a period of several centuries to reach the stage of practical value to mankind.

The discovery of gravity and the laws that govern it, began in the third century BC with Aristotle and then, notably through Copernicus and Galileo in the sixteenth and seventeenth centuries, to Newton in the eighteenth century. Likewise, it was Thales of Miletus in 600 BC who made the first known observations of the properties of electromagnetic fields, which were progressively developed through the centuries by Pliny, Gilbert, Volta and a number of others, until Faraday discovered the dynamo in the nineteenth century.

A longitudinal view of the development of the understanding of the mind and the method of psychoanalysis will show that it too has been achieved through a similar process of successive adjustments over centuries and in parallel with the great discoveries of the material world.

Interest in and observation of what was later to be known as the unconscious mind and its properties, goes back at least to the third century BC when Socrates proposed a scheme designed to remove the 'veils that kept the truth hidden'. The process, called maieutic, is described thus:

> The maieutic art of Socrates consists, essentially, in asking questions designed to destroy prejudices; false beliefs which are often traditional or fashionable beliefs; false answers given in a spirit of ignorant cocksureness. Socrates himself does not pretend to know... Thus Socrates' maieutic is not an art that aims at teaching any belief, but one that aims at purging or cleansing the soul of its false beliefs, its seeming knowledge, its prejudices. It achieves this by teaching us to doubt our own convictions.[16]

Its similarity to the psychoanalytical method in several aspects is striking.

In the seventeenth century, Bacon proposed a process which he called 'Induction', said to be similar to Socrates' maieutic, aimed at freeing one from bias and prejudice in order to ensure that experimental observations were pure.[17]

The seventeenth, eighteenth and nineteenth centuries saw a great revival of interest in the understanding of normal and abnormal human behaviour. A variety of theories such as 'Magnetic fluid theory', 'animal magnetism', 'hypnotism' and 'spiritism' were postulated, criticised, corrected and abandoned. Amidst great rivalries and disagreements between the Continental, English and American schools, and individuals in each of them, the concept of 'rapport' between the patient and the therapist was re-established and a procedure called 'psychotherapeutics' was developed by Bernheime, of the Nancy school. Janet postulated a method called 'psychological therapy'. Many eminent men – Mesmer, Charcot, Breuer and others, including Freud himself – made exhaustive studies and theorised erroneously on phenomena which were inadequately understood until Freud finally made the crucial discoveries and rediscoveries which led to the method of psychoanalysis.

It is of particular relevance that one of the best known and most significant turning points in the history of psychoanalysis, was a typical 'Popperian event', best described by Ernest Jones.[18]

> But up to the spring of 1897 he [Freud] still held firmly to his conviction of the reality of these childhood traumas… At that time doubts began to creep in… It was the awful truth that most – not all – of the seductions in childhood which his patients had revealed, and about which he had built his whole theory of hysteria, had never occurred. It was a turning point in his scientific career, and it tested his integrity, courage and psychological insight to the full… It was at this moment that Freud rose to his full stature… [in Freud's letter to Fliess] he ruefully reflects that, now that he has to renounce his key to the secrets of hysteria, his hopes of becoming a famous and successful physician are dashed to the ground… [in Freud's own words] 'to be cheerful is everything'… 'Tell it not in Gath, publish it not in the streets of Askalon, in the land of the Philistines, but between you and me I have the feeling of a victory rather than of a defeat'… Well might he be elated, for with the insight he had now gained he was on the verge of exploring the whole range of infantile sexuality.

CONCLUSION

Indeed, both the history of the development of psychoanalysis and the method of psychoanalysis itself, closely subscribe to Popper's formula. Naturally, Popper's credentials in the scientific world are uniquely impeccable; Sir Herman Bondi, the distinguished astronomer and mathematician, is quoted by Magee as having said, 'There is no more to science than its method, and there is no more to the method than Popper has said.'[1]

And while Popper himself has been acclaimed as the greatest philosopher of science the world has ever known,[1] – which alone is enough to validate psychoanalytical therapy – what is more important is that his method, so clearly and simply expounded by him and Magee, stands out as a self-evident truth, which has been developed and extracted from a welter of confused thinking and impasse over many years.

Complementary to this and of great significance, is that the psychoanalytical method essentially involves a relationship which so closely resembles the most natural, recurring and lasting relationship in the world – that between mother and baby. (Its similarity to the relationship that is said to exist between Christ and man is perhaps a subject for a different type of paper and a different audience.)

The material of psychoanalysis is derived from the laws of human nature, as science is from the laws of nature; and even though the experience is subjective, it is possible to achieve a degree of objectivity of interpretations, which is as reliable as in experimental science (see Chapter VI).

Psychoanalysis can affect and alter the effect of material things on the mind and it can change the course of material things, where the mind affects such events, as in known psychosomatic conditions.

All these considerations, I believe, do place the psychoanalytical method in a unique position, which merits respect at every level. It would seem as if psychoanalysis straddles the abstract world as science does the material world; far from being in conflict with or contrary to the scientific world of material things, it seems to run in parallel with it, complementing it and making an essential contribution to the formation of a consistent whole.

One of the serious anomalies in the practice of psychoanalytical psychotherapy today, is that anyone without a day's authentic training in the method can put himself up as a therapist, practise anything he wants and call it Psychoanalytical therapy. I have no doubt that this widespread practice both within and outside the National Health Service, has made a considerable contribution to the disrespect in which psychoanalysis is held.

REFERENCES

[1] Magee, B., *Popper*, London, Fontana Modern Masters, Ed. Frank Kermode, 1986, p.9. Ibid.pp.65–67.
[2] Medawar, P.B. FRS, *The Hope of Progress*, London, Methuen & Co, 1972, pp. 57–68.
[3] Magee, op.cit. p.44.

[4] Freud, S., *Constructions in Analysis*, 1937, in *Psychoanalytical Clinical Interpretation*, London, Ed. Louis Paul, The Free Press of Glencoe, Collier-MacMillan Ltd, 1963, p.67.
[5] Popper, K. R., *Conjectures and Refutations, The Growth of Scientific Knowledge*, London, Routledge & Kegan Paul, 1972, p.37.

[6] Magee, B., op.cit. pp.46–47.
[7] Popper, K. R., op.cit. p.190.
[8] Bolton, S. K., *Famous Men of Science*, New York, Thomas Y. Cromwell.
[9] Magee, B., op.cit. p.33.
[10] Joad, C.E.M., *Philosophy*, London, The English University Press, p.46.
[11] Magee, B., op.cit. p.60.
[12] Magee, B., op.cit. p.21.
[13] Ibid, op.cit. p.26.
[14] Strachey, J., *The Nature of the Therapeutic action of Psychoanalysis*, 1934, in *Psychoanalytic Clinical Interpretation*, ibid. pp.1–41.
[15] Magee, B., op.cit. pp.30–31.
[16] Popper, K. R., op.cit. p.13.
[17] Ibid. p.13.
[18] Jones, Ernest, *Sigmund Freud, Life and Work*, Vol. 1, pp.292–294, London, The Hogarth Press, 1953.

Chapter VI
OBJECTIVE-SUBJECTIVISM

ACCURACY OF INTERPRETATIONS IN PSYCHOANALYTICAL THERAPY

In psychoanalytical psychotherapy it is recognised that the communications of the patient come from two sources – from the conscious experiences of the external world, which contain both objective and subjective elements, and from the abstract inner world, which contains experiences which are entirely subjective. The problems with regard to accuracy of interpretations in psychotherapy concern the largely subjective nature of both types of communications and the fallibility of the therapist, who, however well trained and analysed he/she may be, will be yet subject to natural human biases and can only use his/her own subjective experiences to understand, and interpret.

It is well recognised that subjective observations say more about the observer than of the thing being observed.[1] All this, at first glance, and at the very outset, would seem to throw the entire process of psychoanalytical therapy into discredit.

In attempting to understand the patient and interpret his/her communications, the therapist must use ideas gained from a variety of sources from his total life experience, which include his natural understanding of himself and of human nature, his previous experience with other patients, his knowledge of various psychoanalytical theories, his own personal psychoanalytical experience, his supervision experience, discussions with other therapists, all of which may contribute to flashes of intuitive understanding. The conscientious therapist will always bear in mind that every patient is a unique individual, similar but not identical to other human beings, and examine every situation in its own right. He will recognise that it is the direct communications of the patient which give the only real clues to the events of the unconscious inner world, through what is actually uttered by the patient, free associations, dreams, the transference and not least the counter-transference experiences. He will therefore not simply apply onto the patient, as the truth, either a theoretical concept or any other experience from his past. These will be used by the therapist experimentally in his own mind or in discussions with the patient for the purpose of error elimination while progressively arriving at the particular meaning appropriate to that particular patient, in the particular situation under consideration.

So there are two types of interpretations used in the psychoanalytical method:

1. Those that are tentative, which are used experimentally for the purposes of error elimination and further understanding.

2. Those that are used as a definitive understanding.

It is the latter, which leads to the solution of the particular problem under consideration, which then produces other different problems, which require resolution. It is to this type of interpretation that I draw attention in this paper.

I shall show that there is a way of recognising the accuracy of an interpretation, which draws on experiences from both the inner abstract, subjective world as well as from the outer objective world, and is as accurate as one can achieve through objective, empirical observation.

OBJECTIVISM AND SUBJECTIVISM

The terms 'objective' and 'subjective' have come to be regarded as synonymous with accuracy and inaccuracy respectively. A closer look at these notions, I think would make one less certain about such clearly defined distinctions.

In the scientific world, where 'objectivity' i.e. 'accuracy' is generally assumed because the five senses are used in the empirical method, the influence of subjectivism has been well recognised. Bacon, one of the most ardent supporters of empiricism, postulated a method of 'induction' in an attempt to ensure that scientific observations are not distorted by the subjectivism of the observer.[2] Popper's view of the objectivity of the most successful and important scientific theory for over two centuries, is expressed in his comment:

> If Newton's theory is not a body of truth inherent in the world, and derived by man from the observation of reality, where did it come from? The answer is, it came from Newton.[3]

IS SUBJECTIVISM USED IN PSYCHOANALYTICAL THERAPY?

James Strachey, I believe, has made the most valuable contribution to the achievement of accuracy of interpretations in his paper on the Mutative Interpretation.[4] He has shown that a complete and effective interpretation which engenders change incorporates three elements.

1. The experience of the current situation which the patient brings into the psychotherapy session.
2. Its relationship to the past experiences of the patient.
3. Its relevance to the transference relationship with the therapist.

While there are several corroborative ways in which the accuracy of an interpretation may be supported (circumstantial evidence), the value and importance of these three elements in accurate interpreting is well recognised, and they are used in a variety of direct and indirect ways in good psychoanalytical therapy.

In the following paragraphs I shall attempt to describe in, mechanical terms, how what I shall call *Objective-Subjectivism* may be achieved in a psychoanalytical session. I shall put certain mental processes in concrete terms, in order to illustrate the objectivity that is used.

OBJECTIVE-SUBJECTIVISM

The question to be looked at it is, is there a way in which the therapist can discover whether a particular interpretation of the patient's utterance or behaviour is accurate?

In order to achieve objectivity, the selected interpretation must conform to a meeting point of lines drawn from the three relevant elements pertaining to the problem or the statement presented by the patient, i.e. lines drawn from:

A. The patient's own conscious feelings about the current situation as presented by the patient.
B. The history of the patient, and
C. The relationship with the therapist.

For example, from a case in therapy with the author:

Patient M, a young aspiring actor, had been in once-weekly therapy for about a year and had recently started twice-weekly sessions. He had been trained at RADA, at a particularly young age, and was regarded as a gifted young actor.

In this session he expressed severe disappointment about being offered only a very small part in a play directed by R, the most prestigious Director in London, for his next assignment. He had also been offered a leading role in an alternative play by a less important Director, C. M had had discussions with the therapist, on previous occasions, about the importance of working with R, how beneficial it would be to his career and how fortunate he was to have got a foot in his company.

M had often wondered whether he was liked by R. He wanted to be R's favourite. He sometimes felt that R disliked him and became depressed. The actor who shared the dressing room with him, somewhat more experienced, had been offered a more important role by R. M was angry and said he felt like saying 'Up you' to R and taking the alternative role with C. He had discussed the situation with his agent who had said, 'I don't blame you.'

What can one make of this communication? Why did he want to leave the most prestigious company, in favour of a leading role in a lesser company? What significant aspect of his personality was he expressing? In other words, how can one interpret his communication in such a manner that significance is not being attributed by the therapist, subjectively, but that it is the significance being presented by the patient, consciously and unconsciously, which is being recognised?

The meeting point of lines drawn from each of the three different areas of significance can lead the therapist to achieve this objective recognition.

A. LINES FROM THE CONSCIOUS REALITY RE THE CURRENT SITUATION

These point to several different possible characteristics; for instance:

1. He was a young man who was developing confidence in his identity as a good actor and had the courage of his convictions.
2. He had intense feelings of rivalry and an inability to accept defeat gracefully.
3. He wants a special relationship with R and/or the authority he represents.
4. He wants a normal good relationship with authority.
5. He is a fighter against injustice.
6. He cannot tolerate his appropriate position of being a beginner.

An imaginative mind I am sure can attribute significance to several other characteristics to which this story may point.

Diagram 1. TWO-DIMENSIONAL

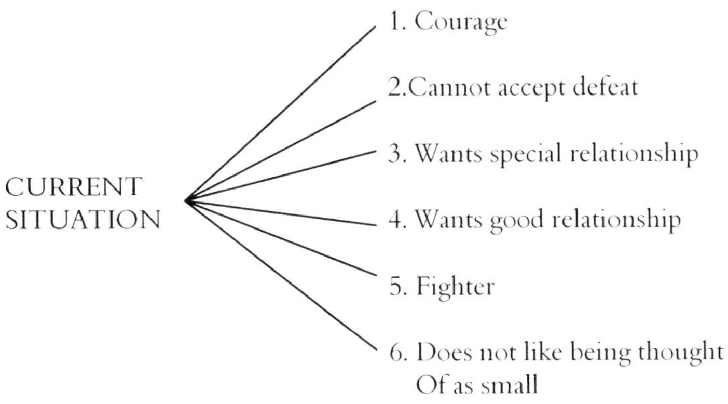

CURRENT SITUATION
- 1. Courage
- 2. Cannot accept defeat
- 3. Wants special relationship
- 4. Wants good relationship
- 5. Fighter
- 6. Does not like being thought Of as small

B. LINES FROM VIEW POINT OF HIS HISTORY

In his history, as told by M is:

His parents had divorced when he was four years old and he had grown up with his mother for five years before she remarried. He remembered feeling contented as a little boy till his mother's remarriage to 'I', when he began feeling deprived of a special relationship with her. He had grown up regarding 'I' as his natural parent. He remembers being very discontented as an adolescent and particularly resented the disciplining he received from 'I', his stepfather, even though he recognised that the disciplining had not been particularly harsh. He had frequently got into trouble at home and in school. All this had led to M having a poor relationship with the teachers in school, and with both his mother and his stepfather. 'I' stayed away from home periodically on professional assignments. M thought his mother used to flaunt herself before him in a partially drunken state, in his stepfather's absence, and had felt awkward and embarrassed. He had left home at the age of seventeen and had virtually cut himself off from his family.

The current situation looked at from the viewpoint of his history could point to the following significant characteristics:

1. M is distressed and angry because he thought he had failed in achieving a special relationship with R who represented 'I'/Authority, which he had always wanted as a boy – same as 3 in the first diagram.

2. He is distressed because he thought he had failed in achieving a good (normal) relationship with Authority which he did not have either with his stepfather or his own father, whom he never knew, i.e. the same as 4 in the first diagram.

3. He is distressed and angry because he was not allowed to feel bigger than he really was. As a little boy he had in fact felt bigger than he really was before his mother's remarriage, during the time he was alone with her; he resented being 'relegated' to being a small boy, i.e. the same point as 6. in the first diagram.

C. LINES FROM THE RELATIONSHIP WITH THE THERAPIST

The relationship with the therapist has two elements in it – the real natural relationship between the two, and the transference relationship which keeps changing with the state of the patient's mind. Distinguishing between the two and recognising the transference relationship is crucial to the understanding of a communication by the patient.

M had always tried to have an easy-going 'friendship-relationship' with the therapist. Initially the therapist himself responded in a like manner, making it clear to M that he (the therapist) was quite comfortable in such a relationship – *the real relationship*. In recent months M's friendly overtures had taken on a clumsy and awkward turn on a few occasions and the therapist had taken up the inappropriateness of what M was trying to do, in a non-threatening manner; M had felt hurt, rejected and insulted, and at times had reacted angrily, almost abusively. M always apologised very quickly – apologies which seemed to arise more out of fear of retaliation by the therapist rather than out of any real understanding. Discussion of these incidents had led to M disclosing that he often felt small and helpless in the presence of the therapist, that he resented the unequal roles, in which he had to say everything about himself while the therapist discloses nothing about himself. M could recognise that what was happening during the therapy sessions was indeed exactly according to the agreement made between them and which M himself wanted as some level. He could recognise that the therapist had in fact always spoken to him politely and on equal terms, without the slightest use of authority, yet he felt resentful of the unequalness in the relationship – *the transference relationship*. Past unrecognised childhood feelings were being brought into consciousness through the transference relationship with the therapist.

From an understanding of the difference between the real relationship and the transference relationship between the patient and the therapist, it seemed clear that the most significant experience and feeling M had at that time concerned his feelings of 'smallness' and resentment that he was not equal to his therapist, i.e. he was not allowed to be bigger than he was meant to be, i.e. point 6. in this diagram; yet he also had an easy-going friendly relationship with the therapist.

Diagram 2. THREE-DIMENSIONAL

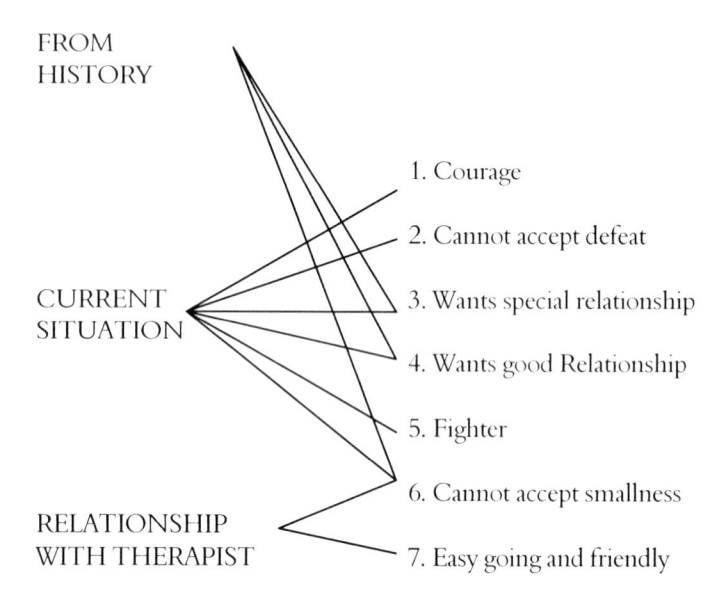

FROM HISTORY

CURRENT SITUATION

RELATIONSHIP WITH THERAPIST

1. Courage
2. Cannot accept defeat
3. Wants special relationship
4. Wants good Relationship
5. Fighter
6. Cannot accept smallness
7. Easy going and friendly

The only point at which the three lines meet is at 6 – the characteristic of being unable to tolerate being small.

It is noteworthy that an accurate understanding of the patient could not have been arrived at without the recognition of the transference.

In this particular case, the transference was relatively simple and direct. In the more severely disturbed patients, manifestations of the transference can occur in fragments and take subtle and abstruse forms.

The therapist's comment to M was, 'It seems as if it is very difficult for you to recognise your true position and be a small boy.' M became very resentful and angry at this. The therapist had not given him a complete or mutative interpretation.

In the following session, a few days later, M broke down in tears and said that he had rejected the role in the play directed by R and accepted the lead role with C. He felt he had destroyed his life. The therapist reminded M that he had said 'Up you' not only to R but also to the therapist's suggestion. M became even more distressed and amidst heart-rending sobs he told the therapist that he had telephoned his mother before he made the decision and his mother had advised him to stick to R and had said, 'You must learn to walk before you can run.'

It was only at this stage that the therapist gave M the complete mutative interpretation, which linked his present experience with his boyhood feelings and his current feelings about the therapy situation.

The session ended with M recognising that he had always 'known' that he wanted to work with R and stay in his company; he saw that it was not too late to change and accept the role with him (which was easily done the next day through his agent). He saw that the practicalities of the current situation did not merit the intense distress he had felt. He realised that the distress really belonged to similar past situations concerning his family life, which he was beginning to recognise and explore for the first time. It is significant that M was very pleased with himself for a few sessions for having chosen to stay with R, and then began to regret what he had done. He discovered after a while, that feeling like a small boy, staying with it and dealing with the feelings he had as a child, was not pleasant nor easy, but he did it.

The therapist had every reason to believe that his interpretation had been accurate; it was also supported by corroborative evidence. The accuracy was achieved by drawing three straight lines which met at a single point. The process was three dimensionally determined, and included subjective information gained from both the inner abstract world of the patient as well as his external world.

In practice psychoanalytical therapists do not draw lines. They are trained to go through a similar process mentally. An experienced therapist often takes a few seconds to arrive at an objective conclusion or what may be regarded as an inspired interpretation.

REFERENCES

[1] Joad, C.E.M., *Philosophy*, London, The English University Press, p.31.
[2] Popper, K.R., *Conjectures and Refutations*, *The Growth of Scientific Knowledge*, London, Routledge & Kegan Paul, 1972, p.31.
[3] Magee, B., *Popper*, London, Fontana Modern Masters, Ed. Frank Kermode, 1986, p.29.
[4] Strachey, J., *The Nature of the Therapeutic action of Psychoanalysis*, 1934, in *Psychoanalytic Clinical Interpretations*, London, Ed. Louis Paul, the Free Press of Glencoe, Collier-Macmillan Ltd, 1963, pp.1–41.

Chapter VII
INDIVIDUAL PSYCHOTHERAPY WITH ADOLESCENTS

SUMMARY

Even though the aims of psychoanalytical psychotherapy with adults, children and with adolescents are basically the same, there is a substantial difference between each of them, in the process which must occur between therapist and patient.

As with adults and children, the immediate anxieties and concerns of the adolescent must be recognised and dealt with as they arise for progress to be made in the therapy. These anxieties of the adolescent are very different from those of the adult and the child, in their nature, in the way they are experienced and in their manifestation.

In this chapter I will attempt to illustrate some features of adolescence which affect the technique in psychotherapy.

INTRODUCTION

> If unconscious fantasy is constantly influencing and altering the perception or interpretation of reality, the converse also holds true: reality impinges on unconscious fantasy. It is experienced, incorporated and exerts a very real strong influence on unconscious fantasy itself. (Segal, from Melanie Klein.[1])

A youngster once hurled a heavy ashtray at me during therapy. Fortunately it missed. For that patient and for me, that ashtray ceased to be an ashtray, it had became a dangerous weapon. I discreetly put it away for the next session, out of sight. The patient looked around for it but made no comment, neither did I. (This was bad technique.) We discussed the entire episode in the following session, when the patient acknowledged his own fear of the ashtray. I resurrected it and we both had a cigarette using it as an ashtray; it lost its fearsome quality and was restored to its original form.

Having grown up in a world which tends to give exclusive importance to the experience of the five senses, i.e. our external reality, we must be wary of our adolescent rebellion against the traditions of our upbringing. It will be useful to remind ourselves periodically of the views of Melanie Klein herself, who emphasised the importance of both, external reality and the internal world and the influence they have on each other.

PSYCHOANALYTICAL PSYCHOTHERAPY

The term 'psychoanalytical psychotherapy' may be defined as a process which recognises the unconscious mind and its properties – resistance, transference and other mechanisms, as originally described by Freud and further developed by others. It could also be defined as a method of treatment which classically follows a certain well-recognised code of practice, involving certain attitudes on the part of the therapist. These two definitions have a functional relationship with each other, the classical code of practice being designed to best deal with properties of the unconscious mind in the adult patient.

However, there is a great inherent difference between adolescents and adults. Adults have gone beyond the stage of being the victims of biological forces that necessarily cause them to have identity and sexual confusions, poor ego strength, inability to make decisions about what is good and bad for them, and other phenomena peculiar to adolescence. In adults, the structure of the personality has crystallised, whilst in adolescents the personality is essentially in a state of flux; they have not yet built into themselves the tough exoskeleton of a semi-successful defence we see in ourselves and in our adult patients, which we find so difficult to go beyond. Adolescents, when they feel comfortable enough, will express themselves as they feel – this is the most refreshing aspect of work with them. All this makes the psychotherapy of adolescents both more rewarding and more difficult.

The process of psychotherapy can be divided into three stages, the *beginning,* during which the therapeutic alliance is established, the *middle,* during which the problems are dealt with and the *end,* during which the patient is helped to depart. There is, of course, an overlap and blending of the functions of the different stages. Often the most useful work is done during the end phase, and sometimes the patient gains the greatest conscious benefit only after the therapy is over.

THE BEGINNING

THE THERAPEUTIC ALLIANCE

The first and most important task of the therapist is to interact with the patient in such a manner as to enable him/her to keep coming, which requires the establishment of a positive relationship with the patient – the therapeutic alliance. This is perhaps the most difficult stage in the psychotherapy of adolescents and often involves the therapist having to contend with external and internal forces acting upon the youngster and the psychotherapy situation.

EXTERNAL FORCES

The therapist cannot have the luxury of being free of all the conflicts and practical problems in the adolescents life, which would allow him to get on with the exclusive task of dealing with the mind of the patient. It is in adolescence that the statement by Melanie Klein, quoted above – 'if unconscious fantasy is constantly influencing and altering the perception or interpretation of reality, the converse also holds true; reality impinges on unconscious fantasy. It is experienced, incorporated and exerts a very strong influence on unconscious fantasy itself' – comes into full realisation.

In treating an adolescent, involvement with several people in their lives, such as parents, care workers, probation officers etc., is necessary, not only because they are in authority over the youngster and can create insuperable impediments to the therapy, but because the adolescent has an important investment in each of them. The different workers and parents often find themselves in conflict and confusion over the youngster. Opinions about the most appropriate way of dealing with a disturbed adolescent differ and are held with conviction. Objectivity often becomes elusive, and feelings can run high.

Adolescents will never be able to settle into useful therapy at more than a superficial level if they feel that the adults involved with helping them are working at cross purposes and do not get on with each other. Parents are of particular importance; even though they themselves may not get on with parents, they do want the parents and the therapist to approve of each other. Psychodynamically it is very appropriate that the therapist is involved in bringing together the conflicting views of all those involved with the youngster; it is invaluable for the psychotherapeutic task of bringing together the splits in the mind of the patient.

The negative influence of peers, who may taunt a youngster in therapy with being sick or 'nutty', often presents as the adolescent's own wish to get away from therapy and is best dealt with as it arises in the course of therapy.

Thus, the therapist working with adolescents must become more involved in the life of the adolescent than is necessary with the adult, and therefore will inevitably have to reveal more of himself than is necessary with an adult patient. Does all this interfere with the transference? This is an important question which will be discussed later on.

INTERNAL RESISTANCE

The initial effect of therapy on the youngster is often felt as if life is being made even more difficult for him; he is, as it were, being forced into owning unpleasant – perhaps frightening – feelings, the very thing he has been avoiding and hopes to escape from by coming for treatment. It is rare for adolescents, particularly those who require the services of a psychotherapist, to be capable of postponing immediate gratification in favour of long-term gains. They are in a stage of development in which they do not have enough of an identity, ego strength and judgement to say to themselves, as adults can, 'Psychotherapy is sometimes painful and unpleasant, but it is good for me and I must therefore attend regularly.'

The therapeutic alliance is influenced most strongly by the personality of the therapist. The therapist must be comfortable with his own adolescence and his understanding of the adolescent process; when, a natural relationship would develop between them.

AN EASY NATURAL RELATIONSHIP

A relaxed natural relationship which is of value in any psychotherapeutic interaction is of vital importance in the psychotherapy of adolescents. Adolescents are usually in a stage of identity confusion and awkward in their relationships. They invariably fear that there is something wrong with them and are sensitive about it. They watch keenly for the reactions of grown-ups through which they judge themselves, and often react in panic if the 'message' they receive is confusing or frightening. They are easily overawed and frightened by the 'Professional stance', as advocated in formal training, and cannot tolerate silences and 'stone walls' for long. They demand genuine reactions, safe and comfortable ones. They want the truth from adults and they want it in a way that does not frighten them nor reduce them to helpless children. They want to know from their own personal experience that this adult – the psychotherapist – is comfortable and relaxed with them, is honest and reliable, is not put out or shocked, can take their nasty bits with comfort, and cares for the whole of them. Yet, it is important for the therapist to know that it is the caring for the therapeutic process, rather than directly for the patient, which is crucial to the success of the therapy.

Such an easy relationship is possible only if the therapist is able to recognise his own weaknesses and 'bad aspects', and his own adolescent problems and difficulties, and knows how to deal with them. Such an adult feels relatively comfortable in almost any situation and with all types of people. The therapist who has this natural ease and ability to make friendly, robust relationships will find it easy to establish the therapeutic alliance with adolescents.

It is quite true that the therapist should not simply 'be himself' in the psychotherapy situation. Important considerations regarding this question in relation to the dangers of self-disclosure and the transference in adolescence are discussed later.

VOLUNTARY ATTENDANCE.

Even though many adolescents are seen in psychotherapy as 'voluntary patients or clients', it is not often that they actually have a choice.

Their initial attendance is often because they are compelled, by the situation they are placed in, because they want to please some adult in their lives or because they have been threatened or 'blackmailed' into it. (Vide Chapter X, the case of K.)

Even though the patient comes for therapy under compulsion, he can gain much from the sessions if the therapist recognises that his 'voluntary' attendance is only a 'pretence', and that the patient is indeed angry about having to come. The anger with the authorities that have placed them in the position of having to attend for treatment is invariably displaced onto the therapist. It is only after a period of attendance at therapy and if the therapy has effectively dealt with the immediate anger and anxieties of the youngster that he can develop the concept of having a choice and can take the risk of not attending. Once the possibility of non-attendance has been established between the patient and the therapist, the therapy becomes more rewarding, for both.

Once the youngster has gained the freedom to not attend, the only thing that will keep him or her in psychotherapy, is the experience of the therapy being satisfying, the burden and responsibility for which rests with the therapist.

A LASTING RELATIONSHIP

Though planned short-term psychotherapy can be of great value for the relatively mildly troubled youngster, the more severely disturbed adolescents generally want to feel that the relationship with the therapist is going to last for ever, before they can make their own personal commitment to the therapeutic alliance and to a serious relationship with the therapy and the therapist. This is particularly true of youngsters who have been repeatedly deprived of a consistent caring relationship. This tendency, which is really a manifestation of the pathology of a particular type of youngster, is so common amongst adolescents who need psychotherapy, that one will not be far wrong in regarding it as a feature of adolescence. Some who have been trained in the traditional methods, try to conduct the therapy through stated verbal contracts with the youngster for defined periods. Adolescents may agree to such arrangements but will rarely stick to them – it is not because of their unreliability.

One does not have to make any promises to the patient about the length or strength of the relationship, the therapist must simply recognise the feelings in the youngster and make the relevant comment or interpretation. Sometimes making no comment, but simply resolving within oneself that *you may need to stay with a youngster for ever if necessary*, can make a dramatic difference in the patient's keenness to relate to you, his ability to attend and in the progress in therapy. Of course, this does not happen through some magical process, the intention is conveyed by a whole range of subliminal cues.

Example:

> When Jon came to me for psychotherapy, I was tired. I had taken on too much work and I told myself that I would make this a short-term case. The psychotherapy went fairly well up to a point, but he would not enter the area that was clearly the most important for him – his feelings about his mother. He had the most intensely ambivalent relationship with her. He had no other family. His father had died when he was about nine years of age and his mother had suffered a serious stroke shortly after; she was in a wheelchair. Initially, the mention of his mother was enough to make him abuse me and leave the session, this gradually changed to his being able to remain in the room without abusing me, but there was no chance of his feeling safe enough to think about or verbalise his feelings about his mother.
>
> After a while I recognised my 'disinterest' in him, by which time also some of my other patients had left, and I decided that I would have to stay with Jon in therapy for an indefinite length of time; I found that I wanted to, there was no hurry. This tacit change of attitude on my part made all the difference in the therapy; no doubt it was reflected in my behaviour with him. The pace of the psychotherapy slowed, and Jon went smoothly and naturally into discovering more and more of what he felt about his mother. He loved her and needed her, he was very disappointed that she was ill and in a wheelchair, and was very angry about it; he felt it was he who had caused her illness. The

sight of her in a wheelchair was almost too painful for him to bear. It was his guilt that troubled him the most. He had pushed his mum out of the wheelchair as a boy of twelve and had been assailed by the Social Services for his cruelty to her.

Discussion:

For adolescents, talking about an event or a feeling often makes it as real as if it is actually happening. Feelings become concretised. Jon was scared of his anger with his mother. He dared not allow himself to experience any of it and talk about it, for fear of losing her and being left utterly alone. He was able to do this only when he had established a trusting relationship with the therapist, which he felt was strong enough to survive his feelings and last for ever – he was not alone.

In practice there is no danger of youngsters 'clinging on' for too long; if the therapy is good, they will stop or let you stop when they are ready. In fact, if the therapy has dealt with the problems effectively, the change is permanent; then the relationship with the therapy (and the therapist) does indeed last forever, and is felt as such by the patient.

THE MIDDLE

It is during the middle phase of therapy that most of the general and specific features of adolescence emerge most clearly. It is in this phase that the deeper manifestations of the individuality of the patient emerge.

GENERAL

THE ADOLESCENT PROBLEM

The adolescent is chronologically between a child and an adult, in a kind of 'no-man's land'. In this 'no-man's-land' one finds both a child and an aspiring, thwarted adult. Because adolescence is considered a passing phase, and not easily understood, the adolescent's troubles are easily neglected, avoided and denied, by parents, the authorities, society and even the psychiatric establishment; the youngster often feels lonely and neglected.

Within the adolescent, all the biological, intellectual and social forces are driving him towards adulthood, independence and a responsibility for which he has a powerful attraction. This drive is coupled with disappointment and anger with parents whom he/she has loved, while there is also a strong pull to remain a child with all the peaceful safety of dependence. There is what Keats called 'The fierce dispute betwixt damnation and impassioned clay'.

The adolescent feels in a trap and is generally miserable and resentful. The resentment is invariably directed primarily towards the parents, who are felt to be the source of these conflicting feelings, and secondarily against authority figures who represent the parents, and against society as a whole. The youngster does sometimes derive enjoyment from his relationship with his peers, and indeed from his parents, but his chief source of pleasure is through his fantasy life and the hope he puts into the future.

In treating an adolescent, the therapist must take into account the several differing aspects of the youngster; the rapid changes that occur during this period, his pathology, and the effect of the disturbance he creates in those around him, which often rebound on him and the therapist.

The adolescent may experience his changing and contradictory feelings one at a time, or he may feel them simultaneously. He may feel he is going mad, and act it out, giving a good imitation of being psychotic, especially if he has been in touch with such a patient either in his family or during a spell in psychiatric hospital. His identity is changing and does not stay fixed long enough for him to recognise himself; he wonders who he is.

Adolescents act out their multifaceted feelings in the psychotherapy situation. The therapist must recognise and deal with the rapid changes they may make, sometimes in a single session – a switch back to childhood, a jump to 'super adult', a quick display of psychopathology deftly disguised as ordinary adolescent behaviour. They are highly adept at sensing weak points of adults and using this knowledge to embarrass, attack, seduce and manipulate the therapist, and most importantly, they constantly test out the authority of the therapist, until they are satisfied that the therapist is one whom they can respect and trust and feel safe with.

In practice, the adolescent feels hurt and angry if the therapist articulates any ideas that he is like a child or has childish feelings, which are often quite prominently displayed, but feels greatly relieved if the therapist's interactions give tacit regard to them.

All the obstructions to development and pathology developed in earlier years re-emerge in adolescence where there is the best chance for them to be dealt with and corrected. Adolescence is indeed a passing phase. Nevertheless, what happens in this phase is crucial to the future life of the youngster. All of this makes the task of the therapist more complex than with an adult or a child, and carries with it a greater responsibility.

THE EFFECT ON THE THERAPIST

The difficulties that occur because of the nature of adolescence are only one aspect of the problem. A more important factor and the one that causes the greatest problems in dealing with disturbed youngsters is that the intense feelings experienced by the patient are similar to one's own more hidden ones. It is a myth that adults grow out of adolescence into a state of sexual and emotional maturity, with a well crystallised identity. Many aspects of adolescence remain throughout adulthood and when one is confronted by youngsters with problems, one's own adolescent residues are touched – often exacerbating any unresolved pathological aspects of one's personality. It is this that creates the greatest difficulty and confusion in dealing with disturbed youngsters.

It is more difficult for the therapist to separate himself from the youngster and regard him clinically and objectively, than for him to do this with a child or adult patient. Most disturbed adolescents do not look ill and cannot be placed in a diagnostic category with a recognised treatment. It is relatively easy to separate oneself from a psychiatrically ill adult and to feel aloof, calling him ill and oneself well, and to look at him clinically. Equally to separate oneself from a disturbed child is relatively easy; after all, he is only a child and the helper is an adult. But the disturbed youngster is neither a child or an ill adult; he is a youngster who suffers intensely from feelings of depression, anger, fear, guilt, confusion and insecurity – feelings common to all adults. His feelings are so similar to one's own that the boundaries between him and the therapist are blurred. Thus recognition and understanding of the feelings created in one by the patient, and the use of this for interpretation, which is essential for successful therapy, is more difficult with adolescents. Inability to separate one's own deeper feelings from those of the adolescent may result in an 'acting out' and consequently an attempt to get rid of the youngster, or a confused involvement with him that perpetuates one or more aspects of the problems.

SPECIFIC FEATURES OF ADOLESCENCE

ACTING OUT

Adolescents tend to 'act out' and 'act' their feelings, more than adults. '*Act out*' is being used here in its psychodynamic sense, for the expression of unconscious feelings through action, and '*Act*', for the expression of conscious feelings.

Youngsters feel their feelings in an unadulterated, intense form. While possessing a greater verbal capacity than children, they do not believe that their words can adequately express what they feel. (This is common in adults as well, but is felt more strongly in adolescence.) Most distressing feelings spill over into action, often taking the form of a plea for help. Many youngsters have been known to stop their 'misbehaviour' after just one or two meetings together with parents, when they have had their first experience of being listened to and being taken seriously by their parents.

In general adolescents have poorer ego control than adults, and are more likely to express themselves through behaviour rather than through words. Likewise they give greater value to the behaviour of adults (the therapist), than to their words.

Example:

> Jon (the same described above) was as inpatient who had just started psychotherapy with me. He was a sad, needy and awkward adolescent with a hugely distorted self-image and a very poor self-esteem, who could not believe that it was possible for anyone to care for him. One evening, shortly after he was admitted, I saw him in the recreation area with a tin of glue in one hand and a bottle of gin in the other, alternately taking a sniff from one and a

gulp from the other, in full view of staff and patients. He was very well aware of the policy of the unit that patients should not be manhandled by staff; this particular issue had recently been discussed in the community meeting. He was also well aware of the policy that alcohol and solvent abuse were not permitted.

The staff were trying to persuade him to give up the glue and the drink. I joined the staff and added my own persuasions to which Jon responded by taking another sniff of glue.

I then removed the tin of glue and the bottle of drink from him forcibly, with the assistance of some of the staff. He was angry but was easily calmed down by staff – he had not taken enough of either intoxicant to lose his senses.

Jon started his next psychotherapy session, probably the third with me, with an air of injured outrage:

Jon: (in angry tones) 'You manhandled me!'
Myself: 'Yes.'
Jon: 'You had no right to do that.'
Myself: 'Yes?'
Jon: 'You broke the rules of the unit, your own rules.'
Myself: 'It does seem like I did.'
Jon: 'You had no business to do that, we get told off for breaking rules.'
Myself: 'Yes, of course you will get told off for breaking rules. Why do you think I did that?'
Jon: 'I don't know.'
Myself: 'You may know if you try to think about it. You know I do not want you to sniff glue or drink.'

The words were accompanied by a tone of voice and demeanour which was a contrast to his defiant, challenging attitude.

Jon: (after a longish silence and very softly) 'Maybe you care.'

This led to the beginnings of a good therapeutic alliance. I think it was the first time in his life that he dared to conceive of the possibility that he mattered more than a rule.

Jon was a great actor-out. At the age of eleven he set fire to a very precious jacket of his in the view of his mother, who was in hospital, unable to move following a stroke. At the age of twelve he had pushed his mother out of her wheelchair. At fourteen he threatened a priest, who had come to visit his mother, with a loaded airgun and had marched him out of the house, at gun-point. He had been arrested numerous times for minor offences and had been apprehended many times by the police for running away from children's homes.

Discussion:

In this case Jon expressed his feelings – conscious and unconscious – through his behaviour; the therapist too expressed his intentions through his behaviour. This, I think is permissible, and in some cases necessary, in order to make understandable and effective communication with the youngster, and as in this case to prevent something harmful or dangerous. A problem will arise however, if the therapist uses behaviour and actions as the preferred way of interacting, rather than allow and encourage the adolescent to grow into more mature and more satisfactory ways of interacting through appropriate language.

In residential settings, where the therapist is on the staff of the institution, adolescents invariably try to recreate their 'family situation'. They often regard communications to any staff member, whether acted, acted-out or verbally conveyed, as a communication to the therapist. Whether or not the therapist picks up these communications to other staff, is often felt as evidence of the interest and care taken over the youngster. A therapist who does not keep in touch with the conduct and the communications of adolescents in the community and take up with the youngster the issues that arise out of them, in addition to those communicated directly to the therapist in the session, fails the patient, invites the anger of the staff, becomes a victim of 'splitting' and fosters a situation which will inevitably lead to a breakdown of the therapy. In residential institutions where the therapist is not on the staff of the institution, and attempts are made to keep the two separate, the adolescent invariably engineers situations which compel communications between the two.

Acting-out in adults and adolescents:

Adults also could well present their problems through their behaviour, as Jon did, by acting them out; but if they do, the appropriate response would be entirely different. An adult must take full responsibility for his actions, if there is no reason for his inability to do so, such as an organic brain condition, or an incapacitating illness; the psychotherapy is used entirely for the purpose of jointly understanding and interpreting the meaning of the patient's behaviour in terms of his total conscious and unconscious experiences. An adolescent is in a different position, particularly a disturbed one. By definition he does not know enough of the world or himself to make judgements about what is good and right for him. He is constantly looking to adults (the therapist in particular) for guidance, to learn about himself and the world around him, and to save him from serious trouble – this is not simply a greedy wish on the adolescent's part, it is his need and his right. You help an adolescent to develop responsibility for himself, you do not act as if he already has it.

THE ADOLESCENT AND AUTHORITY

Adolescents have a powerful involvement with authority, on the one hand needing it to feel safe, and on the other, needing it to rebel against, test out, and build their own internal authority. An adolescent who does not have a clear, firm authority over him, to contain him within boundaries of behaviour, will never be able to have that interaction which allows him to truly develop his own authority.

Adolescents often fear and dislike authority figures, yet they want to get close to authority, examine it, test it out, attack it and try to destroy it. This interesting interaction can achieve an alarming intensity, particularly when the adolescents are in groups or in a residential setting.

In the one-to-one situation the interaction usually occurs in a more subdued form, though it can become very distressing for the therapist. The pathology of the youngsters is invariably locked in with this continual interplay. If this pathology is to emerge for understanding and treatment, then that boundary between the therapist representing authority, and the adolescent as the child/adolescent must be maintained.

The key to the exercise of good authority is whether it is Empathic or Coercive. Empathic authority works at an ego-syntonic level, in tune with adolescent confusions and strivings. It is readily accepted. However, coercive authority is in sharp contradiction to the adolescent developmental process; it is at the superego level and tends to increase conflict and rebelliousness.

This difference, the boundary between the adolescent and the adult therapist, can be difficult to maintain. The adolescent often tries to blur the difference and manoeuvre the adult into collusion with him. Some adults and therapists also find it difficult, particularly those whose wish/need to be liked and loved by the patient overrides other considerations. A variety of manipulative devices are used by adolescents, to move into pseudo-adulthood or to bring the therapist down to their level. It is important that the therapist is comfortable in his position of authority and is able to use it appropriately when the need arises, rather than to abdicate it, which is sometimes done on the basis of the classical therapeutic stance.

Example:

> K was a small fourteen-year-old who had been arrested together with a group of much older boys for tampering with cars. He came for his first out-patient session with me, together with a friend, and insisted that his friend remain with him throughout the session. I dealt with this situation carefully and empathically, as best I could, trying to understand why K brought his friend along; I thought he was frightened of the whole business of seeing a psychiatrist, but I felt that I should not say that in front of his friend. Instead, I reasoned with him about how important it was for me to speak with him alone for the sake of confidentiality. K replied that he was his best friend and knew everything about him and there were no secrets between them. I tried different 'psychotherapeutic' ways I had learnt, but was not successful in getting him to see me by himself. I gave him an appointment for the following week.

I was a junior doctor then, in the very beginnings of learning psychotherapy, and was taking all my sessions for group discussion and supervision. In the group supervision many different ideas and ways of dealing with the problem were thrown around, some were helpful and others were too abstruse for my understanding.

K turned up for his next session, again with the same friend. I tried applying as many of the ideas I had picked up from the supervision, as I could, with no useful result. I felt frustrated and humiliated by this youngster whom I had come to regard as an insolent little 'scoundrel'. A further group discussion was equally unproductive.

He came for his third session with a different friend. It was the humiliation I felt which affected me most. I felt he was 'taking the mickey' out of me:

> Myself: 'K, I am afraid you must ask your friend to leave.'
> K:. 'If he leaves, I leave.'
> Myself: 'No you don't, you just remain in your seat and do not move. You [to his friend], I am sorry I don't know your name, please go and wait for your friend in the waiting room. Do you know where it is?'
> He nodded and left. K did not move from his seat.
> Myself: 'What are you trying to do, K? You are already in a big mess with the police, do you want to get yourself in a mess here as well?'

This led to beginnings of a good therapeutic alliance.

Discussion:

My last remark to K was an empathic one. I think he understood that I was trying to be helpful to him. I thought his behaviour in bringing a friend with him the first time was indeed mainly out of anxiety and fear. But this rapidly changed to 'testing me out', and then triumph over me and the grown-up world I was representing (he already had this tendency to be bigger than he really was, mixing with older boys), and finally to the beginnings of contempt, as he sensed that I was not in authority; It was the group supervision which was, which I recognised through recognising the feelings within me.

I learned later that I was not using the group supervision properly; good supervision does not attempt to teach you what to do or say in the next session, it should help one to think about and understand what was wrong or could have been better in the previous one.

DECISION MAKING

Decisions are not easy to make. Much information about the various factors involved, together with a capacity to think clearly, are required in good decision making. Such knowledge and capacities are not available to adolescents, many of whom are confused about their own identities and have no way of knowing what is good for them.

Adolescents often demand that they be allowed to make their own decisions. The more severely emotionally disturbed ones have invariably become suspicious of adults making decisions on their behalf, often justifiably – parents have separated, schools have been changed, they have been moved from children's home to children's home, or from one foster parent to another – all of them decisions made by adults without consultation with them, decisions which have been harmful to them, as well as painful; often they have been lied to about the reasons for such decisions. It is not surprising that they want to make their own decisions; it is also for them the 'adult thing to do', a sign of being grown-up and independent. Yet often, they do not have the capacity to make their own decisions, and feel too ashamed and frightened to admit their own inability.

It is easy for workers of all disciplines, including therapists, to collude with the adolescent's demand he should make his own decision, particularly when the decision is a difficult one. This allows the worker to abdicate responsibility for a difficult decision, leaving the responsibility and the consequences to be carried by the youngster, who already has a huge burden of his own problems to carry.

Some of these decisions concern life events of great import. The intimate knowledge of the youngster gained by the therapist is of immense value in contributing to appropriate decision making. It is part of the therapist's role, I believe, to make use of this knowledge and help with good decision making on behalf of the youngster.

Example:

> Kr, a spirited, intelligent, seventeen-year-old girl, in care from the age of four, had been admitted to an Adult Psychiatric Hospital following a bout of drinking, smashing furniture in her foster home, slashing herself and glue sniffing. She was a large girl with close-cropped hair. She wore trousers and gave the appearance of being a tough, robust, 'dangerous young man'. She had been in

the ward for about three weeks from where I had seen her about six times as an outpatient.

Kr had made it clear to me that underneath her tough-talking robust exterior she was a frightened and confused little girl who felt very dependent on the adults around her. She was now more settled and the time had come for a decision to be made regarding her move from hospital.

The decision was a difficult one for the workers.

1. Kr had had several moves to and from children's homes virtually all her life, without being able to settle in any and make a consistent relationship with an adult. It was believed by the social services that what Kr needed most was a foster home with a kindly foster-mum, who would tolerate a certain amount of acting-out and would keep her for a long period and establish a consistent, trusting, relationship with her. They thought they had found such a foster home.

2. Just prior to her admission to hospital Kr had stayed for about twelve months with that particular foster-mum, – the longest period in a single relationship. Foster-mum had idealised their relationship and had made out to Kr that her home was Kr's home for ever, and that she could stay with her until she [Kr herself] wanted to leave, after which they would remain friends for ever.

3. Foster-mum had become frightened by Kr's violence (described above), and had told Social Services that she would not have her back.

4. Kr had expressed her wish to go back to her foster-mum's. She was beginning to believe, for the first time in her life, that adults could be trusted after all.

5. Good foster-mothers are difficult to find and this one was about the best the Social Services knew; the Social Services did not want to lose her.

6. Kr had been promised a flat by Social Services when she was ready and responsible.

7. Kr was an intelligent girl, who became very distressed when

any adult in authority displayed the slightest evidence of hiding the truth from her. She had complained frequently and loudly about the Social Services lying to her.

8. The hospital ward was pressing for a quick discharge.

During a decision-making meeting with Kr and all those involved with her, including foster-mum, Kr asked why she could not go back home to foster-mum. She was told some complicated and unconvincing story, of her foster-mum's father-in-law, who lived several miles away, being unwell, and the extra work foster-mum would have to do and therefore her inability to have Kr staying with her. Kr's puzzled questions about how this would affect her staying in her foster-mum's home, especially when she was willing to help foster-mum with any extra work, were met with even more confusing and unconvincing responses.

Further discussion (non-discussion) of this question left Kr looking distressed, unwanted and fed up, at which point she was asked what her own choice was, and she immediately said she wanted to move into the flat which had been promised by the Social Services. I thought she meant 'it is better to move into a flat and away from dependence of the sort I have just experienced'.

I suggested that Kr was not ready to live independently, and that I would be willing to get to know her real mum, who lived only a few miles away, and assess the possibility of work with her and Kr. Kr's face beamed brightly for a second and then she said, 'No, everyone has tried with my mum, she doesn't want to know me,' while looking at the social worker as if to try and win her approval.

Kr finally did move into a flat; it was her decision. Her stay in the flat lasted two days, she drank, sniffed glue and took drugs together with a group of squatters who had rapidly gathered. She cut herself and got herself back into hospital, from where she moved into a halfway house.

PHYSICAL CHANGES

Rapid physical growth and body changes together with the development of secondary sexual characteristics alter the body image. These engender feelings of awkwardness and embarrassment for a while in normal adolescents who adjust to the changes relatively easily. But in some, those who have had traumatic childhoods, the altered body image becomes easily identified with bad feelings within, they feel ugly, and the natural adolescent feeling of awkwardness may become prolonged and intensified. Youngsters who have been severely deprived and have been living with unconscious 'ugly' feelings, may feel misfits and unacceptable wherever they are. Resolution of the problem will occur only when the ugly feelings within – especially anger with parents and the authorities and accompanying guilt – are recognised, understood and worked through.

It is important that the therapist recognises that acceptance of the 'ugly' physical body has a significant bearing on the patient's ability to recognise, accept and work through the ugly feelings within. Here again Melanie Klein's statement about the relationship between fantasy and reality, quoted above, is relevant:

Example:

> Some months after I started therapy with Jim, a severely emotionally deprived youngster with an appallingly low self-esteem, reflected in his appearance and his demeanour, he told me about the damage to his finger, which he had sustained some years ago. He was being chased by the police, when he fell down, was caught and in the struggle one of his fingers was damaged. He had complained about it but nobody had taken any notice; he was locked up for several weeks. Some months later a doctor had told him that his finger had been fractured and would be permanently disfigured. He held out his hand to me quite spontaneously to show me the broken finger, and I, equally spontaneously, took his hand and examined his finger as a doctor would. It was only after it was all over that I realised from the look on Jim's face and his behaviour that he had had a significant experience of being accepted by me, who had by now acquired a very significant role through the transference – I had actually touched his damaged finger without recoiling in horror, and had felt quite comfortable doing it. There was a marked increase in his ability to talk about himself and his 'bad' aspects.

Discussion:

In this case a significant step towards acceptance of the 'damaged' body was achieved through chance, spontaneous, physical contact. I believe it was the spontaneity which was of the greatest value here.

Physical expressions of acceptance I think are on the whole inappropriate in the psychotherapy situation, and indeed are usually ineffective for the intended purpose. With adolescents in particular, they can create sexual excitement, and because of the transference, are apt to be misunderstood and confused with expressions of sexual interest by the therapist. Acceptance of the body should be achieved through interpretive statements which are far more effective than any physical manoeuvres.

SEXUALITY AND ADOLESCENCE

Sexuality can only be discussed in the knowledge that it defies comprehensive understanding. It is a part of the process of man's creation, and bigger than man. We can but comprehend only some of its aspects. Of all human activities it is the most precious and yet the most common; the most mysterious and yet the most ordinary. It is the activity around which the world revolves and survives.

Sex, the most sensitive and powerful medium for the expression of human feelings, is also the most susceptible to misuse, abuse and exploitation. It can involve one's noblest nature and also one's basest.

> The expense of spirit in a waste of shame
> Is lust in action; and till action, lust
> Is perjur'd, murderous, bloody, full of blame,
> Savage, extreme, rude, cruel, not to trust;
> Enjoy'd no sooner, but despised straight;
> Past reason hunted; and no sooner had,
> Past reason hated, as a swallow'd bait,
> On purpose laid to make the taker mad:
> Mad in pursuit, and in the possession so;
> Had, having and in the quest to have, extreme;
> A bliss in proof – and prov'd, a very woe;
> Before, a joy propos'd; behind a dream.
>   All this the world knows well knows; yet none knows well
>   To shun the heaven that leads men to this hell.'

Shakespeare (Sonnet 129)

Shakespeare, one presumes, is not talking about the kind of sex that is involved with one's nobler aspects. Bad sex is evacuatory in nature in which one temporarily gets rid of bad feelings, impulses and bits of one's self. It is impulsive and compulsive.

Sexuality is sometimes split off and experienced as apart from the rest of the personality. In the normal condition of an emotionally whole person, it forms part of the whole of an interaction between two people.

THE ADOLESCENT AND SEX

Sex, which in the child is no more than a curiosity becomes a powerful driving force in adolescence. Its general direction and manifestation acquire the characteristics of the only such feelings that have been experienced – infantile and little child ones; but they will be governed by the main developmental task, which in adolescence is concerned with renegotiation of relationships.

While sexual interest between two adolescents can sometimes be the beginnings of a lasting love relationship, it should not always be regarded as a premature form of adult sexuality. Adolescent sexuality consists largely of imitative behaviour together with their own particular baby experiences, which may contain pathological elements, modified by their childhood experiences.

Unrestrained, unworked through, indulgence in sexual activity at this stage will inevitably lead to ill-advised undertakings, with consequent damage to the sensitivity and finer feelings in youngsters, and particularly a loss of self-esteem in girls. Adolescents want to engage in sexual activity for a variety of confused reasons often long before they are ready for it. They often imagine that sex will solve their feelings of adolescent loneliness and depression. Others are goaded into sex by their mates who boast of their imaginary sexual exploits and don't feel accepted by the gang or respected if they are still virgins.

'I feel used', 'I feel guilty' and 'I feel bad', are the commonest comments by adolescent girls after a sexual experience which has been unrelated to a relatively well tried out meaningful relationship. Some who have already split off their sexuality would say, 'I feel nothing.'

Sexuality is an area in which the therapist and any worker interacting with adolescents should have clear objective standards of what is good and bad, right and wrong for adolescents. It is one of those exceptional areas in which value judgements must be made by the therapist. Adolescents do not know about sex, it is new to them and they want to find out. Yet giving direct advice has its disadvantages. The safest communications are through understanding and interpretation of any current anxiety about sex conveyed by the adolescent to the therapist.

Adults who, with the best of intention, give advice and guidance to adolescents on sexual matters often succeed only in disclosing their own sexual attitudes and biases to the youngsters, who pick up the covert messages more diligently and accurately than the consciously expressed advice.

Adolescents are often troubled by their sexuality and want to bring their worries into therapy but feel embarrassed because they do not know how to do it. They often do not know the appropriate language to use, especially when the therapist comes over as 'posh' and the adolescent knows only the common, vulgar sexual terminology. Having finally made some confusing communication, the youngster may feel frightened and embarrassed, not knowing how the therapist is taking the thing. Is the therapist disgusted? Is he embarrassed? Is the therapist enjoying the youngster's embarrassment? Is the therapist being voyeuristic? Is the therapist now going to exploit the youngster, especially if the communication contained some positive feeling about the therapist? All these questions and the sensitivity with which the therapist deals with them are of great importance to what happens after such communications, and whether the therapy proceeds satisfactorily.

Sexual material is often brought into sessions consciously or unconsciously for the purpose of testing out and finding out whether the therapist is a 'safe' person. Adolescents love it and feel very safe when they discover through their interaction that the therapist is thoroughly comfortable with 'sex', and is truly interested in their troubles and in their total development, and not particularly in their sexuality.

I think the most important factor in the psychotherapy of

sexual problems of adolescents is that a communication about the adolescent's sexuality is occurring between an adolescent and an adult who purports to be and is seen by the youngster as a responsible authority on the subject, and not just an adult whose comments can be ignored or laughed at. The attitude of the therapist to the communication is of crucial importance, and is probably the main thing, if not the only one, that will be picked up by the patient.

It is important for the adolescent to know that the therapist is comfortable with his or her [the adolescent's] sexuality and is very willing to listen to the anxieties of the youngster, to take them seriously and try to understand them. At the same time it must be recognised that for adolescents, talking about sex is exciting and is often felt as actually having the experience; clear thinking is impossible at first. Dwelling on sex repetitively, without the discussion becoming open-ended and leading to wider issues and the uncovering of underlying feelings, is of no value to the adolescent; it is often felt by the youngster as the voyeurism of the therapist, or an expression of the therapist's vicarious gratification. Spending time in exploring and trying to understand the underlying feelings and meanings can be of great value.

If it is recognised that sexuality is a vehicle through which one's emotional state and capacity for making relationships is expressed, then one would see that attention given to the nature of the relationship between the therapist and patient can deal with the sexual problem without discussion of details of the sexual activity worrying the youngster. Similarly, the nature and quality of a youngster's relationships with parents and the staff of a unit gives a good indication of his or her ability to have a rewarding sexual relationship.

Example:

> D, a sixteen-year-old was admitted as an inpatient following his arrest for buggery and rape of a fourteen-year-old boy. He came into therapy with me. He denied the offence of rape, though he acknowledged the buggery, which he said happened with the full consent of the boy. He seemed to be well advanced in his homosexual life and was very ashamed and unhappy about it. He

seemed to be genuinely interested in gaining help for his unhappiness.

After a while in the unit, D, who was a particularly intelligent and talented youngster, charming in many ways, was found to be continually quarrelling with staff. He gradually became both a leader and a bully amongst the patients. His bullying was confined to verbal assaults on youngsters who did not accede to his way of thinking and 'toe his line'.

After some months in the unit D became known as the patient who would talk the most in the community meetings, where two characteristics emerged.

1. He would argue with staff fiercely, loudly, insistently and interminably, desperately trying to force in his point of view, and becoming very distressed and angry when his argument was not accepted by the community meeting.

2. The majority of arguments were created by him, by giving a small but significant twist to something staff said and then arguing vehemently against his own twisted version. He made it impossible for anyone in the community meeting to point out to him what he was doing when he was caught up in the throes of his violent arguments.

It was easier to pick up these qualities as soon as they appeared in the therapy, where discussion and clarification were possible. He was able to see that he twisted what he was told to him when he felt frightened of acknowledging the truth of what had been said.

D's complicated behaviour seemed to be related to his babyhood experience of father who beat his mother badly from the time he was an infant. It seemed to be about his fear of annihilation when he sensed or anticipated disagreements, which led him to trying force his point of view, i.e. himself, into the object/person involved – an understandable, self preservative manoeuvre. I believe that all this was acted out in his developing adolescent homosexuality which in his particular case was developing into a perversion, indicated by the twist he gave to some of the staff utterances. The manner in which he tried to force-in his point of view into the audience at the community meeting, I thought showed his tendency to becoming a rapist.

D, who at one stage was very keen on talking about his sexuality in therapy, soon lost interest in the subject. Discussions centred around what was going on in the therapy between him and me. He learned and understood a great deal about how he twisted my words, and was greatly relieved a few times when he truly recognised that he was not fighting me but something that he had created through such a twist.

This was accompanied by an episode of change in his sexual orientation. He acquired a girlfriend and for the first time in his life had a heterosexual experience, which he said he enjoyed.

Discussion:

One of the most striking and rewarding features of psychotherapy with adolescents is that one can observe and work with the process of the formation of pathology which one sees in its fully formed state in the adult. In adolescence the process is clearly seen and is more amenable to change because it has not yet become crystallised. Treatment or even discovery of how the pathology came about in the adult is much more difficult because of the layers and complexities of defences which have been formed.

I think D gave us a clear illustration of how perverse qualities expressed through sexuality are also expressed through one's non-sexual relationships, and how they can be altered by paying attention to the non-sexual interactions; the external reality. Here is another of the many instances where the quotation from Hanna Segal, above is particularly relevant.

Shortly after the episode described above with a girl, D had a relatively minor homosexual involvement with a boy – mutual masturbation. He became very frightened of what he had done, could not face the community of youngsters and left the unit with the agreement of staff on duty after a discussion of his fears. He had told the staff he wanted to leave only for a short while. He saw me several times after that as an outpatient, the purpose of which was to discuss re-entry into the unit. I could not persuade him to be re-admitted. D left too early; he had just begun to change. I thought the staff member had acted incorrectly in agreeing that he left; in so doing he had given truth to D's fears that he had done something irredeemable.

TRANSFERENCE AND SEXUAL FEELINGS

It is said that sexual feelings are often transferred onto the therapist. In my experience it is the deeper feelings of wanting care and affection that are transferred; these can be confused with sexual feelings. No doubt there is a lot of 'excited' talk amongst adolescents about their sexual feelings for the therapist, particularly in inpatient cultures. There is rivalry amongst them about their differing feelings about their therapists, those with the strongest and most intimate feelings being regarded as the most prestigious. Adolescents have a tendency to get carried away by such exciting feelings, and often end up not knowing what they really feel. They may communicate such confusions to the therapist, which could easily be misunderstood as transference feelings by the unwary.

Example:

> M, an attractive fourteen-year-old inpatient, was in therapy with me. She had quite unwittingly incurred the animosity of many of the female staff of the unit who regarded her as a shameless flirt. I thought M had a natural, innocent femaleness and attractive feminine gestures and mannerisms, without the slightest aim of seducing or flirting with anyone. She was only fourteen, had never had any sexual experience, had a very poor self-esteem and was pleading for understanding and help. She had attempted suicide three times. Her own father abandoned her and mother when she was an infant, and mother had cohabited with three other 'fathers' since then. M was a battered baby.
>
> She had been in therapy with me nearly a year, when she knocked on my door one day, out of therapy hours, came in and blurted out, 'I want to kiss you, I want to rape you!' I said, 'Tell me about it when I see you for therapy, don't worry.' She had always interacted with me as a battered helpless infant, who was nowhere near having reached the stage of experiencing genital sexual feelings.
>
> During the next session she went directly into serious distress about some experiences she had had in the unit and she started crying. These experiences were clearly related to the infantile battering she had received. She crossed her arms, hugging her shoulders, and she tossed her head from side to side, saying, 'I can't stand it, I can't stand it, please hug me, please hug me.' I

recalled to myself her history of having her head split open by one of her 'fathers' throwing her against the wall. I, who had always maintained a therapeutic distance from her, left my seat and cuddled her head in my arms. Her tears subsided soon and she smiled faintly.

Further discussion with M about these events showed that when she burst into my room and declared her wish to kiss and rape me, she did not have any such feelings at all. She had contrived them in order to fill the emptiness she had felt when some other girls had spoken about their feelings for their therapists. The thing that frightened her most at the time was the possibility that I might have taken the sexual 'rubbish' she had spoken of seriously. She felt so reassured when I cuddled her head, knowing then that I had no fear of her sexuality and was in touch only with her baby needs.

There was a remarkable change for the better in M after this, in her therapy and in her conduct in the unit. She developed steadily and unbelievably into a stable and fine young girl.

Discussion:

The action of the therapist (myself) in cuddling M's head, I think, must be regarded as a departure from the psychoanalytical code of practice. It does indeed violate a principle on which psychoanalytical thinking is based; that expression of feeling by the therapist in any form is inappropriate. Feelings created within the therapist are meant to be understood, as counter-transference feelings, and used to understand the unconscious experiences and feelings of the patient, which should then be interpreted in a helpful way to the patient.

Whilst one cannot but accept these arguments as valid, as a general rule, one must consider that in psychoanalytical psychotherapy the patient is not seen every day. It is far more difficult to achieve that safe, continuous, ongoing process of interaction between the therapist and patient which obviates any need for concrete intervention. Psychoanalytical psychotherapy in which the patient is seen less frequently, twice a week in this case, is more difficult. One must achieve the same result with less time spent with the patient; short cuts must be taken.

In this particular case the action taken by the therapist dealt with several different aspects at the same time and helped the patient to move on in dealing with her deeper problems. Given that M was very unhappy with what was going on in the unit with regard to her own confused sexual/pseudo-sexual behaviour, and the attitude of some of the staff; given that she was in touch with her inner world and the real concrete experience of cruelty and physical abuse she had suffered as a baby, the action of the therapist could have:

1. Helped her to feel that the same man (her father via the transference) who had caused the wound in her head by throwing her against the wall had healed it. Melanie Klein's views on the mutuality of the relationship between reality and fantasy, quoted at the beginning of the chapter, are relevant.

    At a different level M felt that the therapist understood the intolerable distress she was experiencing, in her inner life as an infant, in the unit and in the therapy. Words, whether the patient's or the therapist's, do not often convey the true feelings and intentions.

2. It demonstrated to her that the therapist was not afraid of her emerging sexuality. Her sexuality stopped being dangerous.

3. It allowed M to move back safely into her infantile feelings with her therapist, without the insistent demand from the culture of the unit and the world outside that she be mature and adult – she needed much more time to work through her infantile traumatic experiences.

Just before M left the unit, she came to wish me goodbye, when she said, 'Dr Perin, I am frightened to ask you this, but I want you to make me a promise.'

Dr P: 'What is it, M?'.

M: 'Will you promise to give me away when I get married.'

Dr P: 'Yes, I will promise you on one condition, that you promise me that you will not hesitate to change your mind if you feel like it.'

M: 'Agreed.'

Eleven months after M left the unit; I received the following letters, one from M and one from her social worker.

From M:

Dear Dr Perin,

I have not seen you for a long time now, I really do miss you. I really do feel better myself but I feel as if I don't really know myself. How are you, I bet you [won't] tell me even though I have asked you. I still haven't forgotten that I asked you to give me away if I ever got married. I am doing well outside in the big world; I take my exams on etc…

From the social worker:

Dear Dr Perinpanayagam,

I am enclosing a paper cutting of M which I am sure you will be delighted to see. It may be that M has already sent you one, however, in this case I am sure you will agree that two is better than one!

M has made great strides and is a different girl. She will be attending college in September to commence a community care type course and still hopes to become a nurse. She has been having Home Tuition and has taken several CSEs. Mrs B seems better able to cope with her own life, has had an operation for removal of scar tissue to her abdomen and she and M have a much improved relationship. It would seem that M's period at Brookside has given her the insight into her own feelings and problems and I hope that she can now build a useful and happy life for herself. At the moment she has visions of being a future Miss World!

The 'transference' sexual feelings that adolescents develop for the therapist or the staff of a unit are often not sexual at all, but feelings of wanting to be close, to be cared for, and to be loved. The sexuality is often made up in order to fill a feeling of emptiness.

IDEALISATION, DENIGRATION AND ROLE MODELS

However good, bad or indifferent parents have been, children generally idealise them. It is the parents who provided everything for the child, and the feeling of being safe. To the child, parents are all-powerful and all good. As the child reaches adolescence, and comes under the influence of the adolescent process – the biological, intellectual, and emotional forces within him – he comes to realise that his parents are in fact fallible human beings. This then leads to a conflict within the adolescent; gross disappointment and denigration of the objects (people) they once idealised; the greater the idealisation the greater the fall and the denigration. But the original feelings of adoration still remain in the preconscious mind. (That is, they are not usually conscious, but are available to consciousness if the effort is made, with ordinary discussion and support.) It would take many years of adolescence and adulthood, to be able to bring together these two opposing experiences into a well-blended composite whole.

Adolescents find it impossible to contain these two opposing feelings. The strength of each of them makes the ambivalence intolerable. So the adolescent separates them (splits his feelings) into the idealised good ones and the denigrated bad ones and projects them into the world outside. If the parents do not get on well with each other, each of them may become the recipients of the projections of the adolescent's split feelings, one of them being felt as all good and the other as all bad.

These split ambivalent feelings about parents become easily attached onto different groups of adults and individuals in the adolescent's life, the bad untrustworthy ones whom he despises and the good ones whom he idealises. Therapists and staff of residential units are common objects of such projections.

In children who have had the experience of parents separating early in their lives, this process of splitting and projection in adolescence also occurs, as it does in the youngster whose parents have provided them with a safe environment throughout childhood. The entire process and the intense conflict of feeling which occurs at an earlier age, in such cases, remains dormant till the emergence of adolescence.

Such splitting and projections can be very useful in this period of their lives because staff who are idealised make excellent role models for the youngsters, if they simply maintain their staff roles responsibly. Youngsters become seriously depressed when they feel let down by the adult (staff) whom they idealise. They expect absolute honesty, chastity, compassion and good sense from staff. The staff person does not have to reach these impossible standards in their personal lives; these qualities are projected onto the staff and remain untarnished if the behaviour of the staff conforms to the acknowledged standards of a good psychodynamically orientated therapeutic unit, where the emphasis is on an honest and responsible relationship between the youngsters and staff, which includes a *professional* distance from the patient (adolescent).

Example:

> 1. Jacky, a girl of seventeen, who had an extremely disturbed family background, had at last settled well in the therapeutic adolescent unit. She was a member of a small group conducted by Alan. She came to see me one morning, looking very troubled, and told me that she wanted to leave Alan's group. She explained that she had overheard a telephone conversation Alan had made in which he had told someone (a girl, she thought), that he would meet her behind a house, late the next night. Jacky told me that she knew that Alan had a steady girlfriend to whom he was going to be married. She told me that she had always believed that Alan was an honest and trustworthy person, but now felt so let down that she could never trust him again.

> 2. I was Mac's group therapist. He felt very safe with me particularly because he felt I was not frightened of his anger and could engage with him comfortably, whatever he said or did. He never failed to attend the groups. I was idealised by him but did not realise it.
> One evening another youngster broke into my car and took an overdose of some painkillers I had left there, foolishly, in full view of any passer-by. This was discussed in the community meeting in which my foolishness was commented on and acknowledged by me. Mac became seriously depressed and refused to attend group therapy with me for several days, he abused me and later wept. He was able to re-attend the group only after he had had a full discussion with me about my foolishness and his fear that I was on drugs.

SELF-DISCLOSURE

There are two types of self-disclosure, those that say something about the qualities and characteristics of the therapist, and those that disclose facts about the therapist. The former are important to the patient. The latter, I believe, has no place in a psychotherapeutic relationship.

It is important that the patient comes to know something of the true qualities of the therapist which are relevant to the psychotherapeutic interaction. For instance, the patient must know that the therapist is honest and reliable and genuinely interested in his welfare and development. This is important for the establishment of the real relationship and the therapeutic alliance. This knowledge of the therapist's characteristics is gained through the normal psychotherapeutic interactions; it does not require any active self-disclosure by the therapist.

Some adolescents are highly skilled at enticing adults to talk more about themselves than they intend to. Therapists who convey their attitudes through statements can find themselves in trouble. For instance, the statement 'I care for you' made in response to a youngster's distress or persuasion, or because the therapist all by himself has had an 'intense bout of caring', which may occur as a transference or counter-transference phenomenon, can be very foolish. Such a statement is usually not believed by the adolescent. Many adolescents would find it tantalising and want to test it out by trying to make the therapist (or staff) prove it, repeatedly. The therapist (or staff member), who has tried to prove it repeatedly and whose patience may have been stretched to breaking point, may be finally forced into acknowledging that it was not really true after all and destroy the possibility of a trusting relationship with the youngster.

There are some who believe that it will be beneficial for the patient to know that the therapist also has problems and difficulties similar to the patient's. This may have value in a GP's surgery, when the doctor sometimes has to quickly reassure a fussy hypochondriac or a hysteric, but it can be most damaging to the psychotherapeutic process. Adolescent patients do not understand psychopathology, and any similar symptom or habit acknowledged by the therapist can only be seen by them as the same as their own similar weakness. Adolescents cannot gain help from someone whom they consider as bad, as weak, or as sick as themselves. They are likely to projectively identify with such a therapist, then believe that the therapist is ill, feel well in themselves and triumph over the entire psychotherapy situation.

Revealing to the youngster any of those aspects you consider to be good or normal is equally unwise – if you answer questions about yourself in one area which you consider to be good, you cannot refrain from answering questions in another area without making it clear you have something to hide.

In fact, any active disclosure to the patient merely *burdens* him/her, and interferes with the patient status. The therapist must allow the patient to be the patient, and he must always remain in role as the therapist.

ADOLESCENCE AND THE TRANSFERENCE

It is well acknowledged that the transference plays a central role in psychoanalytical psychotherapy. Whilst it may be possible to engender some degree of superficial change without making use of the transference, any expectation of making accurate interpretations or engendering deep change will have to be abandoned if the importance of the transference is neglected. It is through the transference that the unconscious feelings and attitudes of the patient are most frequently expressed and understood most clearly.

In emphasising the value and importance of recognising the transference, one assumes that the ordinary real relationship is also being recognised, valued and being used at all times. Thus every feeling that the patient develops towards the therapist should not be regarded as the transference. The patient sometimes becomes angry with the therapist because of the therapist's incompetence or mistakes. The transference is of value only when seen in the context of the real relationship. James Strachey's paper on 'The Mutative Interpretation' shows the crucial importance of both the transference relationship and the real relationship.[2]

It is generally understood that a certain distance and remoteness must be maintained by the therapist in order to mobilise the transference. Therefore when one considers that in psychotherapy with adolescents, the therapist's interactions must go well beyond the classical psychotherapeutic stance with adults, questions about the effect of this on the transference and the effectiveness of the therapy must arise.

Indeed it is important to emphasise the importance of maintaining a professional stance and a certain 'remoteness', a remoteness that is neither rejecting nor arrogant, from adolescent patients. But this is not so important for the purpose of mobilising the transference; though it is of particular relevance to the adolescents' predilection for closing the gap between the themselves and adults, unrealistically and often illegitimately, if allowed to do so. They thereby lose the opportunity of recognising and dealing with the very important problems contained in this gap – the boundary between the child and the parent. The transference, I believe, is related more to the personality and problem of the patient, than to the distance and the enigmatic stance adopted by the therapist.

I believe that the adolescent condition lends itself naturally to the transference, because of the nature of adolescence and the attendant identity problems. Generally speaking, no work needs to be done to mobilise and develop the transference, as it is ever present. Adolescents, and disturbed ones in particular, see all adults, especially professionals, as a homogeneous agglomeration of authority figures, and in this perception all the essential elements of the transference are contained. As the adolescent develops, his perception of adults gradually changes into one of a heterogeneous agglomeration and finally more or less into differentiated individuals of another generation. The last being a state which coincides with the development and crystallisation of the youngster's identity and wholeness – a state of 'enlightenment' which is achieved by human beings only periodically.

The task of the therapist with an adolescent, then, is to allow the youngster to experience the therapist as an individual person, as far as this is possible in the light of the dangers of self-disclosure. It is only then, that the pre-existing transference relationships can be put into use.

I would therefore like to suggest that as far as the transference is concerned, two contradictory situations prevail with adults and adolescents. With adults one of the chief tasks of therapy is to recognise, maintain and develop the transference so that it can be used in conjunction with the real relationship, whilst with adolescents one of the main tasks of the therapist is to develop certain aspects of the real relationship so that psychoanalytical work can be done in conjunction with the pre-existing transference relationship.

A feature of the relationship in the psychotherapy of adolescents, is the creation of an 'Ideal' relationship between the patient and the therapist, which happens nearer the end of therapy, and lasts for a variable period. A transference seems to occur, which contains the expectations of a relationship which is devoid of the fear of all human foibles. A recognition of this allows the therapist to work with the youngster within the fringes of something that is felt to be a much bigger and wider idealism, than can be comprehended or described by either. If the therapist recognises it and allows this aspect of the transference to last as long as it will, the real relationship will inevitably be recognised in due course, but this particular significant experience remains unspoilt. It is in this phase that the therapist has the opportunity to taste and appreciate the purity, the truth and the honesty of youth; it is an experience that makes the therapist feel sure the youngster is on his/her way.

This phenomenon occurs with adolescents who historically have not had anything like a good relationship with their parents. The question then arises, about whether this phenomenon is none other than the usual split-off part object relationship being transferred onto a gullible therapist, or whether, indeed, it is something more than this.

In my experience, it has occurred only after the therapist has repeatedly dealt with the part object phenomenon. Further investigation of this occurrence is necessary, and if, indeed it turns out that there is a difference between the part object transference and the 'Ideal relationship' phenomenon I have described above, occurring with even the most uncared for baby, then the source of such an experience must be accounted for. Is there something beyond the relationship between mother and baby which occurs in the unconscious mind which becomes transferred onto the therapist if the therapy relationship has not been spoilt by the therapist? What are the implications of this? Is this an experience of God?

THE END

The time to stop psychotherapy is often decided by the adolescents themselves. They usually do it unconsciously through a variety of practical impedimenta to continuing therapy, because of circumstances and 'accidents'; the patient is entering university and has to move, or has started work and cannot attend, or has got into some trouble with the law and is put away. Some adolescents get sick of being 'patients' any more and want to give it up – indeed a sign of good health. The more emotionally developed and competent youngster will discuss termination of therapy.

Parting is about the most difficult thing for adolescents, indeed for any human being; if the therapeutic relationship has been long and rewarding, it is also difficult for the therapist.

The parting usually begins with the agreement on a date of stopping therapy. With it a phase of disturbing feelings in the patients occurs; invariably they are about the underlying angry unconscious feelings of being unwanted, and others of a similar nature. If these are not understood and interpreted they may be acted out and the youngster may become destructive to self and others, particularly the therapist. They may feel and behave as they did when they first started therapy, and parents and workers complain that all the therapy has been no benefit at all – 'a sheer waste of time'. This is a neat manoeuvre by the patient which demonstrates vividly and concretely his/her anger with the therapist. The more one accurately interprets the underlying feelings of being unwanted, the fear of sadness and depression, feelings of wanting to hurt and damage the therapist, the better the therapy, and the less acting out.

In inpatient units, it is not uncommon for patients who have been given notice of leaving to escalate their acting out so as to invite getting 'thrown out', – a manoeuvre which allows them to escape the pain of parting. If the patient is not thrown out but allowed to continue with therapy during this vital period it will be of immense benefit to him/her. He/she may then be able to truly work through digest and metabolise, this universal trauma of separation. This often causes disagreements and anger between staff of inpatient units; those concerned with the general organisation and maintenance of the unit would want the patient out and those more interested in psychotherapeutic development of the individual will want him/her to remain, despite the disturbance.

Psychotherapy with adolescents can go on virtually for ever if one's aim is to 'cure all problems', or wait till the youngster crystallises into stable adulthood. This, I believe, is unrealistic. My concept of the aim of psychotherapy with adolescents can be described in terms of a game of football, in which the adolescent is the ball being kicked and buffeted in all directions; when the ball finally reaches a good player, it is directed towards the goal with considerable momentum; the good player has then done his job well; whether or not a goal is scored depends on several other factors. The job of a good therapist is to direct the youngster towards his goal, giving him the momentum to carry on in the right direction. This momentum is the therapeutic experience, which in addition to dealing with any external obstacles to his/her development, principally helps the youngster to mobilise his/her internal resources, in order to deal constructively with future difficulties as they arise. Thus the result of the relationship between the adolescent and good psychotherapy, of which the therapist forms an integral part, lasts forever.

EXAMPLES

MU

Mu wanted to stop when he felt normal and safe for the first time in many years; he had stopped glue-sniffing and cutting himself secretly and felt sure he would not go back to it; it was also the time when he began to be able to interact with his peers as an equal. He wanted to return to college to do his A levels. It was clear to me that he still had problems, which could be helped with continuing therapy, but so does every youngster, and I did not even suggest to him that he continued therapy. I told him that I was sure that he could get on without further help from me, and I suggested to him that if at some future date he felt that he wanted to understand more about himself, he should get in touch with me. I continued the therapy with him for a further six weeks – twice-weekly.

C

C wanted to stop when he got into some trouble at work through trying to manipulate his colleagues and boss. He had developed considerably in therapy and had gained much insight. He thoroughly understood what he had done; it was a replication of the manipulations he had done at home with his parents and siblings. He wanted to pack up his job and go to Amsterdam, where, I understood, he had the opportunity to make good or throw himself totally into the drug scene. I discussed with him, the dangers of what he was doing. He decided to go anyway, and he left promising to get in touch with me on his return.

Jm

Was a fifteen-year-old public schoolboy who asked for therapy because he felt depressed and suicidal. He was a polite, intelligent, good-looking, boy, who was in touch with his feelings and had the ability to express them clearly. He made good use of the psychotherapy and recovered quickly. After about nine months of once-weekly therapy, Jm was ready to leave. He was given two months to prepare for termination of therapy. He was confident about being able to get on without the therapy when the termination was first broached. During these two months I had taken careful note of manifestations of feelings of being unwanted and angry, and had interpreted them effectively. Jm felt greatly helped by the therapy and wondered how it had happened. During the last two sessions he started becoming somewhat alarmed at what he would do if he felt like he had felt when he first came for therapy; and was worried about who he would have to turn to. I went over the sessions we had and the areas we had covered, and pointed out to him that I had not given him any advice nor told him how to deal with any of his difficulties. I helped him to realise that it was he himself who had used his own internal resources to solve his problems.

Further discussion led to my asking him whether he had read the poem 'If –' by Rudyard Kipling. He said he had not. I typed it out and brought him a copy for the last session, it was greatly appreciated by him.

If –

If you can keep your head when all about you
Are losing theirs and blaming it on you,
If you can trust yourself when all men doubt you,
But make allowance for their doubting too;
If you can wait and not be tired by waiting,
Or being lied about, don't deal in lies,

Or being hated, don't give way to hating,
And yet don't look too good, nor talk too wise;

If you can dream – and not make dreams your master;
If you can think – and not make thoughts your aim;
If you can meet with Triumph and Disaster
And treat those two impostors just the same;
If you can bear to hear the truth you've spoken
Twisted by knaves to make a trap for fools,
Or watch the things you gave your life to, broken,
And stoop and build 'em up with worn-out tools:

If you can make one heap of all your winnings
And risk it on one turn of pitch-and-toss,
And lose, and start again at your beginnings
And never breathe a word about your loss;
If you can force your heart and nerve and sinew
To serve your turn long after they are gone,
And so hold on when there is nothing in you
Except the Will which says to them: 'Hold on!'

If you can talk with crowds and keep your virtue,
Or walk with Kings – nor lose the common touch,
If neither foes nor loving friends can hurt you,
If all men count with you, but none too much;
If you can fill the unforgiving minute
With sixty seconds worth of distance run,
Yours is the Earth and everything that's in it,
And – which is more – you'll be a Man, my son!

> Rudyard Kipling

REFERENCES

[1] Segal, Hanna, *Introduction to the Work of Melanie Klein*, 1988, Karnac Books and Institute of Psychoanalysis, London, p.15.
[2] Strachey, J., *The Nature of the Therapeutic Action of Psychoanalysis*, 1934, in *Psychoanalytic Clinical Interpretations, London*, Ed. Louis Paul, the Free Press of Glencoe, Collier-Macmillan Ltd., 1963, pp.1–41.
[3] Klein, M., et al., *Developments in Psycho-Analysis*, London, Hogarth Press, 1948, p.198.
[4] Lewin, K., 'Field Theory', in papers dated 1939–1947, Cartwright, D, (Ed.), New York, 1951.
[5] Hinshelwood, R.D., *What Happens in Groups*, Free Association Books, 1987, p.64.

Chapter VIII
RESIDENTIAL TREATMENT OF ADOLESCENTS

INTRODUCTION

It is in residential work that one faces the greatest difficulties of work with adolescents and where one learns the most; it can also be the most rewarding.

Mistakes, whether they be in management of the internal structure of the organisation, in the handling of difficulties created by external authorities, in the management of staff or in the understanding of the individual and group phenomena in the resident or staff population, are punished most severely by the disruptive behaviour of the resident. The young dependant adolescents are affected by the mistakes of staff and invariably act out their disturbing feelings. Unlike in outpatient work, where it is the community at large and the adolescent himself and his family who take the consequences of the acting out, in residential work, it is the staff who bear the full brunt of the destructive behaviour of the youngsters; a vicious cycle can easily be created.

In residential work, where inevitably there will be a large number of staff having to work together, from different backgrounds and disciplines, and having to interact with a range of professionals involved with the youngsters in their care, there is the greatest chance that the psychodynamic approach will be abandoned for pragmatic solutions and seemingly quick practical measures of dealing with the problems that arise.

The Psychodynamic Method

Psychodynamics is often talked of as if it were a specific form of treatment, like behaviour therapy, but different from it or opposed to it. In fact it is not a single specific form of treatment, it is a logical and reasonable approach to the problems of the youngsters; it is an attitude, a method, which takes into account the effect of relationships with significant people – the relationship with the therapist or the staff of an institution being of crucial importance. Alternatively it could be regarded as a thoughtful response to the behaviour or the communication of the patient / client / offender, rather than a reaction or a retaliation.

Within this broad concept are specific but different forms of treatment such as psychoanalysis, psychoanalytical/psychodynamic psychotherapy, psychodrama and art therapy, for instance, each of which follows a method of its own, all of which aim at uncovering hidden material and basing the therapy on the information this provides.

A significant feature of the psychodynamic approach in the residential setting is that built into the method there is a continual critical appraisal of the responses made by the therapists and the staff. This is of particular importance and value in the residential setting, where much difficulty and deskilling can occur because of the close involvement between staff and residents. This critical look at the professional response is done through continual in-service supervision/discussion, and staff sensitivity meetings. It is a safeguard that is not built into any other kind of treatment. I would advocate supervision or discussion of cases for even the most experienced, because of natural human fallibility.

The most respected axiom in the medical world and indeed in all human affairs is that treatment should be directed to the cause. The cause in adolescent disturbance is well known and widely accepted as predominantly concerned with damaged and distorted relationships with significant people, often the parents and the family. The concept of family therapy, its importance and its development is based on this knowledge. At Brookside, such factors were found in 88% of a random sample of youngsters referred to the unit ([1]Perinpanayagam, 1978a).

Even in those few youngsters who could be described as suffering from a formal psychiatric illness, the effect of their condition on the family and their larger social environment, and the rebound effect on the youngster, are considerable and require attention.

Those who have worked with adolescents in depth know that contributions to the disturbance are made by both the youngster and the environment, so it is the *relationship* between the disturbed adolescent and the family and/or significant people that must be looked at, understood and dealt with.

Examination of the distorted relationship of the adolescents can be made possible only if they are able to relate to those who treat them, in their most natural way – in a way they have related to their own parents, and further, in ways they consciously or unconsciously wanted to relate to them, but did not or could not. Invariably these relationships contain 'bad' elements – anger, murderous impulses, incestuous feelings and fantasies, guilt, fears of madness and confusion. The expression of these by the youngsters is often in a disguised form and requires some unravelling before it can be understood and clearly identified. Expertise in psychodynamics will be helpful for this.

This means that the unit must have a culture which permits the expression of these 'bad' elements. It cannot, therefore, have policies which insist upon 'good behaviour' as a prerequisite and it should not use methods of depersonalising the patient or systems of sanctions and punishments (appropriately used in institutions which treat by suppression of symptoms).

Different forms of treatment and aids to treatment – individual psychotherapy, small group therapy, family therapy, behaviour therapy, art therapy, psychodrama, bioenergetics and a wide range of modified versions of these – can be used effectively in co-operation with the basic treatment philosophy. All of them, apart from certain types of Behaviour therapy, which suppress symptoms, serve to bring out the underlying suppressed and repressed feelings of the patients. When medication is used, it is important that psychodynamic implications for the patient and the community re fears of madness, responsibility for one's actions, control, punishment, staff fear etc., and more covert feelings of the individual patient, be discussed and dealt with realistically.

Whilst the primary task of a treatment unit is to deal with the cause of the problem, there are also subsidiary tasks – care of youngsters, providing for their educational needs and meeting their total development needs. These must be organised in tandem with the primary task of treatment Sometimes (surprisingly, a rare occurrence), there are conflicts between the two, and it requires fine judgement to handle such situations.

'SANCTIONS' AND 'NO SANCTIONS' UNITS

The predominant difficulty in treating adolescents in an inpatient setting is control of their behaviour. This can become the major preoccupation with staff, with consequent loss of attention to the primary task of treatment. Some units have found it necessary to build in systems of 'punishments' and sanctions into their treatment philosophy in order to obviate this difficulty. Others find that sanctions interfere with in-depth treatment, and therefore build into the treatment philosophy and management of the unit ways of 'containing' the disturbed behaviour of youngsters and the difficulties that arise for staff. These different approaches are related to the type of patients admitted, the depth of treatment aimed at, and the training, experience and inclinations of the staff.

A SANCTIONS UNIT

The unit that uses sanctions is a 'safe' unit, and if well organised, is pleasant to work in. The philosophy is easy to understand and implement. The 'bad' behaviour of the patient is well controlled by the sanctions and the staff have only the nicer aspects of the youngsters to relate to. The staff are clearly in charge and they control the youngsters through sanctions. They also have legitimatised opportunities of retaliation through sanctions when the 'badness' of the youngsters offends them or engenders angry or nasty feelings in them. They do not have to carry within them the 'badness' and pathology of the patients.

Patients in such a unit also feel good. They are not in touch with their 'badness' or their guilt, do not fear their own destructiveness, and have a general sense of well-being. The morale in a well-run 'sanctions unit' should usually be high. It has been often found, however, that as the 'well' side gets better, the 'disturbed' side becomes worse by becoming more isolated within the young person and hence more liable to erupt in crises.

A NO SANCTIONS UNIT

In a well run 'no sanctions' unit, the situation is very different for staff and patients. The patients get more and more in touch with their 'badness'; they feel they are getting worse and find it hard to trust staff, who do not take away their bad feelings but seem to make them worse. They are angry with staff, not only because of this, but also because staff, who represent parents and the authority figures in their lives, acquire in their minds the characteristics of their own parents and authority figures (transference), and so they feel and express with staff all the anger they dared not express with their parents and, perhaps, never knew they had. The full pathology of the patients emerges in all its nastiness, and staff can feel attacked. Legitimised retaliation by staff is not possible. The staff must absorb and contain all the badness that is pushed into them. There is no clearly defined special way to relate to the youngsters. Staff can only learn how to respond through a progressively greater understanding of the patients and of the feelings created in themselves. Staff are often frustrated and taken over by helpless and sometimes hopeless feelings. They often feel deskilled and may, sometimes, actually become deskilled for a while. The general atmosphere in the unit is one of thoughtfulness and a subdued doubtful enthusiasm. Staff morale can fall easily.

However, the changes in the youngsters and the knowledge that these changes are from within, not imposed, and are therefore likely to last, bring rich, long-term rewards for staff.

In a 'no sanctions unit', containment, internalisation of controls and self-discipline are achieved very effectively through what could be understood as a combination of behavioural and psychodynamic principles – in the usual 'Reward and Punishment systems', a painful experience is dispensed for bad behaviour; in a 'no sanctions unit', where such systems are not used, the painful experience within the patient is uncovered. Staff strive, through discussions, to enable the patient to recognise and experience the internal pain he creates for himself through his actions, in terms of his relationship with others in the community. This internal pain, usually accompanied by guilt, is far more troublesome to him than any form of external punishment. These feelings are invariably linked to deeper feelings related to the primary source of the problem – the relationship with parents and the family; it sets the scene for further psychodynamic work and deeper changes (²Freud, 1961; Winnicot, 1965).

It is the author's experience that systems of sanctions can be used beneficially on selected patients, within the context of a 'no sanctions unit', after careful thought and discussion with staff and the community of patients. Indeed, it is necessary, if the unit is to operate on admission policies that are not too restrictive. But the reverse – the therapeutic value of 'no sanctions' on selected individuals, within the culture of a 'sanctions unit', cannot be achieved.

AUTHORITY AND THE ADOLESCENT

A key feature in a unit that attempts treatment in depth is the difference between staff and patients. The staff are distinctly 'grown-ups', irrespective of their age, and the patients 'children', irrespective of theirs. This clear distinction must be maintained if one hopes to reach the long forgotten childlike and baby feelings that contain so much of the pathology of the patients.

In maintaining this difference, staff acquire the position of authority figures. Adolescents have intense conflicting feelings about authority. They hate it, but need it. They want to get close to it, examine it, mock it, test it out, attack it and try to destroy it. If they do succeed in destroying it, even for a short while, they panic, and either try to restore it, or become triumphant and overwhelmingly destructive. This interesting and sometimes dangerous interaction can achieve very great intensity and become seriously distressing for staff. The pathology of the youngsters is invariably locked in with this continual interplay.

It must be remembered that the very authority in their lives – their parents – has, at least partially, contributed to their pathology, and they have incorporated a pathological authority or superego. It is this pathological superego that they project onto staff.

The task of staff could be seen as allowing this to happen,

enabling the youngsters to experience and examine their multifaceted feelings about authority, and through their responses, helping the patients to modify their superegos and the authority within themselves.

DEVELOPMENTAL TASKS AND DRIVES

The basic treatment aim should be seen within the context of the normal adolescent process. The adolescent is between child and adult, in a kind of 'no-mans-land'. Because adolescence is considered a passing phase, something peculiar and vaguely threatening, it is neglected and avoided by society (and even the psychiatric establishment). In this 'no-mans-land' one finds both a child and an aspiring adult. All the biological forces and social forces are driving him towards adulthood, independence and a responsibility which he wants so much, yet there is a strong emotional pull to remain a child with all its safety. There are several rapid changes going on within him – physical, biological, intellectual, as well as the expectation and responses of his environment. He is confused, does not know who he is and wants to learn about himself. The adolescent needs guidance, support and encouragement in this drive towards adulthood. In some the drive is powerful; they are in a hurry. In others it is more subdued. The pathology of the disturbed adolescent acts as an obstruction to his or her progress towards emotional adulthood.

Working with the adolescent process may seem to be in conflict with concepts of discipline and good behaviour. It is not really so. Staff learn how to say 'no' to the youngsters and yet not come over as authoritarian but as a safe authority. Staff discussions are useful in dealing with any confusing issues. The staff of the unit need to continually learn how to distinguish between normal developmental and pathological behaviour, each of which will be presented in an endless variety of ways. Staff must have the capacity to recognise that in some areas the developing youngsters may be equal to or better than them; enjoy with them their delight when they have won an argument, legitimately 'scored one over the staff' or shown up staff to be stupid at times.

'You sometimes feel like a child or a baby, but you are neither; you are nearly a grown-up and can become as good as, or better than, me – if you take yourself and the work here seriously.' This should be the staff's most important attitude.

GENERAL ORGANISATION OF THE UNIT

A no sanctions unit

There are many different undertakings in the unit. Some are specifically concerned with the treatment of patients – the psychotherapies and special treatment programmes, and others concerned with the various aids to treatment and development of the youngsters – activity programmes, education, community meetings, staff meetings and more specific staff training programmes.

All the different disciplines working in the unit, whilst having their own specialist functions, also have the common task of working together as a team, offering and receiving mutual support in the interests of the philosophy of treatment. This means discussion of disagreements, doubts and feelings of anger about the philosophy in staff meetings, rather than suppression of such contradictory and conflictful thoughts and feelings.

The staff team should not be seen as a homogeneous mass, but as individuals with their own separate qualities, abilities and identities as they really are, who are working together for a common purpose; so that the different inputs, from individual staff can enrich the totality.

The staff meetings attended by all staff are the 'heart', 'brain' and the power behind the operation of the unit.

The unit would have different conceptual aspects to it: a Psychiatric Hospital, because it treats the mentally ill; a Family, because of the family feelings of the patients, and sometimes those of the staff, are 'transferred' into the unit. It is a Democracy, in that freedom of speech and expression of ideas is encouraged; and an Autocracy, in that decisions are not made on a one-to-one vote, but on the basis of discussion, understanding and the responsibility of the Manager or Medical Director of the unit. It is a Community, in which efforts are made to use the creative potential of all the staff for the benefit of the patients. I will not risk calling it a 'Therapeutic Community', as this term has popular connotations that may not apply to a service for adolescents.

Total staff participation

Ideally, all staff are involved, and consulted, when any task or activity is discussed and arranged, even if only a single member of staff is to undertake it. Such total staff participation ensures the best chance of support from all staff, and success for the project. This is also important because ideas and interventions from the highest to the lowest grade of staff, and new staff, can be of equal value.

Subsidiary task orientated committees

Arising from discussions in total staff meetings, it is sometimes necessary to appoint individuals, by mutual consent, to undertake special tasks. It is also sometimes necessary to form special groups to tackle special problems.

A task should not be left to a group without a leader of that group being agreed on, otherwise the task will fall between several stools, particularly in a unit where levels of stress are expected to be high. Sometimes well-planned schemes do not operate effectively. It is then necessary to understand why this has happened, to look at whether or not the scheme was good, and then either change the scheme, or recognise and deal with the causes of the failure.

Community/House meeting

The daily community/House meeting which is attended by all staff and patients is for the discussion of any relevant issues in the community. It has the function of emphasising and re-emphasising repeatedly the philosophy of the unit; not by lectures, but through the way staff behave and interact with the patients and with each other.

Experience that the youngsters have had in the community meeting and material produced by them in this meeting, is further developed in small groups and individual psychotherapy and, sometimes, 'on the floor' if it is a practical matter pertaining to activities.

The nursing staff or Care workers

The greatest number of staff in the unit are the nurses, in an NHS unit, or Care workers in a Social Services unit. It is the organisation of these staff which plays the most important part in the successful functioning of the unit. The Senior Nurse (Nursing Officer) or the most senior Care worker in charge, or the House Manager, plays a vital role in this organisation and in creating feelings of safety among the staff. He, or she, is in authority over all the staff and should be seen as comfortable in this authority, patently fair and equally concerned about all of them. The staff's realistic needs and rights must be ensured.

The arrangement of staff duties, rotas and activity/training programmes, should be organised in such a way as to recognise the talents, strengths, preferences and healthy rivalries amongst the different grades and individual staff. There should be an awareness of the unpleasant and status-symbolising duties, and care should be taken in their distribution.

THE UNIT AS A SINGLE ORGANISM

The general aim of work in the community is to encourage 'normal' behaviour. This means that staff notice and 'pick up' 'bad' or 'pathological' behaviour. The manner of 'picking up' will depend on the circumstances and the situation, and on an understanding of the youngsters concerned; it can vary from confrontation, at one extreme, to mere eye contact with the youngster concerned. This behaviour may be dealt with on the spot, or left for discussion later and, if necessary, brought into the community/House meeting. If slight deviations from the expected norm are left unnoticed, they eventually escalate into larger and more widespread difficulties. This type of work is called 'on the floor work' in this document; it incorporates structured activity programmes and structured periods for unstructured, spontaneous, creative ventures.

A well-organised unit should operate as a single organism with all its different parts and functions acting upon the other to form a whole, (Systems Theory). Thus, activity programmes are related to psychotherapy, with good staff discussions, good care of patients, and resulting high staff morale forming a whole. The entire system will be affected by inadequate functioning of a part. The principles used are as follows:

1. 'No sanctions' does not mean 'no limit setting'.

2. Adolescents need firm limit setting – especially in a 'no sanctions' unit.
3. They must, and will, rebel against authority – let us keep the threshold for rebellion at a low and manageable level.
4. They do not know what they want, pretend that they do – but look to adults for guidance. The best way to ensure that patients are not neglected and feel cared for, is through well-organised activity programmes.
5. If they are allowed a short while without this guidance, they will get into a mess – 'Act Out'.
6. Acting Out has a specific psychodynamic meaning. It should be prevented if the deeper unconscious problems are to emerge for understanding and resolution. The phrase 'Acting Out' is often used loosely to describe destructive behaviour. It is used here in its psycho-analytical meaning, i.e. some action not necessarily destructive, which serves to release an uncomfortable pressure of unconscious material threatening to emerge into consciousness ([3]Freud, 1955, 1958).
7. Prevention of Acting Out should not, and cannot, be done effectively by force. This can lead to violent eruptions, anger and cracking up – patients cannot think about and deal with these feelings effectively.
8. Acting Out should be contained through the structure organised for youngsters. If the activity programmes of the unit are well recognised and respected by staff, and seen as a very important part of the organisation, the youngsters use their own controls over the urge to 'Act Out' in order to join in the activities and be accepted by the community.
9. If the Acting Out has been contained effectively, then the psychotherapy is enhanced by the emergence of unconscious material into discussion. If the psychotherapy is good, then more unconscious material will threaten to emerge and there will be a tendency to Act Out further, which when contained, will further enhance psychotherapy – the 'pressure cooker model' – an idea first mooted with regard to psychoanalysis in the prison services, by Dr A. H. Williams, Director of the London Clinic of Psychoanalysis, ([4]Perinpanayagam, 1978b) which has been modified for use in any psychodynamically

orientated unit. The 'prison' in such a unit is formed by staff interactions with youngsters; a gentle/tough but flexible wall, which does not crack like glass, nor hurt the youngsters like a brick wall when they bash against it. This kind of wall can only be formed by staff having a genuine trust and confidence in each other, and, again, can only occur if there are 'free-for-all' open staff meetings with honest expression of feeling.

10. 'Psychotherapy' which is unrelated to life in the unit is empty, useless, and is not a true psychotherapy.
11. The activities programme is the hub around which a unit of this sort should function.
12. If the activity programmes are chosen appropriately, the staff morale goes up because all staff will have a clearly defined task and role which is valued and supported by the total staff team and responded to by the youngsters.
13. By 'activities' is meant all non-psychotherapy functions such as work rotas for the youngsters, games, individual and group creative activities, and other aids to development.

The concept of activity programmes being the hub around which the unit revolves is difficult to hold on to, because of 'elitist' value judgements placed on the different tasks in the unit by the staff. Activities usually come fairly low on the scale. It is, therefore, important that the Medical Director or House Manager and all disciplines become involved in the planning, and, therefore, the support, of activity programmes.

The problem of psychotherapy

A major difficulty that arises is to do with the concept of 'psychotherapy'. It has a mysterious quality to it, a specialness about it, and is conducted in privacy. The non-psychotherapy staff, naturally, have an envy of this special thing done by special people. The psychotherapy staff often tend to keep it that way, in order to enhance their self esteem. Many of the psychotherapists have worked hard and spent many years obtaining this special training, and cannot bear the thought of not being considered special, and tend to emphasise the distinction and the division.

This source of inter-staff tension, often concealed, must be recognised and constantly dealt with. Psychotherapy must be conducted in *privacy*, but not in *secrecy* as far as the staff are concerned. Psychotherapy sessions should be brought into open discussion at staff meetings. It is not a mysterious thing, and can be understood at certain levels by any interested human being.

This source of potential staff conflict can be minimised by fostering the understanding and the use of psychoanalytical psychotherapy across discipline boundaries. Capable care staff or nurses may be encouraged to undertake psychotherapy with selected patients under supervision.

THE RISKS OF RUNNING A UNIT OF THIS TYPE

The organisation and management of such a unit which primarily brings out the 'bad' feelings can be a risky business, for those who do not recognise and understand the difficulties that can ensue.

The risks are twofold – the overt and the covert.

Overt risks

These are easy to envisage. They include different forms of disturbed behaviour in the patients and the effect on these on staff, the institution and external management.

Covert risks

These are difficult to imagine and are usually recognised only in the experience. In a good treatment unit, the full pathology of all the patients will emerge. There will be no built-in obstruction to this emergence. Indeed, the unit will encourage the experience of their deeper 'bad feelings' in such a way as to help the youngsters to feel relatively safe with their own 'badness' – the first and essential part of the treatment.

Ideally, the youngsters should express their 'badness' not through action, but through conveying the feelings to staff in non-destructive ways. In practice, it sometimes happens that initially the youngsters will express 'bad' feelings in action, until they learn how to convert their actions into feelings and thought. There is often a constant struggle in staff, between wanting to suppress even the verbal expression of 'badness' in the youngsters and recognition that this is not in their treatment interests.

A large part of the in-service training of staff involves training in methods of dealing with the disturbed behaviour of the patients in such a manner as to enhance and develop their ability to convert actions into feelings and thought.

Staff experience hurtful and bad feelings as a result of the actions and behaviour of patients. As retaliatory anger is not encouraged, staff must develop the ability to contain the pathological behaviour of the youngsters and respond in such a way as to not damage them any further, but to enhance their development. It means containing the disturbing feelings put into them by the patients, understanding them, making them better and returning them to the patients who will now be able to understand the feelings their disturbing feelings which have been made better by the staff.

This process of taking in and containing the pathology of the patients causes great stress to staff, and may touch off hidden suppressed and repressed feelings and pathology within staff, engendering an overreaction.

Sometimes the hidden pathology of staff can lead them to over identify with the patient, and to encourage their disturbed behaviour. This is particularly relevant when staff anger with their own authority within the unit, and in their personal lives, has not found expression and resolution. The feelings created in staff often give clues to the covert pathology of the patients.

The degree to which staff are affected will depend on their own hidden pathology. In an institution which works in a different way, for instance, one which deals with problems intellectually, or by suppressing symptoms and behaviour, one could envisage a situation in which only good aspects of staff and their strengths are evident and available for work. This cannot be in a unit which works psychodynamically. Staff disturbance must emerge, and there must be a forum in which staff can get together and feel free to express and unload the bad and engendered feelings within themselves. This forum is the staff meeting. Staff must contain themselves and interact properly and safely with patients. *They cannot and should not be expected to do this in staff meetings.* One of the important events therefore, are 'free-for-all' staff meetings, where staff can feel safe to express themselves freely and know that they will not be penalised or condemned for it.

The task of the leader, is to enable this by example and by

facilitating it in others. This is also important for staff development and in-service training, because they, in turn, progressively become comfortable in similar 'free-for-alls' with the youngsters. They learn to deal with such situations through their own live experience in staff meetings. The only real learning is done through experience.

STAFF STRESS

The only way in which the appropriate climate for the youngsters to experience and express their 'bad' feelings can be achieved, is through the total staff ambience in the unit. This is of vital importance in a good treatment unit for adolescents, and staff stress and staff difficulties become the pre-eminent consideration.

Staff stress arises from four sources:

1. From patient disturbance – overt and covert.
2. From poor internal organisation.
3. From sources outside the unit, usually external management.
4. From within oneself – from one's own hidden pathology and personal life, often touched off and exacerbated by the other three.

If staff stress arising from these areas is not accurately recognised and dealt with, the staff will be too stressed to engage effectively in their primary task, which in itself is inherently stressful.

The stress arising from patient activity is of the sort that staff should be prepared to encounter if they choose to work in this type of unit. It is of a kind, which if understood and dealt with correctly, leads to an understanding of patient pathology and development of staff. Stress arising from all quarters should be minimised. Stress arising from within oneself is also inherent, is common to all staff and peculiar to each individual, but should progressively diminish in a good treatment unit, if the staff concerned are of the type who are able and willing to look at themselves and acknowledge their own difficulties.

Sources of stress outside the unit

External administration can thwart the good work of the unit by neglect or by active hostility. It is the duty of both external administration and the Head of Unit to ensure that this does not occur.

The Head of Unit should act as 'buffers' between external administration and staff, allowing an appropriate filtering through to the staff, in such a manner as to mitigate, as far as is possible, the stress caused by the actions of external administration.

Staff meetings

'Free-for-all' meetings must be looked at closely. Are they damaging for staff? Are they going to eventually enhance staff development in the long run, even though they may be traumatic initially? Are staff contributions undermining staff morale and the work of the unit? Are they going to allow staff to speak?

It requires training and experience to be able to judge these questions and know how to intervene and deal with the individual and group dynamics which arise, in such a way as to enhance staff development. Sometimes, an apparently harsh statement can lead to great staff development.

Some staff have an initial difficulty in speaking freely in staff meetings – a natural phenomenon in unfamiliar gatherings where robust exchanges take place; it is also often related to unconscious anger in the staff member concerned. Attempting to deal with such a situation by modifying the usual natural process in staff meetings, by acceding to suggestions that staff should speak to each other politely and gently, can lead to staff being afraid to say anything in case it does not fit into the expected requirement and make the situation worse. A community that modifies its standards to meet the needs of the 'weakest' is not a progressive one. A sensitive awareness of such difficulties in staff, and a genuine wish to hear the opinions and ideas of all the staff, invariably results in the development of staff and resolution of such difficulties. The acknowledgment of personal discomfort and difficulties in different situations in the unit by senior staff and the Head of the Unit himself creates a climate in which it becomes progressively safer for newer staff to recognise and if necessary bring out their own difficulties.

The pathology of staff emerges in staff meetings; sometimes as an acknowledged difficulty and sometimes in projected form, when the difficulty is genuinely experienced as outside oneself, as a problem in the unit or in some other significant staff member. This latter phenomenon is very difficult to handle as the staff member concerned does not invite support. It requires firstly, that the phenomenon be recognised by several staff and then sensitive discussion, in order to enable the staff member concerned, i.e. the 'projector', to appreciate what he or she is doing. In such circumstances, it is a disadvantage for a single staff member to spot the phenomenon earlier than others and articulate it. Because if he does so, he immediately becomes the 'projectee', or one in collusion with the projectee. He must wait until several staff recognise the phenomenon of projection if it is ever going to be handled effectively. (See later under 'Philosophy of Staff Management'.)

When the pathology does emerge as a self-acknowledged experience, it should not be dealt with as a 'problem' belonging to that single individual, with the others rushing in to 'support' and help and advise with 'sympathy' and 'compassion' (i.e. treating him or her as a patient), but rather as an ordinary phenomenon common to all staff; which indeed is true, because no one can truly deny having aspects and bits of pathology and psychological defence mechanisms, common to all human beings. This is *true support*, for staff, as opposed to treatment of patients.

Several other psychological phenomena emerge in staff meetings which should be handled in a similar manner.

THE PHILOSOPHY OF STAFF MANAGEMENT

Staff management should be based on understanding and discussion and not on the possibility of disciplinary action. This enhances the work of the unit. Human beings have a strong tendency to pass on their emotional experiences. This is a well-known phenomenon, seen very clearly in families and family disturbances. Those who are experienced in family work repeatedly come across parents who are determined not to bring up their children in the way they have themselves been brought up, but find that they have indeed quite unconsciously transmitted their own growing-up experience to their children, who as adolescents repeat the same patterns of behaviour as their parents did. If we then attempt to deal with staff difficulties by disciplinary methods there is no hope that staff would in turn be able to use discussion and understanding in the way they work with the youngsters. Staff difficulties must be dealt with in the same manner as one would expect staff to deal with the difficulties created by youngsters.

There is one person in an organisation of this sort who cannot afford this 'luxury' of being treated in the way that will be passed down the line – the leader. The leader has to face the world outside and his own employers and administration, who often do not deal with him with understanding. He must be able to absorb this bad experience, contain it, digest and modify it before it is passed on to his/her subordinates.

In a bad organisation 'kicks' are passed down the line and juniors get the worst of it. In a good organisation it is the senior staff who should take and adsorb the 'kicks' that come from both outside the organisation and from within, and deal with all this through understanding and discussion.

In a treatment unit for adolescents the junior nurses receive the most painful 'kicks' from the patients. These must progressively be passed upwards to the senior staff and finally to the Head of the Unit, who must be strong enough to deal adequately with them.

All staff in such a unit must be chosen carefully for their temperamental ability at look at themselves, acknowledge their difficulties and work with them privately or openly. There are some staff who find their way into such units who do not have this capacity. They will leave after a while (disciplinary action should not be taken against them). If such a person occupies a senior staff position and is unable to leave then the senior staffing patterns of the unit will play an important part in the successful handling of the situation. A sufficient number of experienced senior staff can help to recognise, compensate for and mitigate the difficulties that ensue.

Authority and decision making

It is said that authority should be passed down the line. This does not merely mean that senior staff give junior staff instructions and the authority to get on with a particular job. It means that all staff in the unit must carry authority within themselves, and be in charge of themselves in any situation. Adolescents have an intense and ongoing relationship with authority; they test it out constantly, and feel safe only when they discover that the authority over them is strong, caring, reliable and good. They find out about the authority in the unit through their interactions with individual staff, all of whom occupy positions of authority.

Staff must feel safe or be able to cope in their authority roles, which are invariably involved with making decisions. The decision making, however, should be within their capacities and designated staff roles. For instance, it does not in the least diminish a staff person's authority to tell a youngster, 'I cannot make that decision, I must ask the senior staff,' and then to ask a senior staff member and communicate the decision to the youngster. The staff person concerned had been in charge of himself, and the situation; further, he had also conveyed to the youngster that staff work together and thereby has enhanced his own authority and shown his ability to fit into his position in an authority structure – an excellent role model for the youngster.

An important aspect of decision making is that the decision maker takes risks and must be open to criticism in staff meetings. In this way staff are constantly being trained and develop not only in the understanding of adolescence, but also in their own personalities.

Important decisions such as policy matters should be decided in a total staff meeting with the Head of the Unit taking responsibility for such decisions. Authority within one is involved with:

1. Knowing what is right and why it is right and therefore being able to argue it out with the adolescent and other staff.
2. A trusting and good relationship with their own authority within the unit – so that they feel they will not be let down or undermined, which is different from being criticised. (Sometimes not being criticised is felt as being let down.)
3. The relationship with the authority in their past life, which will influence their relationship with authority within the unit.

IMPLICATIONS OF WORKING IN A NO SANCTIONS UNIT

Staff in a good dynamically orientated 'no sanctions' unit are essentially alone in their interactions with the youngsters and in their positions of authority. The unit philosophy forces them into positions of authority over adolescents, but it does not provide for staff any built-in policies and structures to support their claim to authority, except the obvious fact of being staff, and joining staff meetings away from the adolescents. They have no special uniform, no special ways in which they are addressed such as 'Sir', 'Miss', or 'Doctor'. There are no authoritarian structures to support the authority that the staff are expected to have. The authority of the staff must come from within themselves and it is expected to be strong enough to stand up to the battering it gets from the disturbed youngsters, sometimes one at a time, sometimes in groups, and sometimes from everyone at once.

All staff are supposed to get and give support to each other in this difficult situation. But there are inter-staff tensions and this support is not always available. Sometimes staff want to give each other support but do not know how to, and sometimes staff do not know how to gain support. It can be very difficult, confusing and traumatic. The key to the solution of this difficult situation lies in the daily staff meetings. If these meetings are open and honest, the difficulties for individual staff are greatly reduced.

After a while in the unit, staff learn that one of the main common roles of all staff in the unit is to act as *containers* for the feelings generated in them by the patients. Inputs into each staff container come from different sources – patients, staff conflicts, bad management, misunderstandings, and from one's own pathology and personal life. The containing capacity of staff varies. An important function of staff meetings is to 'catch and contain' the overflow from any staff member's personal container, thereby creating joint staff containers. This can also happen 'on the floor' and between any two or more staff.

The value of containing bad feelings and experiences is that, in a relatively sane mind, with minimal help, these difficult feelings become more digestible, thus leading to an increase in one's containing capacity and further development.

Rules and expectations

As mentioned earlier, it is very important to have strict rules and expectations in a 'no sanctions' unit. 'No sanctions' does not mean 'no rules and no limit-setting'. Adolescents must test out and resist authority in different ways, if they are to develop towards achieving their own individual authority. The threshold for rebelliousness must be kept at a very low level and must be confined within the unit. When an expectation or rule is broken the staff must take the trouble to bring it up for discussion. This has value even if the youngsters do not engage in the discussions. The fact that the staff have observed their act against authority allows the adolescents to feel that their rebelliousness was effective and important enough to cause trouble to the authority. They will then have no need to escalate their behaviour or to take it outside the unit, in order to engage with and test out authority.

Adolescents often do not want to discuss their 'bad' behaviour, especially in public. But the fact that staff want to discuss it, rather than simply punish them, allows them to experience and introject a different kind of authority to the one invariably represented by their superegos; furthermore, it allows them to retain any guilt they may have about their behaviour and any emerging bad feelings that have lead them to commit the act. The retention of guilt and bad feelings affords the opportunity for these to be discussed, understood and interpreted in the appropriate setting. (See 'Guilt and Interplay'.)

If they do engage in thoughtful discussion, it is a step forward and it can lead to further and deeper changes.

There are many reasons why youngsters break rules. It is our task as professionals, to pick up the most important of these, for the benefit of the adolescents in treatment with us, and indeed for our own survival. The most important element in their rule breaking, invariably, has to do with the adolescents' anger against the staff – which is invariably present as a transference from their parents and other authorities in their past lives. This may not be initially obvious – when they break our rules – but it causes us one form of trouble or another because we have a 'responsibility relationship' with them; they are just 'acting out' unconscious feelings. If staff can understand what the adolescents are doing, then with time and adequate discussion the youngsters also will understand and eventually recognise why and where the anger comes from. Attempted discussions greatly diminish rule breaking.

The 'acting out' type of youngsters who come into a 'no sanctions' unit may at first tend to run wild and indulge in an orgy of anti-authoritarian behaviour. They can become a nuisance to staff and the other youngsters. The attitude of their peers to their behaviour would influence their behaviour greatly. Reacting to them in the natural way, showing anger and showing displeasure, is very appropriate at this stage and is a part of the psychodynamic approach; it does not contradict the 'no sanctions' policy. These same youngsters, after a while in the unit, often plead for punishment and feel cruelly treated by the staff, who merely want to have a discussion with them instead. They have every opportunity to discover the cruel and self-punitive aspects of themselves (their superegos and introjected authority).

It is important that the rules be meaningful, intelligent and intelligible to staff. Otherwise, any discussion that staff will invite will be a farce and will lead to youngsters developing or intensifying their contempt for authority. Staff who do not know or fully understand the meaning of the unit rules place themselves in a very difficult position, they will invariably earn the contempt of the youngsters, not only for themselves but for the rest of the staff and the authority they represent.

There are times when staff become obsessed with authority issues and can overdo the 'picking up of anti-authority' behaviour and thereby earn the contempt of the youngsters for themselves and the philosophy of the unit. For example, picking up an adolescent for rocking on a chair in a community meeting, right in the midst of an interesting and important discussion in which the youngster may be participating. This can convey to the adolescents the wrong messages about the unit's sense of values and about what is important in the unit. In this kind of situation other staff can ease the difficulty for everyone by intervening in such a way as to keep the community discussion going without humiliating the staff concerned. After some time staff learn how to weave in the confrontation of such doubtful anti-authority behaviour into an ongoing discussion without destroying the latter.

There are times when we, being human, become punitive. We

must therefore be able to acknowledge this, know that it has gone against the treatment plan for the youngster, and discuss it amongst ourselves and then with the patients. It is of great value to the youngster to know that his or her behaviour had the effect of turning us temporarily into the kind of people we do not want to be. Much can be gained by such an honest discussion.

THE DIRECTOR'S ROLE

The primary role of the Head of the Unit is to minimise or resolve the obstacles to the work of the unit – practical and psychological, external and internal – and constantly look to its development. His or her role is complex, especially if he/she is also the Consultant Psychiatrist.

In some units the two roles are split. The Consultant Psychiatrist advises on patient treatment and related issues, whilst the Director will carry out his treatment policies or not, as he chooses, and take responsibility for it. The combined role is more advantageous than disadvantageous, but is infinitely more difficult. The greatest advantage is that a high standard of treatment becomes possible.

The Medical Director/Consultant Psychiatrist must be versatile, and be able to change his stance or his 'hat' quickly. With patients, he must at times be a very firm authority – an immovable object – and be able to change that in an instant when he sees a change in a patient, and a sensitive soft approach is needed. He must, at different times, be a 'policeman', a 'teacher', a 'parent', a 'friend' and a doctor to the youngster.

The role of the head with staff should vary, from a firm authoritarian stance at times to a less dominant, unobtrusive role at others, depending on the total staff ambience and how they are working as a team. The dominance of his role must necessarily vary in inverse proportion to staff cohesion, if patient safety and good treatment is to be ensured. He must be 'a man for all seasons'.

The adolescent aspects of staff are often touched in such a unit, and the Head of the Unit acquires, in the eyes of the staff, characteristics of each of their own parental and authority figures, and his actions and behaviour are often misunderstood (Transference). It requires sensitive staff discussion for such phenomena to be sorted out. It will be advantageous for the Head to shed any 'big-shot' postures with staff and always interact with them as an equal in order to minimise this transference phenomenon. He often becomes the target for staff frustration and anger and must be able to accept this without becoming a victim of his own insecurities and weaknesses. He steps out of his role and indulges his real weakness, at great risk to himself and the workings of the unit.

In this difficulty and lonely position, he must look to staff criticism of himself (besides patient improvement and long-term staff development) as the indicator and source of support regarding the correctness or incorrectness of his actions. Staff criticism of the Medical Director is of vital importance and must be encouraged. Of course such criticism will be multiple, and will be made for a variety of reasons. The Director must be able to understand the motives of staff behind these criticisms and accept what is good and deal helpfully with what is bad or ill-motivated in terms of the total welfare of the unit and its work.

Most of all the Head must be able to look at himself/herself. A good personal psychoanalysis will be very helpful. In this task, where no simple rules and 'management procedures' can be used, it is necessary for the Head of the Unit to constantly watch his or her own motives and check whether he/she is acting for the total benefit of the Unit or indulging in one's personal weaknesses.

The Head should be accountable to management for everything he or she does. His/her daily presence and discussion at staff meetings and community meetings ensures that personal accountability to staff and patients is built into the management structure. Kurt Lewin's 'Field Theory' (°Lewin, 1951) is very relevant to the work of the unit and particularly the role of the Head of the Unit.

CONCLUSION

Interacting well with the youngsters can be complicated, confusing and difficult. *It is not possible to have a clearly defined code of practice.* It can only be developed by a gradual understanding of the youngsters and the feelings created in one by them.

Effective work in a psychodynamically orientated unit can be achieved only if there is a well-ordered tight structure for staff, in which the staff know what they are doing and are in charge of themselves. The picture is of all staff together forming a tight boundary around the youngsters. The boundary made up of a good staff structure, good staff knowledge, confidence in each other as good human beings. Within the boundary the youngsters have the freedom to interact with each other and with the staff. They will often crash against the boundaries set by the staff and when they do so, they should find that the boundary is neither too brittle, which cracks like glass, nor too rigid which hurts and damages them like brick. It should be like rubber which cushions the crash and gives a little but remains whole.

After a while of working in a psychodynamically orientated unit the whole thing becomes much easier for most staff, because some simple truths are recognised:

1. That we cannot control anyone or anything, either in the unit or in the outside world.
2. That it is very difficult to control and be in charge of ourselves, but this is the only real thing we can achieve in our struggle to manage and help the disturbed youngsters.
3. That we can have clear opinions about some of the things that are good and bad, right and wrong for the youngsters, and when these opinions are unambiguously expressed without staff 'splitting', the youngsters invariably comply.
4. That the only kind of consistency we can have is the consistency of always being thoughtful about each youngster and each situation.
5. That 'authority within oneself' is concerned with ones relationship with the current and past authority and a belief in the correctness of what one is doing or saying.
6. That we do not really work for the patients, the National Health Service or the Authority above us, but for a common idea an ideal within ourselves. We fall short at many times.
7. The satisfaction of working in such a unit is in the long term and deep. One recognises after a while that what we do is real, it is truly creative and it is good.

REFERENCES

[1] Perinpanayagam, K.S., *British Medical Journal* 1, pp.424–425, (1978a).
[2] Winnicot, D.W., *In the Maturational Processes*, London, Hogarth Press, (1965).
[3] Freud, S., *Complete Psychological Works*, Vol. XVII, p101, London, Hogarth Press, 1955.
Ibid., Vol. XII, p.151, 1958.
Ibid., Vol. XIX, p.49, 1961.
[4] Perinpanayagam, K.S., *British Medical Journal* 1, pp.563–566, (1978b).
[5] Lewin, K., 'Field Theory', in papers dated 1939–1947, Cartwright, D., (Ed). New York, 1951.

Chapter IX
SOME COMMON PHENOMENA
WHICH OCCUR IN A GROUP OR INPATIENT SETTING FOR ADOLESCENTS

It is in the inpatient setting that one learns most about adolescents and the nature of their disturbance. It is where the greatest problems arise and where they can be resolved. There are several phenomena which may be regarded as typical of adolescents.

PEER-GROUP RELATIONSHIPS

Peer-group relationships are very important for adolescents. They greatly value the opinions, friendship and esteem of their peers. Making relationships with peers forms part of their natural adolescent development towards independence. They need to learn how to make proper friends and be a proper friend. They need support for their ventures into the unfamiliar world of adults.

However, the emphasis in a unit for disturbed adolescents must be on their relationships with staff. This may sound contradictory, but it is not so. Disturbed adolescents cannot make proper relationships with their peers until they are able to feel comfortable in their relationships with the staff – the parental figures in the transference. Otherwise much of their 'getting together' will be an expression of their conflictual relationships with parental figures. The most common feeling shared by adolescents is anger against parents and authority figures. This often makes them identify with each other and gain support from each other in groups and gangs and engage in some defiant behaviour, which if handled incorrectly can escalate into dangerous proportions.

A simple but very effective manoeuvre when this kind of

grouping occurs is to remind and help them to realise that each of them are individuals, with their own problems and their own individuality. When done appropriately the gang mentality melts away with surprising ease.

Example:

Jim, Peter, Mark and Danny were in the community room watching television and defying the staff request to go upstairs to bed. It was 12.30 a.m. and well past the scheduled bedtime. The programme they were watching was not of any serious interest to any of them. Jim had had a confrontation with staff during the day, which had not been resolved to his satisfaction.

The staff on duty had tried every manoeuvre to get them to go to bed and had failed. The youngsters had each defied the staff in different ways. Staff felt humiliated and angry. When one of the staff had tried to put off the TV he had been threatened with physical violence by one of the bigger youngsters.

I was telephoned. The frustration and anger of the staff was such that they and I feared the whole unit would explode into violence. I decided to go into the unit essentially in order to give support to the staff. I was prepared to fail to get the youngsters into bed as the other staff had failed, and then together with them to decide 'what next'. I knew something of these youngster's problems and families, and I had been informed of the latest events in the unit.

I arrived on the scene and I walked into the community room and asked the youngsters what they were doing, breaking the rules of the house and being up so late.

> I said, 'You have caused enough trouble already, I have had to come here all the way to sort this out.'
> One of them said, 'What a shame.'
> Me: 'Who said that'? Silence. 'Come on, have you not got the courage to own up'.
> Mark: 'I said it.'

I now knew that I had got through their gang mentality. But I consolidated what I had started:

> Me: 'I am surprised, Mark. You are a chap who is always so

thoughtful about others and about your mum and dad. You, Jim, I can understand you being angry and trying to make trouble. I heard about what happened this afternoon. You can deal with all that in the house meeting tomorrow you know. We will all be there. You, Peter, you have always got into a mess by joining others. Danny, I don't know what to say to you. I need to talk to you more and understand what you are doing here. Don't all of you waste your time like this. You must all be tired. I am going to the staff room. If any one wants to talk to us come to the staff room. Otherwise go to bed and we will meet you all tomorrow.'

I left them and went to the staff room. The TV was put off within ten minutes, and they went to bed.

Never should staff create a situation in which an adolescent 'loses face' in the presence of his peers. Staff should never stand over them and demand or expect action. Statements should be made and then staff should move on leaving them to think and feel that they have done it thoughtfully and voluntarily.

Some of them do develop the beginnings of real friendship with each other and love relationships in the unit. We must be able to recognise these and deal with them sensitively.

Helping Each Other

Youngsters often try to help each other and do not do it properly. They almost invariably end up exacerbating each other's problems or in some form of identification with each other. If Projective Identification occurs one of the youngsters may carry the problems of both. They can become mutually destructive of each other. Many attempted and real suicide pacts between 'friends' or lovers have been formed through this mechanism. Projective identification is far more difficult to deal with than the simple identification described above.

Adolescents trying to help each other should be discouraged. Each of them is there to be helped by the staff and to help themselves. Yet they can be of immense help to each other. Some thought and discussion will show that the only way to ensure that they will influence each other for the better is to ensure that each of them is paying attention to and dealing with his or her own difficulties.

Youngsters who pay attention to their own difficulties and gain help for them from staff become the greatest allies of staff, the greatest help to other youngsters in the unit, and contribute to the high morale in the unit.

MANIPULATION AND BLACKMAILING

'Manipulation', 'blackmailing', and 'bribery' are closely allied phenomena which occur as part of normal adolescent development. I would regard them as pathological, only when they are taken to extremes. They are probably the commonest currency of interactions in residential settings of adolescents and in the parental home.

Most youngsters usually learn from their parents that it is normal to manipulate, blackmail and bribe, in order to control people and compel them to do what you want. I think all adults will remember having been told by their parents, something like 'You will not go out to play until you have finished all the vegetables on your plate,' or 'If you are a good boy I will buy you a bicycle for your next birthday.' The former is 'blackmail' the latter is 'bribery'. The controlling is done either by the threat of something unpleasant or by the promise of something pleasant. Children learn from their parents that this is an effective way of achieving the desired result and unconsciously build this apparently effective way of controlling their environment into their repertoire of social interactions. Since adolescents often believe that they cannot really give adults and their carers anything that is pleasant or worthwhile, the usual method adopted by them is to threaten something unpleasant. 'Blackmail' is preferred to 'bribery'.

The statement by parents, 'If you go out without your pullover you will fall ill, I do not want you to do it,' or the advice from a doctor 'If you do not take this medication you will get worse,' are of a different nature. They are statements that give realistic information. But to a youngster who has been subjected to a great deal of blackmail, they also have the quality and power of blackmail.

A common manifestation of blackmail by emotionally deprived youngsters is to demand care, with the threat of suicide, some form of self-damage, or a lesser form of trouble for the adult concerned. Much of the interaction between staff and patients in a residential setting involves these kinds of interactions. Sometimes the lesser form of trouble is more difficult to handle than the clear direct threats of suicide or self-damage.

Example – Sandra:

Sandra, a very deprived girl of sixteen, resident in an inpatient unit, often found it difficult to go to sleep at nights. She would then go to the nursing station and want to talk with the night staff – really wanting the night staff to talk to her as a sign of their acceptance and care of her. But unlike some other youngsters who came out to talk to staff if they could not sleep, Sandra would not go back to bed and try, nor would she take any night sedation to help her with her sleeping. She would want to remain with staff the whole night, making it impossible for them to engage in their other duties. If finally the night staff managed to persuade, coerce or threaten her into leaving the nursing station, she would sit outside and repeatedly strike a piece of wood against the wall or walk round the inside of the unit banging on all the windows and doors, disturbing the entire unit and generally making it impossible for staff and the other patients. The other patients never protested about Sandra's behaviour – she was a charismatic and popular girl.

Sandra's behaviour continued unabated, until she met a therapist who understood that she was a borderline psychotic who was operating on psychotic mechanisms, which made her convinced that she was uncared for if she did not feel she was inside the staff or her therapist. Her experiences were accurately interpreted and she settled down smoothly.

Adolescents who manipulate and blackmail always respond to realistic confrontations which have a 'blackmailing' quality to them.

Trudy:

Trudy, a charming, intelligent and helpless-looking sixteen-year-old, had spent several months in the unit manipulating and blackmailing the staff, despite the most thoughtful and caring discussions with her. She had promised several times that she would not leave the unit without staff permission, but would repeatedly wander out at nights and telephone staff about her fear that she might kill herself or get raped. She kept doing this despite the most caring discussions staff had with her. Her behaviour created havoc through the feelings she engendered in the staff. Staff on night duty invariably panicked, the doctor on call was often nonplussed and had to go to the unit, simply to support the night staff and to see Trudy when she finally returned. She was making life very difficult for the staff. Each time she promised that she would talk to staff instead of going out. The efforts of staff with Trudy seemed quite ineffective.

I then called a special meeting with Trudy and her parents and told them that Trudy had been trying very hard to talk to staff when she became distressed instead of leaving the unit at night, and it had become clear that despite all her efforts, she was unable to do this. I told them it was clear that our treatment was not working and that it was dangerous for her to remain in the unit. We therefore had no other option but to ask her to leave, while we sought a secure unit for her. In the interim, they or we could hopefully find alternative help for her. Trudy nearly leapt out of her seat and vigorously swore that she was able to stay in the unit and talk to staff rather than wander out at nights. I told her I did not believe her, because she had really tried to do this very thing and had failed; eventually I relented.

She was a changed girl after that and never repeated that particular form of demanding care.

Manipulations that are not involved with blackmailing or bribery, consist of using tricks to fool staff and obtain what they want. Many deprived adolescents do not believe they can get what they want, even if it is rightfully theirs, by being straight and honest. Most of them have had very real experiences of being deprived of love, care and normal needs, which any child should receive in the natural course of events as their right.

Adults often are very sensitive about being made a fool of by an adolescent, and staff who discover that they have been manipulated may feel humiliated and deny it. They can become unduly wary of manipulations and thereby lose opportunities to build a trusting relationship.

There are times when it is most appropriate to 'give in' to manipulation.

Samantha:

Samantha, who was temporarily discharged for not committing herself to treatment in the unit, came to the unit for an outpatient appointment, out of her head on drugs, making it clear that no one was looking after her properly. She had no parents and was staying in a community home, where the staff were unable to help and understand her. She had run away from there and was living in a 'squat' with some other drug taking teenagers. She was fully aware of our conditions for re-admission. That she should commit herself to serious treatment. Samantha refused to acknowledge that she needed our help and that she wanted re-admission, yet she made it impossible for me to send her away. It was the most elaborate manipulation to get me to re-admit her to Brookside without having to make a commitment to 'working' properly. She seemed to be demanding unconditional love.

I re-admitted Sandra, making it clear to her that I understood what she was trying to do. We worked on this problem after her re-admission.

Successful manipulations, with which staff have unwittingly colluded, are marked by a sense of well-being (triumph) in the youngster followed by an escalation of bad behaviour and further attempts to manipulate.

Manipulations of all varieties should be handled with the greatest sensitivity. Simply 'calling their bluff' because you know it is a manipulation is not good enough.

William:

William, a fourteen-year-old, threatened his mother with having his legs run over by a train if she did not comply with his wishes. (This peculiar threat had a deeper specific meaning for him.) Mother, who had been advised by the Social Services, refused to be blackmailed by him. William went to the railway track, after having telephoned his mother, informing her of his intention of placing his legs under the 2.15 train unless she dropped everything and came immediately. He gave her just enough time to reach him. Mother did rush out to the railway track to him, but she went to the wrong railway track. William lost both his legs and was referred for specialist psychiatric treatment a year later.

The first stage of treatment consists of establishing a safe and caring relationship with the adolescent, and then gradually moving into 'calling their bluff', in the most caring and rational manner, whilst at the same time interpreting to them what they are trying to do. Blackmailing behaviour can be so irritating at times that one can easily slip into an angry reaction, inviting them to get on with their self-destructive threat. A common story heard in casualty wards from youngsters who have recovered from serious overdoses, is of one of their loving but exasperated parents telling them to 'do it, but do it properly this time'.

The aim of staff interactions with adolescents should be designed to undo the damage that has been done by the interactions with parents, often in good faith. Never should staff interact using 'blackmail', i.e. threats or bribery. 'Rewards and punishments' used in a behavioural programme are rightly interpreted by youngsters as bribery or manipulations by staff.

SEXUALITY

The sexuality of adolescents can only be discussed in the knowledge that man does not have the capacity to understand sexuality in its totality. It was there before us, a part of the mysterious process that created us. We can but comprehend only some of its aspects. Of all human activities it is the most common yet the most precious, the most ordinary and yet most mysterious. It can be an expression of man's noblest nature and also his basest. It is the activity around which the world revolves and survives. Man can at times be a helpless victim of this powerful creative drive.

Bad sex is evacuatory in nature, in which one temporarily gets rid of bad feelings, impulses and bits of oneself. It is impulsive and compulsive. Good sex is born out of love and a lasting relationship.

Adolescence and Sex

In thinking about adolescent sexuality, it becomes clear that it is one of the areas in which value judgements must be made. It is an area where questions of what is right and wrong, good or bad, and normal or abnormal are most frequently raised. It is important for us to have criteria outside ourselves and outside society – a conceptual ideal which we can all use as a frame of reference. Using one's own sexuality as a criterion of normality leads to great blunders and a lot of discomfort for the staff concerned.

The accepted Christian or psychoanalytical ideal of sex with a single partner (at any one time period) of the opposite sex, within the context of an ongoing, loving, whole object relationship seems good enough.

Adolescent sexuality is most often not a premature form of adult sexuality, though it can sometimes be the beginnings of a lasting love relationship. It consists largely of imitative behaviour and elements of their own particular infantile and childhood experiences. Active sexual experience for adolescents can be distorted, confused and frightening and can result in a crystallisation of their sexuality in distorted patterns. In adolescence they have a second chance to correct their distorted experience through their fantasy lives.

Adolescents engage in sexual activity for a variety of confused reasons, often long before they are ready for it. They are often lonely, confused about themselves and depressed. They may engage in sexual behaviour with themselves (masturbatory) or with others because it excites them and makes them feel better for a while. Those who do not understand their feelings of loneliness, girls in particular, also hope that sex will win them companionship for ever and drive away their feelings of loneliness. They often feel used, and guilty afterwards, and their already low self-esteem is lowered even further.

Many youngsters today are goaded into sex by their mates – you are not 'in the gang' or respected if you are still a virgin. Others are driven to it through their interaction with adults lacking in insight, who identify with youth and want to display their 'sophisticated modern' thinking; being unable to tolerate the image, and perhaps taunts of the youngsters, about being dull, old-fashioned and 'past it'.

Adolescents are highly sexually excitable, and adept at covering up or disguising their sexual excitement. Even talking about sex is enough to excite them sexually, particularly if they are attracted to the person they are talking to. Sex education in schools 'so that they do not get into trouble', is advocated by those who are extremely naive or by those who gain vicarious gratification from adolescent sexuality. Adolescents become highly excited by sex education classes and are more likely to act out their sexual feelings because of them. Any sex education should be undertaken at a pre-pubertal stage.

Any discussion of sex with adolescents should consist essentially of listening to their anxieties and confusions without displaying any embarrassment or voyeuristic interest and without trying to offer any reassurance or advice. Any advice offered is likely only give them information about your own sexuality. True reassurance about sexual anxieties can only be given through understanding the underlying meaning of their anxieties in terms of their relationships with their parents and their peers and probably best left to those trained in psychotherapy. It must be remembered that we are not in the business of helping adolescents to accept and become comfortable with their difficulties or abnormalities. Our efforts should be directed towards bringing about changes in them so that their difficulties or abnormalities are effectively resolved.

WHITEFRIARS

In Whitefriars, an Adolescent Unit in Westcliff, Essex, sexual activity is prohibited on the basis that the youngsters are not ready for sex – described to them in different ways at different times, depending on the context in which the question arises, as 'You are too young for sex,' 'You are too confused,' 'You are here for treatment, not for sex,' 'You do not have a relationship with him', 'You do not love each other,' etc.

BROOKSIDE

In Brookside Young People's Unit, the Regional Adolescent Unit for the North East Thames region, (during the period 1975–1985), the pill was never prescribed for girls, sometimes against parental wishes. The staff believed that they would have been contradicting themselves, confusing the youngsters and failing in their primary task of treatment if they did prescribe or recommend any form of contraception. They took on grave responsibility and great risks through this policy. But thoroughness in dealing with the underlying causes of adolescent sexual acting out was equally great. Every one of the girls who initially argued vigorously for the pill being prescribed – and some who even threatened the staff with becoming pregnant – expressed their satisfaction and gratitude for the policy after a while at Brookside.

Hugging

Hugging, which purports to be a gesture of casual, good-natured friendliness can easily become a part of the culture of a residential unit, if one is not aware of its anti-therapeutic effect. Hugging should be discouraged in any residential unit, especially between staff and patients. The essence of the meaningful *therapeutic relationship* between patient and staff is lost if random hugging and similar gestures go on, and worse, if it is done as part of a special relationship. It must be remembered that adolescents are both children and growing adults, with powerful Oedipal elements characterising them.

That very important *therapeutic relationship* between staff and patient, with staff always as adult authority figures and the patients as children, is of vital importance in a psychodynamically orientated treatment unit. *It is in that gap between child and adult that much of their pathology is felt by the patient and seen by the therapist.* Patients use many different devices to close that gap and get over the uncomfortable feeling of *difference between them and staff*. Manipulative youngsters build up and elaborate on their Oedipal fantasies and their pathology by manoeuvring 'innocent' hugs and cuddles from staff. In so doing, they are also treating the very staff they presume to like and hug with the greatest contempt, as objects they can use in whatever way they please.

Maintaining that boundary between staff and patients can be difficult for both. Hugging, and similar physical gestures, can be given innocent interpretations and may easily become misused and lead to failure in treatment.

A firm rule prohibiting staff from hugging youngsters is not established at Whitefriars because there are instances when a comforting arm round a seriously distressed youngster can be meaningful and therapeutic.

Repression and Projection

Feelings and experiences which are feared or forbidden become repressed, i.e. pushed into the unconscious mind. This is the commonest mechanism we recognise, and is the basis for many of the other psychodynamic phenomena.

When the repressed unconscious material threatens one from within, the inner experience can be acted out, denied or pushed out – projected – into the world around and experienced as outside oneself. Anger projected in this way is the most frequently occurring mechanism in agoraphobia. Many other kinds of phobias are formed by similar mechanisms. Repression occurs far more frequently than one usually notices, in both patients and staff.

Patients often complain of being in a 'shitty place' and fail to recognise the 'shitty' feelings within themselves. Staff sometimes become angry with patients who say this, because they themselves feel the unit to be 'shitty' and keep this feeling a secret even from themselves. Patients frequently attack the building, secretly, because they have projected their 'nasty' feelings onto the unit as a whole and are frightened to tell staff what they think of us and the unit.

Splitting and Projection and Projective-Identification often occurs without repression in psychotics or as a psychotic mechanism even in the normal neurotic

Splitting

This can be most conveniently described as occurring in two dimensions – the horizontal and the vertical. The horizontal occurs within one and results in repression and other defences of the split-off part. The vertical occurs when two opposing aspects of one are experienced at different times and is reflected in the patient trying to recreate these opposing factions in the external world. Therapy attempts to remove both kinds of splits and bring the opposing forces of the repressed and conscious parts together to create an integrated whole.

Acting Out

A mechanism used to dispense with and dissipate unconscious feelings that are threatening to emerge into consciousness. It is done through an action which is often, but not invariably, destructive. It renders the youngster unable to give any real explanation for his or her behaviour and, when pressed for an explanation they invent some plausible reason and may be attacked by insensitive staff for lying.

Acting out is a very revealing and useful mechanism for those interested in understanding the unconscious, because careful examination of the act, its implications and its effects, invariably reveals the nature of the unconscious material that has been dissipated. 'The acting out bears the hallmark of the unconscious.'

Example:

Shortly after Brookside was opened the staff found that the youngsters were regularly visiting the local pub, even though they were underage and it was prohibited by the unit staff. Staff noticed that many of the adolescents were not the worse off with drink and some did not even drink alcohol. But all of them joined in in behaving as if they were drunk and made a nuisance of themselves to the neighbourhood.

All means were tried, to stop them from visiting the pub, including visiting the landlord and informing him of the age of some of the youngsters and the danger to him. The younger ones argued that they did not drink alcohol.

When the meaning and implications of what they were doing were observed, it struck the staff that the only thing the youngsters were achieving was to inform the neighbourhood that the youngsters in the care of the unit were not well looked after.

Following a staff discussion, the question of how much the youngsters felt cared for or not cared for in the unit was brought up in the community meeting. There followed a vigorous and fruitful discussion. The patients had found it difficult to 'accuse' staff of not caring till it was brought up for discussion by the staff. The feelings and comments of the youngsters were taken on board by the staff. The visits to the pub ceased.

Acting out is usually of no value to the actor out because it merely prevents or postpones some relevant unconscious material emerging into their conscious minds, where thought and development become possible.

Sometimes partial acting out can be useful to a really hard-working patient, because it may decrease the intensity of a particularly frightening or powerful feeling and therefore, permit its entry into consciousness in a less frightening form.

A major part of 'On the floor' work (daily-living interactions), consists of devising ways of preventing acting out, without putting too much pressure on the youngsters. Organised activities through which the acting out can be either prevented or allowed to emerge in a more easily understandable and non-destructive form is very useful for this.

The greatest value of preventing acting out, besides the peace that ensues, is that it allows unconscious feelings to come into consciousness, or to remain just below the surface for further interpretive work in an appropriate setting. The combination of prevention of acting out and interpretive work acts as a 'pressure cooker'(ref).

IDENTIFICATION – PROJECTIVE IDENTIFICATION

There are different types of identification, the simplest being something similar to 'hero worship', where a youngster tries to behave as someone he admires. Identification with good staff behaviour, for instance, can be useful as a short-lived transitional phase in a youngster's move into adulthood.

The converse, i.e. staff identifying with adolescents, is also common. Staff who are able to put themselves in the situation of the youngsters and feel their experiences are the most empathic and the most sensitive to the problems of the adolescent. This kind of identification with the patient can be very helpful, but it can also become a difficulty if the staff loose a grip on their reality and their role. Staff may then start behaving like the adolescents, or may put into the adolescent some of their own problems; especially if they envy the youth of the youngster.

Living in such close contact with the raw, deep emotional life of the youngsters invariably touches the adolescence of the staff and brings out the forgotten memories and feelings that some may never know they had. At times the pathology of the youngsters feels as if it were added to one's own difficulties, creating great distress in staff. Knowing oneself and owning one's own pathology is the best safeguard against this. (See below, Projective Identification).

Identification can occur as a defence against anger, guilt or envy involving the other. Such identifications are made unconsciously with the aim of removing any distance or differentiation between each other so as to avoid experiencing feelings for the other. Thus, two siblings who are envious of each other, for instance, could grow up as if they lived in each other's personalities and consciously feeling that they love each other:

> Julie, a very bright girl, had an older subnormal brother who died of chronic leukaemia when she was about five or six years old. She had been intensely jealous of the attention and care her brother had received. Shortly after his death she began deteriorating in school and by the time she came to the adolescent unit she had had many years of being considered 'borderline' subnormal.
>
> When Julie recognised her guilt about her brother's death, of nightmarish proportions, and worked through the jealousy and anger she felt, she recovered her normal intelligence.

This kind of global identification occurs rarely. It is much more common for the identification to occur with bits and parts of the personality.

PROJECTIVE IDENTIFICATION

Projective Identification is a powerful, unconscious mechanism. It occurs so frequently in working with adolescents that I would regard it as one of the features of adolescence. It requires special mention.

The general description of projective identification is that some quality unrecognised by the owner, the *Projective Identificator*, is projected onto another, the *Projective Identificatee*, who accepts and identifies with the quality. This leads to the Projective Identificatee possessing the quality which has been projected. In effect the Projective Identificator loses that quality which is gained by the Projective Identificatee.

The phenomenon is more than projection and stronger than simple identification. It is unconscious and is felt as real.

In projection, the recipient (object) does not accept the quality; he/she may feel irritated about some quality being unfairly attributed to him. In simple identification, only one of the participants actively engages in the process and the identification is shaken off relatively easily. Simple identification is probably preconscious rather than unconscious. In Projective Identification there is *an exchange* of qualities which make the participants become interlocked. That the process is unconscious deprives the participants of insight, and gives it a *psychotic quality*.

The emphasis in the early work on Projective Identification was principally on the understanding of the psychotic (Klein, 1946). Subsequent observations, by several psychoanalysts, notably Rosenfeld, Bion and Donald Meltzer, however, have shown that the phenomenon is not confined to psychotics but is a normal part of the mother and baby interaction, and occurs with all human beings. It occurs far more commonly than was originally imagined, particularly in situations where there are close and intense relationships. The process can be either beneficial or detrimental to the participants. (See the last chapter entitled 'The Alpha-action'.)

In the clinical sphere it can be observed in inpatient settings between patients and patients, between staff and patients, in small or large groups, between therapist and patient and in ordinary life, between husband and wife, between friends and in the 'lynch mob' mentality. Suicide pacts between two relatively mildly disturbed youngsters, or the suicide of the less depressed, have been known to occur in inpatient settings where the phenomenon has not been recognised and dealt with.

The effect of the projections on the prospective projective identificatee, what he does with the projections, and how he deals with himself when threatened by the process, is of the greatest relevance to adolescents and staff who work with them.

I have observed that the projective identificatee, is usually one who, unbeknown to himself/herself, possesses characteristics similar to the projected ones, which are seeking a 'home' as it were. They become ready recipients for the projected material because they are not aware of possessing some of the very same quality. They do not know themselves well enough and are not fully aware of their identity.

In exceptional circumstances, forceful projective identification with an entirely unwilling and unlikely object can occur in a sado-masochistic relationship, in brain-washing and in prisons. In floridly psychotic patients the projections can be so strong that inanimate object can take on the quality in the eyes of the projective identificator. (See the case of JL below.)

PROSPECTIVE PROJECTIVE IDENTIFICATEES

The recipient of the projections may react or respond in different ways.

He may simply accept the quality and take it into himself, in which case he would become the projective identificatee.

He may take the projection into himself, and if it is a disturbing one, he may metabolise it, modify its quality and return it to the projective identificator in a more acceptable form, thus replicating the interaction between mother and baby. He may do this consciously or spontaneously. Which of these things he does will depend on his knowledge of himself and his capacity to contain and work with disturbing feelings. Good psychotherapists do it consciously with the projections of their patients.

A recipient who recognises within himself the quality similar to the one that has been projected, and has the emotional capacity to metabolise it, does not take on the projected quality; whereas one who is less integrated, who has not recognised his own qualities, and is therefore confused about his own identity, will be more prone to take on the quality and the identity that had been projected.

Thus adolescents (and staff of adolescent units), who experience a multiplicity of confusing feelings and are usually in a state of not quite knowing who they are, are easy victims of almost any quality that is seeking a temporary 'home'. They can become projective identificatees relatively easily and engage in the most unlikely behaviour.

Identification with the projected quality depends on

1. Whether or not the prospective projective identificatee possesses a little bit of the quality, and
2. Whether he/she recognises the quality in himself. (Exceptions

as above.)

Two examples below are from experiences of staff, which I have chosen because discussion with them was possible in order to verify the process that occurred. Staff working in close relationships with adolescent patients, in a non-punitive, psychodynamic setting, often get in touch with their own adolescent confusions.

Examples:

A and KY.

A was an intelligent and keen nurse in the unit. She was a relatively new staff member who was drawn to work in the unit because of its psychodynamic orientation. She was fascinated by what she was learning and was keen to learn more and more. She loved the work of the unit. One day she did not turn up for work following what was described by the other staff as an argument with KY, one of the inpatients, the previous evening. This argument had ended with A becoming extremely angry with KY and telling her off in a manner which was non typical of her. Some staff witnesses did not think there was anything really awful about what had happened, but A felt she was carrying a huge burden and could not come into work that day because she did not think she could face a staff meeting. I had a discussion with the senior nurse, who telephoned A and persuaded her to come to the staff meeting. One of the topics discussed at the staff meeting was the incident between A and KY. It transpired that KY had been very abusive of the work of the unit and the nonsense that was spoken by staff. It was this that triggered off the intense anger in A.

I suggested that what we spoke of most of the time would seem to be nonsense in the face of what we observe with our five senses, and that some of us did indeed really talk nonsense some of the time. This enabled several staff, including A, to acknowledge that they also had similar feelings – feelings which KY had spoken of the previous evening.

A left the meeting a transformed person. She had come in looking very depressed, ashamed of herself and heavily burdened, and at the end of the discussion she appeared bright and light-hearted and said she felt much better. She was not angry with KY anymore and did not feel bad about herself.

Discussion

It was evident from the discussion we had that A identified with a projection from KY, because she had not recognised a feeling within herself that was similar. She then became burdened with a combination of her own angry feelings about the work of the unit and the feelings projected by the girl. It was too much of a burden for her to carry. As soon as she identified and owned her own similar feelings, she was able to recognise herself and the projected material lost its grip on her.

S and J

J was a delinquent inpatient. Repeated staff discussions about his behaviour in the unit made it progressively clear to all of us that there was a 'Policeman-bully' within him as his superego.

S, an intelligent and enthusiastic charge nurse who was very fond of J, was always having trouble with him. There was constant friction between the two. After a while J began to call her 'Margaret Thatcher', whilst S found it increasingly difficult to maintain her calm and warm responses to him. She was offended by the comparison to the notable lady, and her anger with J was progressively increasing. She seemed to be the only staff person having this kind of bad interaction with him; she was very distressed and felt that she could not stop herself from shouting at him in a 'strident voice' which was really unlike her usual self.

Being a thoughtful and insightful young woman, she was able to take note of the discussion we had had about J projecting his 'Policeman/Margaret Thatcher' superego onto staff, and apply it to herself. J had on one occasion playfully placed mock handcuffs on my wrists. We discussed how staff who had a little bit of this quality in them can become easy victims and identify with the projection, causing the particular quality to be magnified in them many times over.

The next day there was a striking change in S. She interacted with J in the community meeting with a depth of understanding and sensitivity that was quite remarkable. There was a visible softening of J's responses and behaviour at the community meeting. It was a significant experience for him, because, at that particular stage, he had localised in S all the bad cruel qualities of all the staff, as well as his own. J was clearly changing, he became less irritable and generally easier to get on with.

Discussion

We learned later that S had had a very troubled night after that staff meeting, before that good community meeting, during which she had felt a lot of guilt, about her own attitudes and behaviour. She felt guilt not only about her behaviour with J but with members of her own family. I believe she had identified those qualities within her that were called 'Margaret Thatcher'; her thoughtfulness and inherent capacity allowed her to metabolise the projective identification and give back understanding to J.

Adolescents, who by virtue of their adolescent condition have a poor identity, are the easiest victims of the projections of others, including those from staff.

The case of JL

JL had a schizophrenic type of psychosis. She was in psychotherapy five times a week with me. She lived in a third-floor flat. She did not arrive for her session one day, turned up the next day and said she had not come the previous day because she had been convinced the lift had turned into a roaring lion. On the day she came she also felt the same, but she said she managed to rush past the lift and came down the stairway.

During the session she came to realise that she was extremely angry with her mother, and had been angry with her for many years, from the time she was a little girl. I suggested that her anger was like a roaring lion. JL left the session having had a very full discussion about the anger with her mother she had been harbouring for so many years, and totally convinced that the lift was a lift and nothing more.

Discussion

JL was a very loving girl who hated the idea of being angry with her mother. Her mother had turned a blind eye to father's sexual abuse of the little JL and well deserved the anger of JL. It was JL's love of her mother which made it imperative for her to deny and split-off the anger of which she had been reminded that night, which then became projected onto the lift in the form of a roaring lion. I did not investigate why it took the form of a roaring lion. It may have been some association with a visit to the zoo or seeing a film with a roaring lion she had seen on TV the previous night.

That an inanimate object became the projective identificatee indicates the intensity of the anger and the forcefulness of the both the denial and the projection.

Projective Identification with the punitive Superego

The mechanism of Projective Identification operates frequently with conduct disordered and delinquent youngsters. It is common for such youngsters to be suffering from excruciating guilt and to have within them a tyrannical superego which they have not recognised. They often project this superego onto staff who can become gripped by a very punitive attitude which they find hard to shake off.

Sometimes staff gripped by such a projection may wish to invite the Police to deal with the offending youngster. Police intervention at staff instigation has no part in a good dynamic treatment unit. If and when this happens it is a clear indication of failure (temporary) in the treatment plans for the youngster concerned.

It must be understood that the occasional failure to contain the feelings created in one and to exhibit an angry reaction does not damage the youngster. The adolescents who reach the residential services have been damaged long before. An opportunity to help them to move forward just a little bit has been postponed. If the dynamic described above is indeed true for the particular youngster it will be repeatedly reproduced in the unit, providing numerous opportunities for further good work.

Real damage occurs when the Projective Identification becomes institutionalised. This can happen when the Head of the Unit, together with the rest of the staff, become victims of the mechanism.

Guilt

Guilt is one of the most devastating phenomena. It is at the root of a great deal of misery in adolescents, staff, and in all ordinary human beings, manifesting itself in a variety of different forms with which the links are not obviously discernible; such as feelings of inferiority, depression, some types of violence, delinquency, self-mutilation, suicide and others. It plays an important part in almost every type of psychopathology.

The relevant guilt is often deep seated and it takes a very safe environment and a very trusting relationship to permit its emergence into consciousness. The guilt that is experienced is invariably not about actual deeds committed, but about feelings and fantasies that have been experienced by the youngsters in their early years. There are two important facts about one's baby years which must be borne in mind:

1. That the baby's perceptual abilities are rudimentary, whilst its ability to feel is as acute as ever. As a result it will naturally become very muddled about the reasons for its suffering and emotional pain.
2. That a baby confuses its reality and its feelings and fantasies. A feeling it has had is as good as reality.

Therefore, if a baby has felt angry enough with mother so as to blot her out, it is felt as having killed its own mother, and so on. If the baby's or child's future interactions have not mitigated these experiences, they remain unaltered or intensified by further bad experiences, which are nothing but feelings and fantasies which create the most appalling guilt.

Adolescents, and in fact any human being, will resist reaching and recognising their own guilt only because it is unknown and vaguely threatening. Adolescents use a variety of techniques to resist reaching their guilt. These techniques and their interplay with staff responses form the basis of a large part of staff interactions with the youngsters. They require special attention.

ATTEMPTED EXPIATION OF GUILT

Adolescents who have a deep sense of guilt from time to time experience vague unpleasant nagging feelings of emerging guilt which they may try to get rid off by inviting punishment. They would engage in some form of behaviour which would normally lead to being told off by staff. Then when they are told off, instead of accepting the correction, would argue or create even more trouble and get into a 'battle' with staff until they feel they have received sufficient telling off, (beatings), then settle down quietly until they begin to experience the nagging feelings again when the same pattern of behaviour would be repeated. Freud has described how this mechanism operates in recidivism in his paper, '*Criminals from a Sense of Guilt*', in which he describes how the feelings of guilt precede the commitment of the offence ([1]Freud).

If staff react in the invited way, all that is achieved is an unpleasant experience for staff and collusion with the youngster in his attempt to get rid of the bad feeling in him caused by the emerging deeper guilt. This would prevent the youngster from progressing towards the emerging guilt in psychotherapy and moving closer to dealing with the real source of trouble.

In a unit where true psychodynamic work is done staff learn to respond to the behaviour of patients rather than react to it.

Example:

> Doreen, fourteen years, was well known in the unit for starting and dragging on endless, pointless, loud arguments, as if to invite attacks from staff. After total staff discussion all the staff had learnt to tell her, 'Doreen you know what you are doing is wrong, we are not going to tell you off or argue with you, you can stop the behaviour yourself.' After a while she gradually gave up this habit and instead took her bad feelings into psychotherapy and told me that she had hit her mother in the abdomen when mother was large with her second baby. It was said as if to inform me of the kind of nasty girl she was. She was a girl who had extreme feelings guilt about jealousy and constantly got into trouble with her peers as a result. She became aware of her jealousy.

We could not help her to get rid of her jealousy, but we helped her to realise the cause of her bad feelings which sometimes made her feel she was mad, and to find ways of dealing with this feeling (her jealousy) in a more constructive way, without getting herself into so much trouble with her friends.

PROJECTION OF GUILT ONTO STAFF

Adolescents, particularly delinquent ones, are very adept at shifting guilt onto staff. This manoeuvre is often seen in good Community/House meetings. The guilty offender picks on something the staff mayor may not have done when the topic of conversation moves onto their guilt-making behaviour; if staff react with a sense of guilt, the offender can feel 'let off the hook', whilst the staff 'scuttle for cover'. If the accusations are of 'being uncaring', staff may feel that they have to bend backwards to care even more.

The most important part of the response to this sort of situation is to look at oneself seriously, and quickly acknowledge to oneself any real cause for guilt. Having thus strengthened oneself, it becomes much easier to discuss anything they wish to bring up calmly, and to help them to see their own guilt. If one does not acknowledge one's own shortcomings within oneself, and if necessary with the youngsters, very quickly, this manoeuvre of pushing the guilt back onto to the offender can deteriorate into a situation of two adolescents simply attacking each other and staff either ignominiously loosing face or having to assert their authority by virtue of their staff status; a deplorable situation.

Guilt is a peculiar thing. It causes a lot of suffering, yet it is not true guilt that does this. It is something closely allied to it, something which I would call 'pseudo-guilt'. True guilt is a 'blessing in disguise', it is not persecutory. It is attended by a feeling of calmness and a strong wish to make reparation; a position from which tremendous development is made.

ENVY

This is a powerfully destructive quality. It is experienced as a death-like feeling. It is secretive and not easily recognised. The possessor is himself frightened and particularly ashamed of the feelings within him. It is secretive.

The envious patient is very difficult to treat, because his or her envious and destructive attacks are often directed towards the therapist and therapy. The well known negative therapeutic reaction is most often caused by envy, which increases as the therapy gets better.

Similarly, this quality in staff is intractable. It is well disguised and seen most often as attacks on the institution by staff who find the treatment philosophy attractive but are unable to subscribe to it, as a result of their own personality defects. Sometimes, the envious attacks are directed towards the youngsters when they have youthful qualities and opportunities which the staff can never possess, develop or regain.

REFERENCES

[1] Freud, S., *Complete Psychological Works*, Vol. XIX, p49, London, Hogarth Press, 1961.

Chapter X
SOME INTERESTING CASES

In this chapter I have described three cases of young people, each with different problems which were dealt with effectively. The first case is of a typical delinquent, the second is about the dangers of overzealous investigation of sexual abuse, and the third is about a seriously depressed youngster who changed radically when his murderous anger emerged.

The Mellowing of a Cruel and Punitive Superego

One evening Jim skipped happily past me along the corridor of the unit, joyously and unbelievingly saying, 'Hey Peri, I'm 6 feet 3½ inches tall.' He had just had his routine weight and height measurement. This was perhaps Jim's most striking feature. This tall, strapping youngster felt very little, and underneath a veneer of ordinary, somewhat immature sixteen-year-old behaviour, he acted like a frightened little boy. It took us repeated staff discussions and reminders to hold onto and recognise the little boy Jim. When we managed to do this he made strides of improvement.

Jim lived with his mum and older sister. His father was evidently psychiatrically ill and had an alcoholic problem. He evidently used to beat up Jim's mother. He died when Jim was three years old. Mum had a boyfriend who lived with her for about six to seven years and left when Jim was eleven years old. He also evidently had beaten her up frequently. Jim manifested disturbance from an early age – stealing, temper tantrums and several petty offences in his early teens. His greatest unhappiness was his inability to get on with his mother.

BEHAVIOUR IN THE UNIT

Jim was a pleasant lad who became irritable and angry periodically for no apparent reason. A notable feature of his behaviour was his sudden inexplicable departure from community meetings. He gradually stopped attending these meetings, though he interacted quite easily with staff 'on the floor'. He did not respond to persuasion or firmness. In psychotherapy as well, he would suddenly leave for no apparent reason, despite his psychotherapist being a very sensitive and understanding female, for whom he had a great sense of loyalty.

It took us some weeks to detect that Jim was an unusually aware and sensitive boy, who felt deep guilt and hurt, and could not stand the slightest attack from us, who represented his superego. He could quite accurately sense the drift of a community meeting discussion or a psychotherapy session and leave well before he got hurt, or alternatively become angry and hurt us. This observation led us to think more about what we do in community meetings and how we had unwittingly drifted back into using them as a means of getting back at the captive youngsters – a particularly bad thing in a meeting which was supposed to reflect the total philosophy of the unit. This realisation on our part led to better community meetings.

Jim's first reappearance at a community meeting was preceded by an angry argument with me over some of his behaviour in the unit. He threatened to smash my head in with a pool cue, which he brandished in his hand, saying, 'Unless you piss off from here.' I responded by saying, 'I am going anyway, Jim, but what you've said to me is very important and we must continue this discussion in the community meeting.'

Jim was the first in the community meeting that day, and he named all the staff as we walked in, calling us in mock humour PC Perin, PC Beau, PC Nora, etc. When we took our places I responded to him by saying 'You cannot make us into policemen, whatever you do.' Jim and the other youngsters relaxed and we had a very good discussion on diverse topics relevant to the community, not only on Jim's behaviour.

A few days later, we heard that Jim and his closest mate in the unit Kevin, had rushed around threatening to 'smash-in' the head of the person who had spilt some milk on Kevin's bed. In the community meeting the next day we began to discuss this incident, when Jim left. We continued the discussion till we reached a point when I could clearly point out that Jim and Kevin had been acting as they thought the police do – as if they were policemen. I told Kevin to be sure to convey to Jim what I had said. Later that same evening Jim came up to me and playfully put mock handcuffs on me, saying, 'I am a policeman.' I told him, 'There you are Jim, it's no joke, there is a policeman inside you, that keeps attacking you all the time. It's not us who are the real police, it's you.'

Repeated staff discussions about Jim's behaviour in the unit made it progressively clearer to all of us that there was indeed a 'policeman-bully' within him, projected onto us, inviting us all to bully him. Our continual reminders to each other about the little boy Jim, brought into staff meetings by different nursing staff, made it easier for us to resist responding to him in the invited way, as a rough, tough bully.

PROJECTIVE IDENTIFICATION

In the meantime, Sally, an intelligent, perceptive and enthusiastic charge nurse who was very fond of Jim, brought into discussion her distress about always having trouble with him. There was constant friction between the two. Sally found it hard to maintain her warm responses to him and after a while Jim began to call her 'Margaret Thatcher'. She was offended by this comparison to the notable lady and was very distressed. She seemed to be the only staff member who was having this particular kind of bad interaction with him.

But being a thoughtful young woman, she was also able to look at herself and take in the staff discussion we had about Projective Identification and Jim projecting his policeman superego onto staff; how staff who did not know themselves well enough, and had a little bit of this quality within them, can become easy victims and identify with the projections, causing the particular quality in them to be magnified several times over.

The next day there was a striking change in Sally. She interacted with Jim in the community meeting with a calmness and warmth and depth of understanding that was quite remarkable. There was a visible softening of Jim's responses and behaviour at the community meeting. I believe it was a significant experience for Jim, because at that particular stage, he had localised in Sally all the harsh, punitive superego qualities of the staff as well as his own.

We learned later that Sally had had a very troubled night, during which she had felt a lot of guilt, thinking about her family and friends. She had identified the 'Margaret Thatcher' as Jim saw her, within herself that night, and in so doing had shaken off the projective identification.

Jim was clearly changing, he was attending psychotherapy regularly, staying in all the community meetings, became less irritable and generally easier to get on with.

A 'CRIMINAL ACT'

A while later there was a reported incident of some girls being 'mugged' just outside Brookside. We suspected Jim and another youngster, from the description of the assailants given to the local press. There was a staff discussion about this situation. Some staff felt we should inform the police immediately about our suspicions. Some in the staff group felt identified with the victims; the idea of ones duty to society was prominent in their minds. Others felt that youngsters should not be allowed to take refuge from the consequences of their crimes in our treatment community. Some in the group simply felt angry with Jim, and with me for *being soft with Jim and 'soft in the head'*. Other staff did not like the idea of bringing the police in, they had an intuitive feeling about it being inappropriate. I expressed my own views about what I thought was my duty. I said it was a very difficult problem because one had different types of duties and loyalties and sometimes these were in conflict with each other. I said that I had solved my problem some time ago in a very simple way, by recognising that as a psychiatrist and a clinician my duty in matters concerning my profession clearly was to the clinical needs of the patient. My inclinations to support or go against society I thought should be exercised outside my professional life. Similarly the *police* had a duty to protect society, whilst magistrates and judges were in the most difficult position of all – *they had a duty to protect both offender and society*. The real question for us was to decide whether Jim was a patient in the unit, or really a criminal masquerading as a patient.

This led to a lot of discussion about Jim's behaviour in the unit. There was some confusion about this question. Whilst I was concerned about Jim's behaviour, I became more interested in our [the staff's] attitude, because after a while I saw that *Jim's role in the unit as a patient or a criminal would be dependent on our behaviour as therapists or policemen*. Jim, as a disturbed youngster, had less choice about such matters than we as relatively normal staff. When I articulated all this, all but the diehard 'policemen' amongst the staff saw that we should stick together as therapists and help Jim to move more into the role of patient, if indeed he was not already there.

We did not inform the police. Instead I told Jim that we thought he was involved in that incident and were concerned about him. After a while Jim told staff that he was indeed involved in the 'mugging'. After a few days of us remaining firmly as therapists, while he alternated between seeing us as policemen at times and therapist helpers at others, he solicited our help and support to own up to the police and take the consequences of what he had done. He received our full support for this. A very kind officer from the Juvenile Bureau interviewed him, advised him and did not charge him. Jim, who feared and hated the police, had his first good experience of them.

Jim is improving, discussing his problems more freely, feeling less like a criminal and more like an ordinary boy with troubles. He is spending more of his time thinking about his relationship with his mother and the trouble he has caused her. He can take a rebuke from staff without flying off the handle or running away.

He has other areas of difficulty to solve, and at the time of writing this the most prominent is a powerful Oedipal relationship, manifesting itself through quite intense, special relationships with female staff. It is his clearly expressed fear and anger, that I, the father figure, would interfere and stop it that makes it so clearly Oedipal in nature.

As Jim's superego becomes mellower and kinder, through his

interactions with us (his authority figures), more and more of his problems emerge and are being made available for understanding and help. The modification of the superego is a most worthwhile end in itself; it is also the means to other ends.

The Role of Projective Identification in the Investigation of Sexual Abuse

Summary:

In the paper 'Child Sexual Abuse – 1', in the *British Medical Journal* of 29th July 1989, Frank B.K. Ford and Raine Roberts have said, 'Repeated questioning [of the child] is potentially harmful…'

It has been our experience that repeated questioning of the child about sexual abuse is indeed harmful, and further that any kind of questioning has its danger, unless it is conducted with an awareness of the psychodynamic consequences, and subsequent work is done to mitigate any undesirable effect. The psychodynamic phenomenon involved is one of the commonest in human relationships – *Projective Identification*. It is of relevance to all work with adolescents and of particular significance in the investigation of sexual abuse.

This is illustrated by the case of K, in which a quiet, shy young girl of thirteen quite untypically began inviting 'old men' to have sex with her, following the investigation of suspected sexual abuse by her father. That she was not naturally promiscuous is evident from the letters she wrote to me during and after her subsequent therapy.

I have come across several young girls who rue the day they revealed to some adult an incident of sexual abuse they had experienced, in the hope that they would feel better for it. Apart from the inevitable but well-recognised trauma caused by the necessary legal procedures, often they have had to contend with a whole range of adult intrusiveness of different sorts, varying from over-solicitude with constant unproductive reminders of an experience they would rather forget, to frank adult voyeurism and perhaps vicarious sexual gratification, which is experienced by the girls as unpleasant repetitions of the abuse. These are conscious experiences, which may or may not occur, after disclosure by a victim of actual sexual abuse.

Projective identification, however, is of a different nature. It is an unconscious phenomenon, which can occur after any investigation of sexual abuse; it 'inexplicably' compels the victim of the mechanism to act in a way he/she would not otherwise have done, i.e. *to act in the suggested way*. Youngsters from families in which parents do not get on with each other are particularly predisposed to becoming victims of the mechanism; they are also the ones most likely to be investigated for possible sexual abuse.

PROJECTIVE IDENTIFICATION

The term was originally used by Melanie Klein (¹Klein, 1946) to specifically describe a phenomenon which occurred in psychotic patients. Since then the concept has been further understood and developed both in the direction of the metaphysical as well as the mundane by several psychoanalysts, notably by Bion, Rosenfeld and Meltzer, embracing interactions which occur in all human beings. It is the wider elaboration of the concept which is relevant to this paper.

The significant features of Projective Identification are:

1. Any quality can be projectively identified.
2. One with a strong enough personality or authority must merely project the quality into someone else with a poor identity for the mechanism to begin to be activated.
3. The personality and emotional status of the recipient of the projection is crucial to the fate of the projections.
4. Those who have a poor sense of identity and therefore are also in a state of relative emotional instability are predisposed to becoming projective identificatees; projections are readily accepted by them, especially if they possess something of the quality that has been projected.
5. Thus adolescents who are usually in a state of identity confusion in varying degrees are highly vulnerable. They can become projective identificatees very easily.

The Case of K, thirteen years:

The allegation that K's father had had anal intercourse with her had been investigated by the Social Services and the police, following the discovery that she was bleeding per rectum, after a fall from a first-floor window and a fractured pelvis. The allegation was denied both by the father and by K. The orthopaedic surgeon who was treating her had confirmed that bleeding PR was to be expected with a fractured pelvis and had stated that there was no medical reason to suspect sodomy. Nevertheless father had been taken into custody, had been subjected to the full process of police investigations and had been discharged. K herself had been subjected to the corresponding enquiries. Her parents had not been getting on with each other and her father did not return home.

By the time of her admission to our inpatient unit, which was some six months or so later, K, who had never had any kind of sexual experience before, had been picked up twice by 'old men', as described by her, and had had sex with them; she was not attracted to them and could not account for her behaviour. She had also taken an overdose. When taking her history during admission, she told me how she had waited at a particular bus stop where she had seen some men get off, had plucked up courage and engineered the 'pick up'. She was afraid it would happen again; she seemed to be asking for protection from her own inexplicable impulses.

K had had two admissions to the unit. Within three months of her first discharge she had again picked up a man and had taken an overdose. Each time she was admitted she was miserable at first and changed to becoming trouble-free and happy in a relatively short time. During her inpatient stay she had individual psychotherapy with another therapist. I, as the Consultant in charge, had insisted that she be treated like the little girl she was, which she overtly hated. For instance, I did not permit her to go home for weekends by herself and insisted that her mother accompanied her home and back.

Following her second discharge, the Social Services who had taken her into care were not happy about the changes in her and I undertook to see her in outpatient psychotherapy. Even though I knew her well through interactions in the community and reports from other staff, it was the first time I was taking her on for psychotherapy. She was known to be a particularly intelligent girl.

The beginning of her psychotherapy with me was remarkably informative and interesting. She was around fourteen by then.

Psychotherapy with K:

K started her therapy very angry with me. During her stay in the unit, I had done the thing that adolescents hate the most – I had treated her like a child. I had emphasised her 'littleness' when she was in the unit and had insisted that she should be accompanied by mother during her weekend journeys home, because in my words, 'K was too young to travel by herself'. I had good reasons for doing this. Mother had an unusual attitude to the sexual behaviour of her two daughters, of whom K was the younger – she had said during a family discussion with K that her only concern about K having sex was that she may become infected with venereal disease. I believed that K had been the victim of 'projective identification', which was compelling her to identify with and feel and behave like a much older, sexually mature and promiscuous girl, to which her mother was contributing. Everything possible was being done in the unit to mitigate the effect of this and to restore her to her true status of a vulnerable little girl.

First Session:

She told me she was coming to see me only because the Social Services had threatened her with a secure unit if she refused. She said it was going to be a sheer waste of time because she was not going to discuss anything with me, and she remained silent for the full 50 minutes, making no response to any of the comments I made, which were designed to understand and interpret her angry feelings.

Second Session:

(It is of relevance that there was a policy in the unit that staff should not cuddle patients.)
She brought a book and read, silently at first, ignoring any comments I made, and later she started reading aloud. I kept silent and listened to her reading, which I actually found very interest-

ing. She suddenly threw the book aside and said,

K: 'How can I have therapy with a sex pervert?'

After verifying that she was talking about me, I told her that I found that remark to be very interesting and I wondered why she had said that.

K: 'The rule you made in the unit, that staff should not cuddle patients, shows that your mind is full of sexual thoughts about the patients. You stopped them from giving cuddles and getting close to the patients because of your feelings.'

It seemed as if she was describing a projective process as had happened to her.

Me: 'So your belief, it seems, is that I am interested in you sexually, and that I put my thoughts and feelings into the staff.'

K: 'Yes.'

Me: 'I think this is really clever of you, they told me you were clever; but you are wrong about your conclusions, you know.' Then, after a short silence: 'You must regard yourself as someone very special to imagine that I would be interested in you sexually.' And then very gently: 'Do you really think that you are very special sexually?' After a longish silence: 'It seemed as if you hated me because I was treating you like a little girl, I wonder if that is true? I think I am still treating you like a little girl, aren't I?'

K: 'Yes.'

Me: 'Well, if you think I am interested in you sexually, it is not surprising that you think I am a sexual pervert, it is not normal for grown men like me to be sexually interested in little girls like you.' After a longish silence: 'You must feel that I am like those old men at the bus stop you told me about long ago.'

K seemed to be listening keenly and there seemed to be a slight softening of her face. After a further silence:

Me: 'Okay, then, I know about the part of you that hates being treated like a little girl, but I wonder whether there is also a part of you that likes it and makes you feel safe with me?'

She nodded, with a slight smile.

This was the beginning of the most interesting and fruitful psychotherapeutic interaction which lasted for about two years.

She is now seventeen years old and holding a responsible secretarial job. She is a great letter writer, and in order to illustrate her true nature, which is a contrast to the promiscuity she displayed in the aftermath of the investigation of sexual abuse, I would like to quote excerpts from some of her letters:

1. *Today I nearly fell into a trap. The caretaker was here making a repair to the window and he asked me if I wanted to go out one evening, no strings attached. Fool that I am I accepted, but then a few minutes later I actually told him face to face, that I'd changed my mind. So now everything is straight…*

2. *In practical terms I'm managing well. I have a part-time job… Then I treat myself with a taxi to reach Safeway, where dwells my current 'love-from-afar', which is the closest I'll ever get to what I want. At least he noticed me and for a time we were quite intense without actually touching. But he's already spoken for and now seems to hav forgotten about 'us'. But all in all I'm too busy to think about anything which I feel is good since I'm no longer confused…*

3. *Dear Dr Perin*
   I couldn't wait two weeks to say how good I felt after the last two psychotherapy's. When I got off the bus yesterday I ran home, really happy, and kissed my mum (although I was wound up about Angela.)…

4. *…I've found someone I like. I hadn't met him before this last weekend, so consciously or subconsciously, that's not the reason for me not turning up. Actually I met him through an introduction agency. He wasn't the first person I met, so please don't accuse me of rushing into things. I am trying to be selective, and although I have been tempted, I'm not letting anyone do anything I might regret…*

DISCUSSION

There were several factors that contributed to K's promiscuous behaviour, the most powerful of which was *projective identification*. Other factors such as parental separation and the Oedipal fantasies of a young girl, and simply being an adolescent who by definition is in a state of identity confusion, would act as predisposing her to be a ready recipient of the projections.

Projective Identificators:

1. The person or people who originally made the allegation and every one of the investigating officers, who probably quite unknowingly pushed into her the idea that she was the sort who has sex with old men like her father, and is sexually attractive to them.
2. There may have been some who actually felt sexually attracted to her and unwittingly conveyed the impression to her.
3. Mother was also a powerful projective identificator – Mother's attitude to her thirteen-year-old daughter's sexual behaviour was, 'The only danger is VD.' This would certainly have projected into K the idea that she is the sort who has sex at that age.

Discussions with K's mother showed that she had also been projecting into K her own unfulfilled adolescent desires. In our family work with Mother and K, the aim was to help Mother to re-own her own frustrated adolescent desires and thus draw back the projections into herself.

K made me also into a Projective Identificator through her Projection/Transference, as I discovered in the psychotherapy with her. She had made me into a sex pervert in her mind, who was interested in her sexually, through her interpretation of the rule in the unit, that there should be no cuddling. In view of the fact that I was Director of the unit and held in high regard by the patients, it would have had a very powerful effect. I was also 'the old man' or 'father' of the unit, and it must be remembered that she had powerfully identified with the projection that 'old men' like father, were interested in her sexually.

There were many interesting psychodynamic phenomena operating in her case. I believe the way this was handled in the therapy led K to lose her false identity, allowing her to feel safe and little. She acquired her true identity as a bashful, adolescent girl.

A certain amount of projective identification will inevitably occur in all investigations of sexual abuse of little children. But the dangers can be minimised if professionals are aware of the mechanism and its effect.

A Case of Severe Depression

This is an unusual case of a severe depressive who was also a secret, lone, solvent abuser (glue-sniffer). Formal psychiatry using antidepressants did not help him. Apart from illustrating the well known psychodynamic edict that 'anger and depression are two sides of the same coin', he displayed some common psychodynamic phenomena – 'The transference', 'the Oedipus Complex' and 'Projective Identification'.

We had at one point contemplated acceding to his request that he be sent to a general psychiatric hospital, so that, in his words, '*I can be safely behind locked doors for the rest of my life.*' He had been severely incapacitated for some months in our unit. Our thoughts about sending him to the psychiatric hospital centred around the clear underlying feelings of despair and suicide that came through his plea and our inability to watch over him closely for an indefinite period in our open door (we have twenty-six exits which cannot be locked), psychodynamically orientated unit. He had made three previous attempts at suicide before admission to our unit.

Then we were instructed by management to vacate Brookside – the building – immediately because the roof had been leaking and constituted a danger to the patients. Management were far too frightened of being accused of neglect to even consider delaying the move for discussion with staff and patients. We had no alternative but to move eighteen patients into inadequate and wholly unsuitable accommodation in the main hospital, literally, in one day. I felt helpless. This move stirred up a great deal of violence in staff and patients, who felt that I should have had the ability or the power to do something about this without putting them into an 'impossible' situation. *The way in which M's violence was handled, led to his recovery.*

M had been a patient in the unit for about four months. I was responsible for the 'family' meetings, which his only sibling, an elder brother, could not attend. He was having individual psychotherapy with another therapist. His father had been doing nothing for the past ten years or so. He had become depressed when M was about five years of age, and was hospitalised for several months and put on on-going Lithium. Father was a thorough gentleman, well spoken and courteous. He would excuse himself and leave the room rather than explode with anger at some remark I had made. It was clear from the family meetings that father had been an emotional zombie for many years, a non-man, and automaton who operated entirely on his good intelligence. He was unable to tolerate the slightest emotional stress. The family spoke of him as 'having been ill', and having been made redundant unfairly when he was fully capable of resuming work. His presence in the family meetings was an embarrassment. He was quite useless there, we could not talk to or about him. I spoke with the consultant Psychiatrist looking after him who told me that Mr B was indeed seriously ill, whose fragile emotional balance had to be maintained with drugs. After two meetings Mr B solved the problem by requesting that he be excused from family meetings. All members of the family and I agreed to this.

M's behaviour in the unit was flawless. He was not disruptive, attended every meeting, and gradually became noted for his declaration *'I don't feel anything'*. His quite clever, cynical and contemptuous attacks on staff (particularly at the daily community meetings which I attended), and his attempts at subtle flirtation with female staff, never with girl patients were noticeable. He was an isolated boy, felt ill at ease with his peers, but because of his intelligence and highly developed social skills his lack of peer companionship did not appear to affect him to any significant extent.

M's relationship with me developed into a very strong therapeutic alliance, because of my interactions with him in the community meetings and in family meetings. In family meetings he experienced me as sensitive and caring of all of them, and very respectful of father, who had lost all respect in his family. In community meetings, I interacted with his cynical attacks on me, without retaliatory anger, giving serious consideration to both the content of what he said as well as the underlying anger and contempt. He gradually grew to respect and trust me.

After a while he let us know that he had been a secret glue-sniffer and had indulged in it while he was at Brookside. Having made this known to us he brought his glue-sniffing into the unit. He sniffed alone. Many staff had tried to interact with him and get the glue off him, had failed and had left him to do his sniffing until he virtually collapsed – a very worrying and unsatisfactory situation. He had also started inflicting deep and dangerous cuts on his arms, very different from the superficial self-inflicted scratches of some of the other youngsters.

One evening I saw M sniffing glue, seated alone on the floor near the nursing station. I tried to persuade him to stop and give me the glue. When he said there was no chance that he would, I got hold of his glue bag and took it off him gently, but determinedly, saying that I could not stand by and watch him destroying himself. He threw a few harmless token blows at me and was quite easily calmed down by the charge nurse and me.

M then made a serious request for him to come to me for individual psychotherapy. I believe that he finally felt safe enough with me because he saw that I was not afraid of his anger. I think it was at this point that he projected his feeling of omnipotence into me and identified me as one with infinite power. There was a projective-identification between him and me. I too felt very effective with him and good about my work with him.

As he had reached quite a serious state, I agreed to take him on after discussion with his therapist, who felt he had got nowhere with M after three months of twice-weekly psychotherapy.

Psychotherapy with M was fascinatingly interesting. He was constantly trying to get the better of me. I thought he had great unconscious guilt about his feelings and fantasised damage he had done to his father and was denying this guilt by identifying with his father, saying *'I have no feelings'*, and his strong urge to be admitted to psychiatric hospital as his father was. He was also letting us know how he came to feel such guilt by reproducing in the unit, through the transference, the contemptuous attacks on his father. His relationship with his mother seemed to be a delicate balance of a protective and possessive love, contemptuous intellectual superiority, anger about the power she had over him and unconscious Oedipal love (manifested through flirtation with staff). He both feared and loved the idea that he had no feelings. He claimed that he did not dream. He felt he was different from everyone else; that he defied understanding and was impossible to treat; someone very special.

M's attempts to get the better of me in all areas in his individual psychotherapy failed, and after about the fourth session he declared that all his life he had met people whom he could *'twist turn and batter into any shape I wished';* he was well satisfied to agree that he had at last met just the right person in me who would not allow him to do that. His identification with father appeared in the transference in an unusual form of constantly trying to make out that he and I had the same understanding about diverse topics that we discussed, which I continually picked up and interpreted.

M improved rapidly. Within a month he was a transformed boy; had stopped glue-sniffing and cutting himself, was more alive and free in his interactions in the unit, and had lost his cynical contemptuous attitude to staff. He still insisted that he had no feelings, though this had become something of a joke between us in sessions, because I had picked up his feelings many times. I thought he really meant that he had no feelings about his parents. He did not bring any dreams into psychotherapy. I thought he was too frightened of his unconscious feelings to allow them to emerge even in dreams.

He requested a week's leave during Christmas in order to see if he was getting on well enough to leave. He returned after a week and requested continuing his in-patient treatment because he was still feeling a misfit with his mates and was not sure that he would not start it all again – the glue-sniffing, cutting himself and his suicidal feelings. This time his progress in therapy was much slower. New feelings that he brought into therapy were not being dealt with effectively – homosexual anxieties – brought in by him not for understanding but for protective action; he wanted a side room (single-bedded room) where he would have less temptation to express his homosexual feelings. The therapy was not progressing with the rapidity that had impressed him so much earlier. His respect for me, which had reached a pinnacle was just beginning to wane, when a sudden move (of eighteen in patients) into thoroughly unsuitable surroundings was ordered by the administration.

We had to leave the same day. There was no time to have a staff discussion or any discussion with the patients, and I had no alternative but to pass on to staff and patients the intensive 'kick' that had been delivered. Staff were dismayed, confused and angry. The staff patient structure of the programmes and activities that we had carefully built up over many months in order to achieve our full (twenty) inpatient numbers collapsed at a stroke.

It was in this climate just after the move to the hospital ward that I went into the ward one evening and found the place in absolute chaos. Several youngsters had been slashing themselves, staff had been attacked by some of the youngsters, a female staff member had sustained a fractured arm. I was dismayed, but calming myself, I started dealing with the situation. I had just begun to achieve a semblance of containment in the ward when I saw M seated on the floor apparently oblivious of what was going on around him, sniffing glue. I lost my calm, told him off roundly and grabbed the glue bag from him. All hell broke loose. M went for me swinging punches and kicks and trying to get me at my throat. Two female staff (there were no male staff on duty) threw themselves between and struggled to restrain M. M's anger and energy were phenomenal, he kept going for me swearing that he would kill me, for a good forty-five minutes. The police were called, M was held down by them and he was given a sedative by injection. As he had calmed down after a while and was clearly not a danger to anyone I rejected the offer of the police to keep him overnight at the Police Station and charge him. The unit had become very calm and contained by then. It was as if all the anger and violence of the youngsters and staff had been expressed by M through his attempt to kill me.

M was very subdued in the community meeting the next day, and kept looking at me as if to pass a silent message. I spoke about the chaos in the unit the previous night without highlighting his attack on me and saw him for his usual psychotherapy the next day. This was a most rewarding and productive session.

He came in and tentatively asked me for a cigarette, (something he would not think of doing under normal circumstances – it was well known in the unit that I was a smoker but did not give cigarettes to patients). I unhesitatingly offered him a cigarette which he took with shaking hands. It was an important and meaningful gesture, which meant to M that I understood just how nervous he felt, and also that I was not angry with him. (I was just sore all over.) He lay on the couch and talked as he had never talked before. He cried and pleaded with me to charge him. I told him that, that would not be necessary for him, because…

> 'you have a good mind and are fully capable of taking the consequences of what you have done through discussion with me.'
>
> M: 'I don't know why I got so angry.'
>
> Me: 'It has caused you a lot of distress.'
>
> M: 'Was it because the unit had closed?'
>
> Me: 'I don't know,' after a short silence, 'only you can tell us.'
>
> (I meant him and me, which he understood.)
>
> M: 'You did not run away.'
>
> Me: 'Did you expect me to? It seems like your expectations of me which were quite high at one time have dropped quite low.'
>
> M: 'You were like the captain of the ship who would not leave it till it sank.'
>
> There was period of silence in which he looked preoccupied, after which I said, 'yes M,'
>
> M: 'Grant and I were building a castle with a pack of cards that afternoon and as the pack of cards grew higher and higher I could see in Grant's face that he would go mad if the pack of cards collapsed; so I knocked them down myself.'
>
> Me: 'I think you were very angry that Brookside collapsed, but also because I had collapsed in your eyes. You had built me up to great heights and were very disappointed in me, that I could not stop the administration from making us make that move. You were already beginning to be disillusioned during the last few weeks because the psychotherapy was not progressing as it did at the beginning.'
>
> M: 'There was nothing left for me but glue.'
>
> Me: 'So you had glue instead of the me you had built to great heights?'
>
> M: 'There are only three things I value in the world, this unit, you and my cassette player. I will murder anyone who messes around with my cassette player.'

We then spent some time talking about his cassette player and where he kept it, and whether it was safe or not. I recalled after the session, that M had told me a while ago that his mother had bought him the cassette player for £180. I made that link in the next session.

It became clear, through the transference to me, that M's glue-sniffing centred around the loss of a fantasy relationship with his mother and denigration of her into a thing which he could hold, use and control in anyway he liked, the glue. His depression was around the guilt he felt about the denigration of his mother as well as his contemptuous feelings about his father.

M did not keep his next few psychotherapy appointments with me, and got into a lot of relatively harmless but quite disruptive acting out together with some other youngsters, for the first time. I thought he had begun to feel safer and more equal with his peers. I discharged him from the unit together with two others and offered him continuing outpatient psychotherapy.

He had his first dreams during outpatient psychotherapy. He told me about them partly in order to gain further understanding and partly defiantly still clinging to the special feelings of being different from others.

M: 'I had a dream.'

Me: (keenly interested) 'Yes M.'

M: 'I was smoking in my bedroom.'

Me: 'Yes.'

M: 'That's it.' (Triumphantly.)

I tried every known and unknown method of getting him to work with me on this dream and failed. He had a triumphant smirk in his face when I said, 'I cannot help you with that dream M, let us see whether anything comes up later on about this dream.'

Two sessions later he said he had another dream.

M: 'I was drinking coke in my bedroom. It was very realistic, I could feel the cold tin in my hands and I woke up and tried to take a sip of it.'

Me: 'Yes.'

M: 'That's it, nothing more, you can't make anything out of this either. There is nothing more to this one. I am not allowed to smoke in my bedroom, but I am allowed to drink coke.'

Me: 'That must be quite a bore for you, not being allowed to smoke in your bedroom.'

M: 'Yes it's my father, he is such a stupid man...'

He then went into telling me about all the angry and contemptuous feelings he had been harbouring about his dad ever since he was a child. He did not stop for a second, it was like an abreaction.

He moved forward smoothly from there on, discussed quite freely his angry and contemptuous feelings he had for both his parents and a whole range of ordinary adolescent difficulties.

He rejoined his old school and started studying for his O levels. He stopped psychotherapy with me just at the point where he was beginning to get into his Oedipal feelings for his mother. He claimed he was getting on well and had no reason to continue with psychotherapy.

I thought M may overcome his Oedipal feelings through relatively harmless acting out in his social life, or he may need more psychotherapy later on. His homosexual feelings were never brought up by him.

M telephoned me some four years later for an appointment. He came to see me together with his girlfriend. He was experiencing bizarre feelings and thought he might be going mad. He was working in some semi-skilled job and was afraid of losing it. He was getting on well in every other way. On taking his history I found that he had been smoking a particular kind of Cannabis, called 'Black' which he described as unrefined and very strong. Detailed clinical examination led me to believe that the psychotic symptoms he was experiencing were caused by his excessive smoking of this drug. I prescribed small doses of antipsychotic medication for a limited period and advised him to stop smoking Cannabis. Within a week of starting the medication he felt he was back to his normal self. M did not give up Cannabis smoking but reduced his intake greatly. He stopped seeing me after four sessions.

REFERENCES

[1] Klein, M., et al, *Developments in Psychoanalysis,* p.198, London, Hogarth Press, 1948

Chapter XI
THE ALPHA-ACTION

The Alpha-action is the name I have given to a process, on which, I believe, hangs all that is understood about normal human relationships. (I have borrowed the term Alpha-action from W.R. Bion who used the term 'Alpha particles' in a similar context.) It involves two parts which are interlinked. An *intrapsychic process* and an *interpersonal* one. The Alpha-action occurs between *a normal mother and her baby*. It is Melanie Klein who first described each of these processes separately. They have been further developed by many eminent psychoanalysts, foremost among who are Rosenfeld, Bion and Meltzer. I believe that the processes which take place in the Alpha-action, as it is understood today, can be seen as arising from self-evident truths. It is the prototype of many good interactions that go on between human beings of all ages. While the process occurs far more frequently in a beneficial interaction the elements involved in the process can occur in destructive relationships as well.

I shall first deal with the intrapsychic process which occurs in the normal beneficial Alpha-action.

THE INTRAPSYCHIC PROCESS

The Intrapsychic Process changes the baby's state of mind (or an adult's) from an unhappy persecutory-retaliatory state to one of thoughtful calmness and a feeling of responsibility, from which further development and progress can be made. This change is a part of a to and fro movement between what has been described as the *Paranoid Schizoid Position* (PSP) and the *Depressive Position* (DP), which may occur repeatedly throughout life. The terms 'Paranoid Schizoid' and 'Depressive' are descriptive and bear only a resemblance to similar terms used for psychiatric conditions. This to and fro movement from the PSP to the DP is largely influenced by the interpersonal process which will be described below.

I shall describe the interpersonal process as it applies to the mother and baby. If what happens in the baby and in the relationship between mother and baby, is transposed to adult life, its relevance to almost any situation and any relationship, can be seen. Melanie Klein who first described the process called them 'Positions' – not stages or phases of development, as Freud did with his theory of sexual development, because the 'to and fro' movement occurs with all human beings throughout life.

Melanie Klein's understanding is not a contradiction of Sigmund Freud but a further development of his understanding. Freud's basic personality structure, the id, superego and ego and his stages of development can be seen as occurring side by side with what I have named *The Alpha-action*. I shall describe it as it happens in the baby. See diagram 1.

THE NORMAL MOTHER-BABY RELATIONSHIP

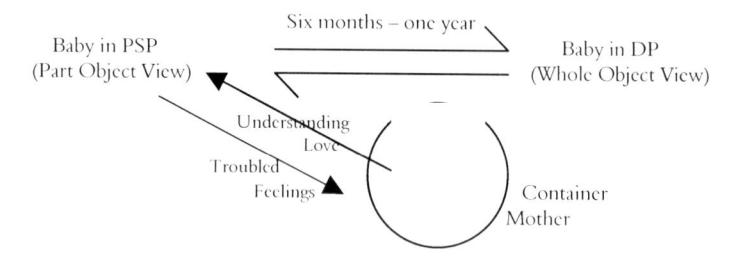

Baby in PSP (Part Object View) ← Six months – one year → Baby in DP (Whole Object View)

Understanding
Love
Troubled Feelings

Container Mother

PSP and DP represent the baby in Paranoid Schizoid Position and in the Depressive Position.
Diagram 1

The newborn infant is in the Paranoid Schizoid Position. It is simply a bundle of reactions (the *id*, in Freudian terms). It is happy when it is well fed and comfortable, as will be observed when it smiles and chuckles. It is angry when it is hungry or uncomfortable and expresses it in angry crying. Its perceptual apparatus is rudimentary and immature while its ability to feel is acute. This combination of immature perceptions and acute feelings is the basis for the development of primitive fantasies.

At this stage because the baby's perceptual apparatus is rudimentary it experiences events and things only partially, as part objects. It experiences things according to the feelings it receives at any particular time. During feeding when the baby feels satisfied and comfortable, the mother, the thing that feeds it and makes it feel good, is experienced as good; *it has a loving feeling about this thing that it experiences and recognises only partially – the good breast*. When mother leaves it and goes away, as all mothers must do at times, it feels *angry, bad and sad*, especially if it is not fully satisfied – *the bad breast*. So mother is experienced as a part object, which is sometimes good (a loving feeling) and sometimes bad (an angry feeling). The intensity of the anger and love will depend on the strength of its natural *id* impulses.

In infants, whose experience of reality is mainly through its feelings and fantasies, and whose emotions are acute, the angry feeling is experienced in its extreme form, as killing mother, especially when she has disappeared for a while.

As the baby grows older, certain changes relevant to its emotional development occur:

> Its perceptual ability develops and matures. By the time it reaches the age of six months to one year, it is able to experience mother as a whole person. Normally, it then recognises that it was angry with and may have hurt (killed) this same person who fed it, made it comfortable, and gave it all the good things, whom it loves. It then becomes alarmed and regrets the angry feelings it had and moves into a feeling of remorse and thoughtfulness and a wish to make up – the *Depressive Position*. In the Depressive Position the infant takes responsibility for its bad actions and tries to make amends to mother – *Reparation*.
>
> While it is in the DP, the infant does not feel persecuted. It is calm and thoughtful. It has taken in a bit of mother's thinking process through projective-identification and is able to develop in its ability to think and feel.
>
> After a while when it has some experience it cannot understand and feels troubled, it may move back into the PSP for a while, and it would cry and scream in anger, when the whole process would be repeated and it would move again into the DP. This to and fro movement between the PSP to the DP occurs repeatedly

throughout ones life. *It is greatly influenced by mother's state of mind in the case of the baby and the baby's own inherent qualities.* In the case of the normal adult it would be influenced by someone, often an authority figure, who plays the part of the container or 'mother' and his/her own qualities.

THE INTERPERSONAL PROCESS WITH INTRAPSYCHIC CONCOMITANTS

The baby's relationship with mother, (Interpersonal Process), facilitates or inhibits the movement into the DP.

The interpersonal process between mother and baby, involves *Containment within* mother of the pain and disturbance of the baby, and *Projective Identification*. In Projective identification between mother and baby the painful feelings and the angry, nasty, feelings of the baby are taken into herself by mother who is then experienced by the baby as bad; bad because she not only causes baby pain, as any mother must, for instance by turning away from it on occasions, but also because she contains the badness of the baby. (More of Projective-Identification is also dealt with further below in this chapter as well as in Chapter V.)

In the normal loving relationship between infant and mother, mother then carries it, cuddles it, makes soothing noises in order to ease the pain and badness and gives it understanding and love. *In effect she takes into herself the pain of the baby, understands something of it, and changes it into a more tolerable feeling and gives it back to the infant with love.* An exchange of psychic material occurs between mother and infant, in which the infant gives mother its badness and mother returns to the infant much of her own love and goodness and instinctual understanding. (Her thinking.) This intimate and powerful process happens unconsciously, through the *instinct of the mother*. It is the identical process described as *Projective Identification*. When this process is repeated several times between mother and infant, it facilitates the movement into the DP. A position, as described above, which is of great progressive value to the infant.

This process has been likened by Bion, to a mother bird who takes out the indigestible worm from a baby bird's open mouth, chews on it for a while, making it more digestible and then returns it into the open mouth of the baby bird, who then is able to complete the mastication and swallow and digest its food.

It is that process of taking into oneself the bad feelings or the troubles of the infant, changing them into something understandable or something more digestible, and returning it to the infant, which helps the infant to grow emotionally and intellectually. *This is Beneficial Projective Identification which occurs in a good container.*

However in exceptional circumstances the process can become deleterious to the baby, for instance, if mother is overstressed or disturbed. Likewise projective identification can be pathological in human beings of all ages. This may be called *Beta-Action*.

THE EXCEPTIONS

1. The over-stressed mother
In some cases mother is not able to act as a good container for the infant because she is over-stressed, through problems in her personal life or because of an illness. Mother's 'emotional/stress container' then becomes too full to allow her to also contain the stress created by her baby. See Diagram 2.

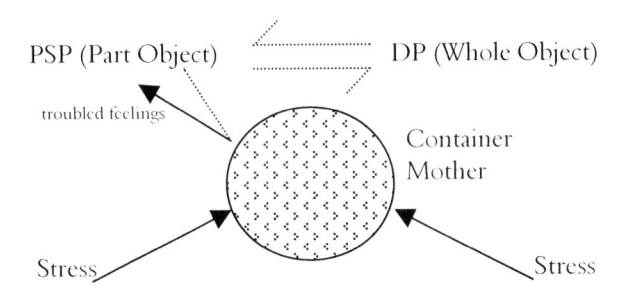

Diagram 2

2. Over-stressed and Disturbed

Sometimes mother is so stressed and disturbed that instead of taking in baby's troubles and making them better she takes them in and makes them worse and gives them back. The Projective Identification then works in reverse. In an extreme case she would beat the baby for making a noise she could not stand. In such a case the movement into the DP will be far more difficult.

The baby may never be able to move into the Depressive Position and may move 'backwards' into either psychosis or psychopathy. (see Diagram 3)

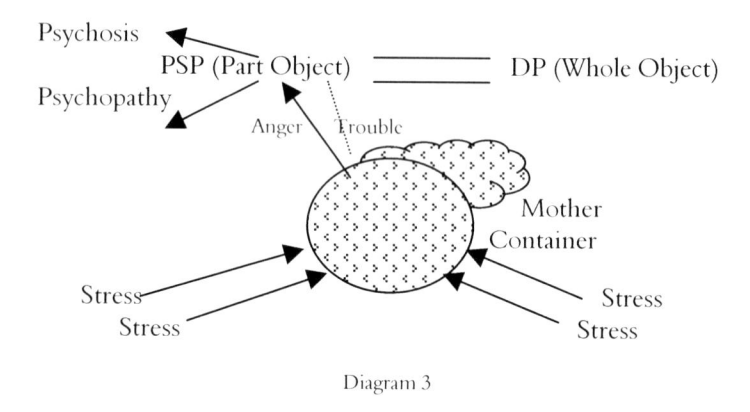

Diagram 3

In these cases the Alpha-action does not occur. We could say that the Beta-action prevails.

3. Inherited Qualities

In cases where the baby has a particularly difficult inherited quality or some other inherent problem, or a physical illness, the movement into the depressive position may become very difficult. Therapeutic work with a child or adolescent with such a problem is more difficult. Such babies may grow into adulthood finding it very difficult or being unable to own to their own mistakes or to make amends for any wrong they may have done. A good psychoanalysis could allow them to recognise the qualities they posses and help them to make conscious adjustments to allow them to live satisfying lives.

THE ALPHA-ACTION IN THE CLINICAL SPHERE

As Therapists

Good therapy uses the Alpha-action beneficially, as the normal mother does with the baby.

It behoves us as therapists to *listen* carefully to patients and to *hear*, and to *take in* what we have heard. We must remember that patients communicate to us in different ways. In order to hear and take in what is said it is important that we are able to put ourselves in his/her position – *empathise*. We should be genuinely interested in his/her troubles and in wanting to work on the problem. Having taken the communication in, we should then make some sense out of it, (semi-digest it as in the analogy of the Birds), and *give it back* to the patient to solve the problem. (Digest it.) It is crucial that the semi-digested problem is given back to him if he is to genuinely progress. (Grow.) Fully understanding the problem may prove daunting, but if it is realised that what the therapist must do is *to honestly make more sense out of it than the patient has*; then he/she has embarked on the first step in the therapeutic process.

When, as therapists, we have done this, the beginnings of a beneficial intrapsychic change occurs in the patient, just as it occurs in the baby described above. The patient who is feeling angry, troubled, confused, becomes able to see more about his situation. (Whole Object View.) He becomes better able to take responsibility for the troubles and often discovers that he is truly able to understand and deal with the problem himself.

It is recognition of the *Transference* that is used by the therapist as the means of recognising the Projective Identification. The transference puts the unidentified, hidden, lost' feeling into the therapist, which a trained therapist will be able to feel and recognise.

Example: The case of J

> J had made a good therapeutic alliance with me in the inpatient unit. He had also made a strong transference relationship with me as his father who died when he was ten years of age. He was frequently unreasonably angry with me. Each time he shouted abusively at me I took in what he said, understood it, and calmly

returned it to him. For instance, I did not turn up for his appointed therapy on one occasion and I could not pass any message to him. He had waited for me. When he saw me next he yelled at me in what I saw as sheer distress, called me names and said *'you tell us off if we don't come.'* The degree of his anger was well beyond what the occasion demanded.

I took in his excessive anger, recognised that he had linked my unexpected absence with his father who had died on him, and I said, *'J you are shouting at me as if I had died or something.'* J calmed down immediately and asked if could see me alone. I agreed. He poured his heart out about his feelings about his dead father whom he had hero-worshipped, and then went on to talk about his plans for the weekend.

In Patients or Clients

Some patients come to you for treatment in the full throes of a Projective Identificatory experience. Others get into projective identification while in therapy, with the therapist or with someone else. If they get into projective identification with the therapist, the best situation for good therapy becomes available, as described above.

It is more difficult when the patient comes to you already in a projective Identificatory relationship. I have had several girl patients who have come to me having already been in projective identification with their mothers for years, identifying with and carrying mother's illness in a Beta-action relationship. In such cases mother remains well as long as the daughter is ill and mother becomes disturbed when the daughter gains her own identity and feels well. Mother may become angry with the therapist and protest that the therapy is bad

Examples:

The case of CL – an intelligent, sixteen-year-old girl.

> CL was admitted to hospital following great concern about her potential for suicide. She was found wandering near railway lines in a state of disassociation. She was depressed. Mother visited her regularly in hospital and showed great love and concern. We did not know what the problem was. She got better while in hospital. We did not know why. When the time came for her to leave

hospital she refused to return home. She could not give any reason for this she just felt frightened

It took several family meetings and 'confessions' from mother that she had had a very unhappy adolescence, *from which she claimed she never suffered*, for me to realise that mother had pushed all her adolescent disturbance into CL, while CL had given all her health over to mother.

Thereafter treatment was aim-directed. CL continued with the her psychotherapy for six months, during which mother was banned from visiting her. Keeping mother away from CL was painful for both. It was painful for CL because she loved her mother. It was painful for mother because she was re-owning her adolescent disturbance and felt disturbed. CL tolerated the pain well because she understood the reasons for the separation. Mother did not understand and was very angry with me. It must be remembered that Projective Identification while being a very powerful mechanism, *is unconscious*.

CL went back home after her therapy was over and has been struggling on with a difficult mother for the last four years.

The case of Ju an honest, intelligent fifteen-year-old

Ju accused her mother of having sexually abused her on three separate occasions in a space of one year. On the third occasion she added father as joining mother in the abuse. Each time she herself went to Social Services, made the complaint and was taken into interim care. Each time after about two weeks she retracted her accusations and returned home. On the third occasion she was referred to me, to the Regional Adolescent Unit. Parents were angry with her and with all of us who wanted to investigate, and refused to co-operate. She was then taken into care. She was in treatment with me for around nine months. Careful clinical and police investigations left us doubtful about the truth of Ju's allegations, till *Ju herself finally acknowledged that she was never sexually abused*. She was an honest girl and was convinced that she had been sexually abused when she made the accusations. Then she became unsure after a period of separation from mother when she withdrew the accusations. Projective Identification is an unconscious process and diminishes in intensity with separation.

Parents were angry and refused to join in any family meetings. Ju had also told me that mother was having an extramarital relationship which she had confided to Ju. Before parents withdrew their support I had two meetings with them in which father angrily stated that mother did have extramarital sexual relationships and that it was none of my business. I could not discover whether mother had been sexually abused by her parents.

My understanding of what happened with Ju is that when mother confided in her about her extramarital affair she pushed her disturbed feelings and guilt into Ju. Ju who was an honest, innocent adolescent just developing in her adolescent sexuality, had natural sexual fantasies about sex with parents which then became confused with the sexual immorality and guilt pushed into her, which she experienced as sexual abuse. In truth mother abused Ju's innocence by trying to make her share and carry her sexual guilt and Ju felt abused. When Ju saw that father supported mother in her sexual immorality she felt abused by father as well.

THE ALPHA-ACTION IN NORMAL LIFE

The Alpha-action is the prototype of all good relationships that go on between human beings. The to and fro movement between the PSP and the DP as described above occurs with human beings of all ages and in almost every situation where there is some difficulty. If one looks at any quarrel or any kind of trouble, one will see someone or yourself in the PSP, in part-object experiences. It may occur in some or all of the participants, together with the attempt to blame someone else as the cause of the trouble.

Somebody then may take on the role of the container, take in someone's trouble, understand it, make it better and return it; when the trouble and the problem seems to melt away. It is this process which facilitates the change from feeling persecuted and being angry and attacking (the Paranoid Schizoid Position) to being more thoughtful and able to take responsibility for your part in the trouble, (the Depressive position), the position from which progress is made.

If one looks at the whole troublesome scene from all points of view, you would reach the whole object position. From this position it will be easy to see one's own responsibility for the trouble. As soon as one is able to recognise one's self as responsible for some aspect of the trouble, two things happen:

1. You are no more a helpless victim of someone else's villainy or weakness.
2. You take responsibility for the troublesome situation and recognise the power you have to make it better. You take charge of the situation and of yourself.

It is important that trouble is taken to make sure that the problem is correctly identified and that you are not taking responsibility for the wrong thing. I have come across honest and good staff who are eager to do the right thing and hasten to take responsibility, alas! for the wrong thing. Problems do not get solved that way. They would be made worse.

Taking into oneself the indigestible, badness of another, making it better and giving it back, is the essence of the 'healing' process. It is what is done in nature, between the normal mother and baby, between the mother bird and the baby bird, between friends, and what is done between enemies if they want to solve problems. It is done without thought or calculation as a natural thing that happens between man and man. It is described as what goes on between Christ and man – *Christ/God takes into himself the sins/misery of man and gives back forgiveness and love.* Man seems to have a natural instinct to behave as Christ/God – *in a small way*.

In psychotherapy it is not just the recognition of what is going on but the help which is given by the taking in of the problem, the understanding, and the giving back of the understood version which is necessary for recovery to take place.

Chapter XII
ABOUT THE AUTHOR

Dr Southy Perinpanayagam, known as Dr Perin to patients and colleagues in England, grew up in Ceylon (Sri Lanka), during the period when it was a colony of Great Britain and its transition to an independent democratic state in the common wealth. He was greatly influenced by the values of honesty, self-discipline and sportsmanship, brought into the country by the English principals of the prominent schools and the Christian missionaries from England and the United States, which he imbibed through his father, a well known school master, in the era of 'Spare the rod and spoil the child' – a policy he used freely both with his five children and the boys in school. Yet, Southy felt enormously loved by his parents. They took trouble over all the children at home and in school.

Sports of all kinds played a significant part in Sounthy's early life. He represented his school in Tennis, Athletics, Rugby and Boxing. He won the Francis Jayawardena challenge trophy for the best boxer in the Stubb's Shield interschool boxing meet and later was the inter-university champion of India and Ceylon. He captained his school and the university in boxing and won university rugby colours. He experienced many of the insecurities and failures and depression and excitements of adolescence that go with engaging in a full adolescent life. Sounthy feels that his adolescence and his upbringing made him uniquely well prepared for understanding the difficulties of adolescents and distinguishing between the training of 'normal' adolescents and the treatment of damaged and disturbed youngsters.

He qualified as a doctor in 1960 from the Colombo Medical School. Having trained in and practiced general medicine, Paediatrics, Surgery and Obstetrics and Gynaecology for four years, he entered the field of psychiatry at the Mental Hospital,

Angoda, Ceylon, which contained around 4000 patients – it was called the 'Lunatic Asylum' in its colonial days – adults and adolescents, where he saw and practiced, the early forms of treatment – Insulin treatment, ECT and drug treatment with Serpasil and also saw the beginning of the change into the Phenothiazines and the modern drugs.

He joined the Royal Ceylon Army Medical Corps (Volunteers) as a captain, when he made an oath of loyalty to the Queen of England. He found the camaraderie and fun of the life of an officer to be luxuriously enjoyable, but the treatment of the other ranks to be indefensibly degrading. He resigned his commission shortly after his arrival in the UK in 1966.

In the UK he went immediately into work in English hospitals, trained for postgraduate exams through the teaching he received from some of his consultants, his own reading and practice, and from discussions with colleagues, and passed the Diploma in Psychological Medicine and the Membership of the Royal College of Psychiatrists.

It was after he joined the Northgate Clinic for disturbed adolescents in 1968, as a registrar, under the medical directorship of Dr Brian O'Connell, and the consultancy of Dr Arthur Hyatt Williams, that he saw the vast difference between formal psychiatry and Psychodynamic psychiatry which attempts a genuine understanding of the human being. It was a culture shock.

He recalls with affection the comment of his friend, Dr Peter Bruggen – '*I don't know Perin, I did not listen, it was so boring*', said with the characteristic 'Bruggenish' brutal honesty, when Sounthy asked for his opinion of his first case-presentation at the Tavistock Clinic, a presentation which was in typical formal psychiatric style. It had the most salutary effect on him. He later joined the Tavistock Clinic Adolescent Department where he was soon appointed as honorary Consultant to the Young Peoples Counselling Service and Tutor in Psychotherapy for the Introductory Psychotherapy Course for doctors.

Shortly after he joined the Tavistock Clinic he had the good fortune to listen to a lecture by Dr P .L. G. Gallwey, of the Portman Clinic whose understanding of sexual perversions and delinquency, Sounthy felt was remarkable. He asked for supervision from Pat Gallwey, which eventually led to Sounthy becoming a founder member of the Group of Senior Forensic Psychiatrists at the Portman Clinic, started by Dr Gallwey.

Sounthy was accepted for training at the British Institute of Psychoanalysis, in 1971 and went in for a personal training Kleinian psychoanalysis. After about two years of psychoanalysis he discovered that he was much more interested in and adept at applying the psychoanalytical method in a practical way to work with disturbed adolescents, than in sitting behind a couch in psychoanalytical practice. He resigned from the training while he continued with the personal psychoanalysis to its termination.

Although he has been steeped in Psychodynamic work for many years he has retained his belief in formal psychiatry, and has continued to use it in those suffering from a formal psychiatric illness. Dr Perinpanayagam believes that every psychiatrist should have training in both, Psychoanalytical work and formal psychiatry if they are to be able to make appropriate differential diagnoses and provide an effective service.

Sounthy Perinpanayagam feels the greatest learning and changes in his thinking were in the early stages of his entry into psychodynamics at the Northgate Clinic, which he feels was the cradle of his development. He feels privileged to have had the opportunity to observe at close quarters, the work of Dr Brian O'Connell, whose versatile knowledge and breath of view, set the scene for his further development. Sounthy's greatest gratitude is to Dr Arthur Hyatt Williams who has been his Guide, Mentor and Friend throughout his psychodynamic life, and for his introduction to Dr Donald Meltzer who helped him to round-off, correct and finish the incomplete aspects of the psychoanalysis he had.

There are many others to whom Sounthy is thankful for their supp.ort and friendship during the development of his psychodynamic life – To Donald Bird, Consultant Psychiatrist at the Northgate Clinic and the Tavistock clinic, for the many times they shared dinner and discussions of the difficulties of psychoanalysis, and for the supervision and support he received. The late Jorge Thomas, Consultant, Tavistock Clinic, who

Sounthy considers to be one of the finest human beings he has known.

Mike Brearley, the philosopher, psychoanalyst, and cricket captain of England, with whom he has had many discussions pertaining to psychodynamics, and gained valuable honest opinions. He is thankful especially to Anton Obholzer, Consultant Psychiatrist, Chair of the Adolescent department, and Chief Executive of the Tavistock Clinic and Portman Trust, who has remained a loyal friend and stalwart support from the time they were both junior doctors at the Northgate Clinic. This book may never have come about without Anton's support. He is also thankful to Kabir Padamse, Medical Director, Romford Child and Family Centre, and Tim Kidger, Manager, Drug and Alcohol service Redbridge, for the encouragement and support he received in attempting this book. Sounthy also gained much from the friendship and the honest, ruthless criticisms of drafts of the book by Alister Warman, Principal, Byam Shaw School of Art, whose views as a non-medical, non-psychoanalytical layman were invaluable.

All of them were there throughout the difficult times Sounthy had, as a single Consultant, in having to defend psychodynamics and the work he was doing.

In the background was Mano, his loyal and loving wife who gave him unstinting support in his work and psychoanalysis, while tolerating all the idiosyncrasies and eccentricities that inevitably go with the early stages of psychoanalysis.